ECONOMY AND CULTURE IN PAKISTAN

Also by Hastings Donnan

MARRIAGE AMONG MUSLIMS: Preference and Choice in Northern Pakistan
SOCIAL ANTHROPOLOGY AND PUBLIC POLICY IN NORTHERN
IRELAND (*co-editor*)

Also by Pnina Werbner

BLACK AND ETHNIC LEADERSHIPS IN BRITAIN: The Cultural Dimensions
of Political Action (*co-editor*)
THE MIGRATION PROCESS: Capital, Gifts and Offerings among British
Pakistanis
PERSON, MYTH AND SOCIETY IN SOUTH ASIAN ISLAM (*editor*)

Economy and Culture in Pakistan

Migrants and Cities in a Muslim Society

Edited by

Hastings Donnan
Senior Lecturer in Social Anthropology
The Queen's University of Belfast

and

Pnina Werbner
Research Associate, Department of Sociology
University of Manchester

St. Martin's Press   New York

First published in the United States of America in 1991

Printed in Hong Kong

ISBN 0–312–04891–2

Library of Congress Cataloging-in-Publication Data
Economy and culture in Pakistan: migrants and cities in a Muslim
society/edited by Hastings Donnan and Pnina Werbner.
p. cm.
ISBN 0–312–04891–2
1. Migration, Internal—Pakistan. 2. Pakistan—Emigration and
immigration. 3. Immigrants—Pakistan—Economic conditions.
4. Acculturation—Pakistan. 5. Urbanization—Pakistan. I. Donnan,
Hastings. II. Werbner, Pnina.
HB2100.5.A3E29   1991
305.8′095491—dc20   90–8453
                                                               CIP

Contents

Contents

List of Tables

List of Figures

Notes on the Contributors

Akbar S. Ahmed was Commissioner in Quetta, Pakistan before taking up his present position as the Allama Iqbal Fellow/Chair in Pakistan Studies at the University of Cambridge. He has published widely on Pakistan society and is the author of many books, the most recent of which include *Discovering Islam: Making Sense of Muslim History and Society* and *Pakistan Society: Islam, Ethnicity and Leadership in South Asia*.

Hamza Alavi taught for many years in the Department of Sociology at the University of Manchester, and since retiring has served as Visiting Professor at the Universities of Denver and California. He has written extensively on the peasantry and the post-colonial state and has co-edited several books including *Sociology of Developing Societies*, *Capitalism and Colonial Production*, *State and Ideology in the Middle East and Pakistan*, and *Sociology of South Asia*.

Hastings Donnan is Senior Lecturer in Social Anthropology at The Queen's University of Belfast. He is the author of *Marriage Among Muslims: Preference and Choice in Northern Pakistan* and co-editor of *Social Anthropology and Public Policy in Northern Ireland*.

Michael Fischer is Lecturer in Social Anthropology and Computing at the University of Kent. He has written a number of articles on artificial intelligence and expert systems, and on the relevance of these to social anthropology.

Wenonah Lyon received a PhD from the University of Texas at Austin in 1986. She has taught social anthropology part time at the University of Kent at Canterbury, and is now a Research Assistant at Imperial College, London.

Omar Noman is a Research Associate at Queen Elizabeth House, Oxford and Director of the Economic Policy Research Unit, Lahore. He is the author of *The Political Economy of Pakistan 1947–85* and is currently preparing a book on *The Impact of Aid on Pakistan*.

Frits Selier is Senior Lecturer in the Department of Cultural Anthropology/Development Sociology at Free University, Amsterdam. He is the author of *Rural–Urban Migration in Pakistan* and co-editor of *Migration in Pakistan*.

Saifur Rahman Sherani has been until recently a lecturer in the University of Baluchistan, Quetta and is currently a research consultant with development agencies in Pakistan.

Jan van der Linden is Senior Lecturer in the Department of Cultural Anthropology/Development Sociology at Free University, Amsterdam. He is the author of *The Sites and Services Approach Reviewed: Solution or Stopgap to the Third World Housing Shortage?* and a co-author of *Squatter Settlements in Pakistan: The Impact of Upgrading*.

Pnina Werbner is a Research Associate in the Department of Sociology at the University of Manchester. She has written widely on many different aspects of Pakistani life in Britain and is the author of *The Migration Process: Capital, Gifts and Offerings among British Pakistanis*. She is also editor of *Person, Myth and Society in South Asian Islam* and co-editor of *Black and Ethnic Leaderships in Britain*.

Acknowledgements

The editors would like to acknowledge their gratitude to all those who participated in a series of workshops on Pakistan society at the University of Manchester's field-centre in Satterthwaite, over the last three years, for their encouragement and support in preparing this volume. They would also like to thank the Royal Anthropological Institute for permission to print a revised version of Akbar Ahmed's 'Death in Islam' and Patricia McKnight and Lorna Goldstrom of the Secretarial Centre at The Queen's University, Belfast, for their impeccable work in typing the final manuscript.

HASTINGS DONNAN
PNINA WERBNER

1 Introduction
Hastings Donnan and Pnina Werbner

Until recently anthropological interest in Pakistan has been dominated by a focus on the countryside. This is probably as it should be in a country which is predominantly agricultural. However, a growing number of Pakistanis live in cities both in Pakistan itself as well as overseas and very many more have some indirect experience of cities through contact with those who have lived there. Within Pakistan the rate of urbanisation has been rising dramatically, fuelled not only by natural growth and rural to urban migration, but by a massive influx of refugees. Millions of migrant Pakistanis are now also to be found residing overseas in British and Middle Eastern cities. But despite the fact that migration and urbanisation have thus become such a major part of Pakistani life, and although they have been the focus for a number of economic and demographic studies, the social and cultural consequences of these trends are less well understood. This book tries in part to rectify this.

But it is not just a book about Pakistani cities and migrants. It is also a book about how people respond to and deal with the large-scale forces shaping their society, forces for which their behaviour in a radically changing environment is partially responsible. Because some of the forces currently shaping Pakistani society are shared by many other developing countries – migration, ethnic tension, and urbanisation for example – the experiences of many Pakistanis are echoed in developing nations around the world. At the same time, however, they are uniquely moulded by Pakistan's particular culture and religion. Pakistan's claim on our attention is thus twofold. On the one hand, it is important for what it can teach us about the global significance of these forces and on the other, for what is distinctive about it: the particular configuration which these forces take and the ways in which they uniquely combine, as well as the way in which people's responses to them are rooted in Islam.

The contributors to this volume are ideally qualified to examine how ordinary people influence and are influenced by these processes. Most of them are anthropologists or sociologists whose research is characterised by extended fieldwork and an emphasis on the culture or way of life of the people studied. Their research thus provides a grass roots perspective on Pakistani society which complements existing studies of how these processes operate at a more general level. By using case studies the contributors are able not only to offer insights into how such large-scale processes interrelate with each other, but to provide clues as to what they mean and how they are interpreted by ordinary people.

This is not to say, however, that by offering a grass roots perspective the wider contemporary and historical contexts are of no interest or relevance here. As a discipline anthropology has increasingly come to realise the arbitrariness of a focus on a particular community and to recognise the necessity of going beyond this, not least because the horizons of the members of that community have themselves broadened. This is certainly the case in Pakistan where people are now more mobile both socially and geographically than ever before. Large-scale migration and massive urbanisation have exposed many Pakistanis to new ways of doing things and new ways of thinking about their society. Events throughout the Muslim world and its relationship to the West over the last decade have encouraged new ways of thinking about their religion, not only for Pakistan's predominantly Sunni population, but for its many minority Muslim sects as well. Pakistan is clearly a society experiencing massive change and those previously isolated from one another are now coming into contact.

In such circumstances it is easy to emphasise disjunction and transition, to emphasise the novel and the innovatory. We are led to ask questions about how Pakistan has changed, rather than about how it has remained the same. We ask questions about those who have left their home, rather than about those who have remained behind. We ask questions about how new capital or new skills can be harnessed, rather than about how old skills can be developed. By emphasising change and transformation, we can miss the fact that 'tradition' may remain significant, only transposed to new settings or used in new ways. As Rabinow (1975) reminds us, and as many of the chapters in this volume demonstrate, tradition is not necessarily opposed to modernity but may offer a means to integrate, create, and make meaningful new experiences.

Yet the kind of image which anthropologists have so far presented of Pakistan is of an essentially 'traditional' society, a society which is mainly rural, kin-based and governed largely by peasant or tribal values. Much of the existing anthropological research on Pakistan falls easily into the categories of 'tribe' or 'peasant' (see Ahmed and

Hart, 1984 for a summary of the definitional issues here), and although the extent to which this distinction has characterised Pakistani anthropology can be overstressed, it nevertheless has had important implications for the compartmentalised way in which ethnographic research has developed there, as we will see later. Such a distinction, moreover, broadly corresponds to the geographical and administrative divisions of Pakistan whereby 'tribal' is associated principally with North West Frontier Province (NWFP) and Baluchistan, and 'peasant' with Punjab and Sindh, divisions which themselves are a consequence of diverging colonial and precolonial histories. Tribal groups outside NWFP and Baluchistan, such as the Kalasha in Chitral, are only beginning to receive adequate and systematic ethnographic attention (see Parkes, 1987, in press; see also Jettmar, 1986; on Kohistan see Keiser, 1986).

The hub of much of the research on tribal society has been provided by the work of Fredrik Barth in a series of now classic publications on the Swat Pakhtun (see, for example, 1958, 1959a, 1959b, 1960, 1969) and by his editorial contribution to Pehrson's pioneering research on the Marri Baluch (1966). While other early work has provided crucial source material on the Pakhtun (Caroe, 1958; Honigmann, 1958; Spain, 1962, 1963), it has been Barth's analysis of Pakhtun social and political life which has generated most debate and which has perhaps been at least partially responsible for ensuring that the Pakhtun are now the best studied of all Pakistan's tribal populations. One way or another most of this research has been concerned with the Pakhtun political system and with the unique code of honour known as Pakhtunwali which underlies it (see, for example, Ahmed, 1982; Lindholm, 1979, 1981, 1982b, 1986b). Almost all the other interests in tribal society – in its social organisation (Hart, 1985), stratification (Barth, 1960), conceptualisations of women (Ahmed and Ahmed, 1981) – have been directed towards this end or have been an offshoot of it. As a result, Barth's account has been both criticised and extended by, for example, greater sensitivity to the colonial presence (see Ahmed, 1976; Asad, 1972), and by detailed analysis of the logic underpinning the apparently contrasting Pakhtun values of generosity and jealousy (Lindholm, 1982a). Meanwhile, Pakhtun groups other than those in Swat have been added to the ethnographic record (see Ahmed, 1980 and 1983b on the Mohmand and Wazirs respectively and Hart, 1985 on the Afridi), and more recent analyses have endeavoured to grapple with the nature of the relationship between tribe and state (see, for example, Ahmed's

1980 discussion of encapsulation and his 1983a and 1983b discussions of the 'Islamic district paradigm'). For a variety of practical and political reasons the Baluch have been rather less well studied than the Pakhtun. Moreover, no single pivotal monograph has galvanised research there as Barth's *Political Leadership among Swat Pathans* has done for the Pakhtun and although Pehrson's posthumously published book on the Marri Baluch is often cited, it has never generated the same sense of debate (Pehrson, 1966; see also Gardezi, 1968). Again, however, research has focused largely on the political system and an important series of articles by Stephen Pastner documents the central political role played by *pirs* or saints (Pastner, S., 1978a, 1980, 1984a, 1988), while Nina Swidler's work contrasts Baluch and Brahui chiefdoms to the at least nominally egalitarian and individualistic political system of the Pakhtun (Swidler, N., 1977). As Swidler argues, such clearly different political systems may have quite far-reaching consequences for the extent to which each is politically encapsulated by the state, something which has also concerned the Pastners in their work on the Baluch (see Pastner and Pastner, 1977). Other Baluch tribes such as the Bugti have received much less attention (though see Ahmed, 1988).

The study of tribal groups in Pakistan has usually taken place in isolation from the study of other types of community in the country. Since their political and social systems are based on segmentary lineages or on chiefdoms, they bear more obvious resemblances to Muslim tribal groups in the Middle East and North Africa than to the peasant farmers who are their countrymen in adjacent provinces. Consequently, it is to the former that they are most usually compared (see Ahmed and Hart, 1984; Duprée, 1984; Hart, 1985: Chapter 7). Only occasionally have comparisons been drawn between tribal politics and those elsewhere in Pakistan (see Ahmed, forthcoming; Lindholm, 1977), thereby accentuating the sense that tribe and peasant belong to different worlds. It is in this sense that Werbner's efforts in this volume to extend the segmentary lineage model to Manchester Pakistanis of mainly Punjabi origin is thus a useful attempt to draw attention to the many similarities which exist between the political styles of each group.

As already mentioned, other issues of tribal life in NWFP and Baluchistan have been largely tributary to the main concern with political organisation. These have included, for example, some discussion of religion (see Pastner and Pastner, 1972b) and of the ecological adaptation of different groups (see Pastner and Pastner, 1982). But by their nature some of these topics have also more readily invited comparison with other tribal societies in the Middle East and North Africa rather than with the rest of Pakistan. This is true, for example, of the small amount of research on the tribal economy, particularly where this is based on pastoralism (Pastner and Pastner, 1972a, 1982; Scholz, 1974; Swidler, W., 1977). But even where institutions are obviously shared (at least to some extent), as in the case of some kinds of close kin marriage or in attitudes to women and honour, comparisons have not always been made right across Pakistan (Pastner, C., 1974, 1978, 1979, 1981, 1988).

If research on Pakistan's tribal areas is characterised by a comparative orientation towards the Middle East, research on Pakistan's peasant farmers, tenants and sharecroppers has tended more often than not to look in the opposite direction for appropriate comparisons, towards the country's eastern neighbours. (This has tended to militate against the development of a distinctive and coherent body of anthropological scholarship on Pakistan comparable to that for India.) In the case of peasant farmers in Punjab there are perhaps once again sound historical reasons for this, not least the fact that the province was dissected by partition in 1947, when eastern and western Punjab exchanged populations and many people from the former settled in the latter. Similarly, the flow of refugees into rural Sindh at this time, and later from there into Karachi, perhaps also encourages comparison with India, although anthropologists have had rather less to say about this province and have done virtually no field research there outside Karachi itself. With the exception of the Pastners' work on a coastal village populated by Zikri Baluch fishermen, little ethnographic research has thus been published on rural Sindh (Pastner, C., 1979, 1981, 1988; Pastner, S., 1978b, 1978c, 1984a, 1988; though for one brief, early study see Honigmann, 1958).

Anthropologists have carried out considerably more research in the Punjab, where once again an early monograph, while not as influential on the wider anthropological stage as Barth's *Political Leadership*, set the tone for subsequent research. Zekiye Eglar's study of a village in Gujrat in the 1950s, although focusing principally on gift exchange, also touched on many of the subjects to be examined in greater detail by later anthropologists. Like Eglar's (1957, 1960) study, much of this later research was rural based and sought to establish the social and economic bases of village life. Attention focused particularly on kinship ties and on the workings of the *biradari* or 'patrilineage'. There are now numerous accounts of the *biradari* 'system', which among other things look at the gift exchanges which take place between *biradaris* during different life-crisis rituals, or at how they provide a focus for competing claims to honour and prestige (Ahmad, S., 1974; Alavi, 1972; Kurin and Morrow, 1985; Naveed-i-Rahat, 1981; Wakil, 1970). Marriage has also been a major interest, and researchers have tried to identify the many different factors which come into play in arranged marriages, showing for example that there is much more to Punjabi marriage than the preference for paternal kin so often mentioned in the literature (Aschenbrenner, 1967; Donnan, 1985, 1988; Fischer, Chapter 5 this volume). Some of this research on rural Punjab, particularly that on the agricultural economy, has more recently demonstrated its potential value to workers in the developmental field (see Kurin, 1983a and 1983b).

But anthropologists working in Punjab have also been interested in stratification and rank, worrying mainly about whether these are best explained in terms of class or caste (Ahmad, S., 1977; Alavi, 1971; Barth, 1960; Rouse, 1983; Wakil, 1972). Some similarities with caste in India are apparent; hereditary economic ties known as *seyp* which bind service groups (*kammis*) to landowners (*zamindars*) bear more than a passing resemblance to the Hindu *jajmani* system (see Alavi, 1971; Ahmad, S., 1977; Eglar, 1960), and may be reinforced by the relatively strict practice of endogamous marriage. Nevertheless, the range and practice of such groups across Punjab, and the particular theoretical predilections of individual ethnographers some of whom have put more emphasis on class, make generalisation difficult. Moreover, the Indian model of caste, if taken to be tied to ideas about purity and pollution, does not fit easily with Punjabi social life where the hereditary groups known as *qaum* or *zat* mix relatively freely with one another in many different contexts. Certainly, it seems that whatever the rigidity of such distinctions in the past, new ideologies are now more readily available by which such distinctions can be acceptably challenged, and new opportunities have opened up for those hoping to escape from such a system. In cities particularly, as we might expect given the Indian experience, such distinctions must at least be reworked as Fischer demonstrates later in this volume.

One of the things to have opened up rural society in many parts of the Punjab in the last decade has been migration, and although we will look at the nature of this in more detail later, it is worth noting here that anthropologists have so far largely concentrated their attention on the impact which this has had on village life. In some areas the impact of the remittance economy on the day to day life of Punjabis has been enormous (use of remittances has occupied much of the general literature on Pakistani migration, a discussion which has relied heavily on the work of Gilani *et al.*, 1981). Increased purchasing power has led not only to a consumer boom and a thriving trade in smuggled goods, but has also facilitated a set of more widespread social and economic changes which include inflated dowries, withdrawal from agriculture, and increasing seclusion of some (usually young) women (Bilquees and Hamid, 1981; Lefebvre, 1986; Selier and Karim, 1986). The impact of migration on domestic organisation and gender roles is particularly well documented and a number of anthropologists have charted the emergence of so-called matri-weighted families (Naveed-i-Rahat, 1986; Rauf, 1982; though for a contrary view see Gilani, 1983). These are families in which the male head of household is absent for long periods and in which his wife has consequently taken on responsibility for much that was previously his domain, including decisions concerning land, children's education and household finances. Evidence suggests that these responsibilities do not revert to the male on his return. Here it is ironic that while the absence of their husbands has allowed some women greater participation in extra-domestic affairs, the same process with its new prosperity has forced their daughters indoors. Thus paradoxically, while migration has meant radical change for some, it has meant greater conservatism for others. This is a theme which recurs in a number of the contributions here but is perhaps most evident in the chapter by Akbar Ahmed.

Some anthropologists have been equivocal about the advantages of migration and have suggested that the large sums remitted by migrants have actually retarded development in Punjab. The money is used to refurbish dwellings, purchase consumer goods, or languishes idly in bank accounts instead of being invested in the country's industrial and agricultural base (Addleton, 1981, pp. 326–7; Ballard, 1987; see also Ahmed, F., 1976 and Halliday, 1977 who are similarly pessimistic about the economic benefits of migration). This is fine as long as the money continues to pour in, but with high rates of unemployment among Pakistanis in Britain and with signs that the Middle Eastern boom is already on the wane, there may be problems when the remittances cease. However, other observers are more positive about the advantages of migration and disagree that migrants have been just quite so prodigal with their money (see Amjad, 1986, p. 780; see also Guisinger, 1986; Tsakok, 1986). Thus contrary to what Ballard (1987, 1989) and others have suggested, some recent research indicates an enormous level of rural mechanisation and investment in agriculture, with a consequent growth of small-scale service and manufacturing industry (Nadvi, 1989). Nor will remittances necessarily dry up, since as Noman suggests in this volume, reconstruction in the wake of the Gulf war is likely to sustain demand for cheap migrant labour.

As in the NWFP and Baluchistan, so in the Punjab anthropologists have been concerned with politics, especially local level politics. Classically they have focused mainly on politics at the village level and on the factional links between landlord and tenant (Ahmad, S., 1974; Inayatullah, 1958, 1959; Smith, 1952), although like some of the more recent work on tribal politics here too their approaches have become more sophisticated, incorporating insights from political economy and trying to show how village, provincial, and state level leadership articulate at local level to produce specific political configurations (cf. Alavi, 1971, 1973). Religion too has occupied those working in Punjab, but often only in so far as it relates to politics (see Ewing, 1983) and there has been surprisingly little research specifically on religion itself (though see Ahmad, S., 1971; Kurin, 1984). What does exist has been concerned mainly with shrines (Ewing, 1982, 1984a, 1984b; Kurin, 1983c; Lewis, 1985; Mayer, 1967; Hafeez-ur-Rehman, 1984) and has paid much less attention to mainstream orthopraxy, although recent government policy has generated interest in the country's 'Islamisation' programme (see Weiss, 1986). Sherani's contribution to this volume extends this research by examining the relationship between *ulema* and *pir*, as well as their role in the political and social structure of the country.

Much of this research, whether concerned with tribe or peasant, has been oriented inwards towards the study of the community itself. However, changes within Pakistan as a whole coupled with theoretical developments within the discipline have increasingly forced anthropologists to look beyond the local communities that have formed the main locus of their study. As already implied, those studying tribal or peasant politics have perhaps been in the vanguard of this move. This has been reflected in a growing interest in ethnicity and in the relationship of different groups to the state, a focus which distinguishes contemporary research on ethnicity from earlier work which examined its role in relation only to local social or ecological conditions (Barth, 1958, 1969). Recent research has been able to show, for example, how ethnicity in Pakistan is often more complex than demands for regional autonomy may sometimes suggest, since not only does support for Baluch or Sindhi nationalism, for instance, stem from linguistically, culturally and historically diverse origins, but the meaning of certain ethnic identities has sometimes been transformed by changes at state level (see, for example, Alavi, 1988, 1989; see also Ahmed, 1986, forthcoming; Gardezi and Rashid, 1988; Kurin, 1988). Nevertheless, changes at state level alone cannot adequately explain ethnicity in Pakistan, since the state does not penetrate equally everywhere and at all times, and only by working simultaneously at local level and beyond have anthropologists been able to show how programmes and policies initiated at the political centre are inevitably mediated and refracted by local circumstances. As Alavi's chapter on ethnicity in this volume testifies (Chapter 8), it is by offering such a perspective that anthropologists have clearly a unique contribution to make to the understanding of Pakistan society.

Anthropological research in Pakistan thus needs to transcend the study of the local community which has hitherto preoccupied it and to move beyond the tendency to compartmentalise into separate social systems. However refined our classifications of Pakistani social systems may become (see Ahmed, forthcoming), they are likely to fix these social systems at a particular stage in their development and to direct attention away from contact between the individuals who compose them. Such an approach flatly contradicts the realities of contemporary Pakistani life in which previously accepted structures of authority are being increasingly eroded and in which people of widely varied background are thrown together. Two of the processes which have contributed to such changes in recent years, migration and urbanisation, provide a focus for this volume.

I MIGRATION AND URBANISATION

It has sometimes been suggested that migration and mass population movements are deeply ingrained in Pakistan's fabric, these themes being woven through the country's history as well as its religion. Not only is Pakistan's population a blend of the many different groups which swept east in successive waves of invasion in earlier centuries, but its more recent history has also witnessed a series of large-scale population movements. The country's very foundation in 1947 involved a massive upheaval of people and since then millions of Muslims have moved into Pakistan as a consequence of war, communalism or political oppression. Since 1947 many have also moved out of Pakistan as migrant labour to Europe, the Middle East and other destinations. In some people's minds these movements have religious connotations. For the former especially their exodus has strong resonances in religious history, for in Islam too migration is important, Muhammad's 'migration' (*hijra*) from Mecca to Medina in AD 622 marking the beginning of the Muslim calendar.

Like Islam itself, therefore, Pakistan's roots lie in migration. With the partition of the subcontinent in 1947 some 8 million predominantly Urdu-speaking Muslims arrived in Pakistan (then West Pakistan), settling mainly in urban areas of Punjab and Sindh, and remaining a relatively distinct segment of the country's population ever since. These were followed in 1971 by thousands of Biharis fleeing the war in embryonic Bangladesh (previously East Pakistan), and who, like the arrivals in 1947, still feel themselves to be the victims of Partition. Despite the intervening years, both groups continue to be referred to as *muhajirs* (from '*hijra*') or 'refugees'. More recent still are an estimated 3 million refugees from Afghanistan who have settled along Pakistan's western borders and in its major cities.

But just as Pakistan's development has been characterised by a flood of people into the country, so also has it been characterised by a flood of people out, most of them in search of work. This began in earnest in the 1950s when large numbers of Pakistanis began to leave for Britain, following in the footsteps of their pioneering countrymen such as former soldiers and seamen who had settled there in smaller numbers a decade earlier (for a brief summary of labour migrations in the nineteenth and early twentieth centuries see Afzal, 1974, p. 29). Between the mid 1950s and mid 1960s approximately 150 000 Pakistanis (including Bangladeshis, Anwar, 1979), arrived in Britain. Many of these were unskilled or semi-skilled labourers from Mirpur and Punjab (many of them *muhajirs*) who headed for England's industrial north and Midlands where they already had kinsmen who might help them find work. While tougher immigration laws were to curtail this flow from the mid 1960s onwards, many of these men were able to bring their families to join them as they became more settled.

However, tougher laws in Britain did not halt the exodus of migrant labour from Pakistan, which in the 1970s and 1980s merely changed its destination to the Middle East in response to the oil boom. Although reliable data on the size of this exodus have been notoriously difficult to find, and although estimates vary widely, most are agreed that it was very much larger than previous labour migrations. Some of the higher estimates suggest that at its peak in the mid 1980s there may have been over 2 million Pakistanis working in the Middle East (see Ahmed, 1984; Owen, 1985, p. 3), a figure which would represent almost 10 per cent of the country's labour force. Once again this flow of labour did not affect the country evenly with the majority of migrants being Punjabis and a substantial number of Pakhtun and Baluch, but with disproportionately few from Sindh (cf. Addleton, 1984, p. 584–6). Nevertheless, it was not as densely concentrated as the migration to Britain and consequently affected many more people both directly and indirectly. This time it also affected substantial numbers of urban professionals, particularly from Karachi and Lahore, who were nearly as numerous as construction workers in some of the Gulf States (Burki, 1980, p. 55; Ahmed, 1984; Halliday, 1977, p. 289; ECWA, 1982, pp. 719–20) and whose families were permitted to accompany them, unlike the majority of migrants. In contrast to the British migration, however, few of the migrants to the Middle East were permitted to settle permanently or to take on the nationality of the states in which they worked, but were recruited to work for fixed terms after which they returned to Pakistan unless re-employed.

Within their own country Pakistanis are also highly mobile. In addition to those who are more or less permanently itinerant (see Berland, 1982, 1983), substantial numbers participate in a seasonal agricultural labour migration from one rural area to another, as well as in a small but visible urban to rural flow. This ensures that rural areas are often much less parochial than frequently represented. Bureaucrats, businessmen and government officials are sometimes led there by the exploitation of resources (e.g. Sui gas, Baluch coal) and sometimes by the need for political control, while some places have been transformed by the influx of foreign aid and development workers; residents of Quetta, for example, refer to their city as 'little Geneva'. However, it is rural to urban migration which has most dramatically grown in volume and complexity (see Karim and Robinson, 1986 for a review of research on internal migration in Pakistan). Much of this flow is from the north (particularly NWFP) to Karachi, but the large industrial cities of Punjab also draw in workers, both from their immediate vicinity and from further afield.

A new ease of travel characterises these movements with not only many more people moving around than ever before, but with greater frequency and over larger distances. The variety of destinations and the range of people travelling is also symptomatic of these contemporary migrations: 'Punjabis, Pathans and Baluchis are moving to Sindh and Karachi as labourers or businessmen. The intellegentsia goes to Geneva and Washington; the businessmen to anywhere in America or Europe where there is business to be done. And, in the past ten years, millions have gone to the Gulf oil states to make their fortunes' (Duncan, 1987, p. 3). Increased mobility of all kinds is thus bringing apparently different kinds of social system with their associated sets of values into increased contact. The result is a new 'openness' in Pakistani society and a greater awareness of the existence of alternatives. Pakistanis everywhere are being exposed to new ideas, either because of those moving in or returning to their area, or because they have themselves moved out. There had, of course, been contact between these different groups before but either it was ignored or their isolation was overemphasised (cf. Burki, 1974). More importantly perhaps, the contact had never before been on this scale. This is epitomised in the dramatic growth of Pakistan's urban population.

Throughout this century the cities in the area that is now Pakistan have been growing steadily, but the increase has been particularly dramatic since Partition: between 1951 and 1961 the urban population increased by 56 per cent (Gardezi, 1966, p. 68) and between 1961 and 1972 by 75 per cent (Shah, 1982, p. 509). Although the rate seems to have slowed in the next decade (1972–81), Pakistan's urban population has continued to rise at a rate far outpacing rural growth (40 per cent and 25 per cent respectively). Table 1.1 illustrates how these rates of growth have affected the size of individual cities.

Part of this growth has obviously been a consequence of natural increase, but it has also been due to migration. Immediately after Partition an estimated one-third of all incoming refugees settled in urban areas mainly in Sindh and Punjab (Afzal, 1974, pp. 70–5; Kennedy, 1957, p. 82). By 1951, 45 per cent of Pakistan's urban population was made up of refugees and in four out of Pakistan's ten largest cities refugees constituted more than half the population (Wilber, 1964, p. 52; Burki, 1980, p. 66). Since then the consistently higher rate of urban growth indicates that migration continues to be important, particularly rural–urban migration within the country itself. In the mid 1970s, for example, the Karachi Development Plan

Table 1.1 Urban growth in Pakistan

	Karachi	Lahore	Hyderabad	Faisalabad (Lyallpur)
1901	136 000	203 000	69 000	9 000
1951	1 068 000	849 000	242 000	197 000
1961	1 912 000	1 296 000	434 000	425 000
1972	3 496 000	2 148 000	624 000	820 000
1981	5 180 562	2 952 689	751 529	1 104 209

Source: Maloney, 1974, p. 525; Demographic Yearbook, 1988.

(1974) estimated that of the approximately 200 000 people being added to the city's population every year, 45 per cent (90 000) were migrants. So far the proportion has remained very much the same.

Of course, successive waves of migration have not only changed the size of cities; they have also changed their character and composition. This is most evident in the case of Karachi which attracted not only the greatest number of *muhajirs* at Partition (replacing the Hindus who had previously dominated urban Sindh and who now moved in the opposite direction) but has continued to draw large numbers of migrants ever since. Most of these have come from NWFP and Punjab and there have been relatively few from Sindh itself. This has clearly affected the feel of the city and some observers have remarked on how it has a 'cultural flavour of its own' (Qureshi, 1986, p. 88): certainly the city's South Asian character has been altered by the influx of so many Pakhtun and Baluch, giving it a 'tribal' dimension never so evident before. But such changes have not only been occurring in Karachi and many of Pakistan's other towns and cities, which although they draw predominantly on more provincial pools of labour, are now similarly characterised by ethnic diversity to varying degrees (for small town growth see Burki, 1974; see also Belokrenitsky, 1974, pp. 244–5). Many Biharis, for example, settled in Lahore in the 1970s, while more recently Peshawar has had to absorb large numbers of refugees from Afghanistan.

Because of the heterogeneous origins of the inhabitants, many of Pakistan's cities thus display a mix of cultures from urban north and central India, and from village and tribal Pakistan. Their former homes remain important for many of these people but in slightly different ways. The *muhajirs* still remember homes in what is now India or Bangladesh but as refugees their ties to their place of origin have been necessarily severed in most cases. For them their new home is a place of exile and this tends to give them a different outlook from those who always lived in what is now Pakistan. For labour migrants who have always lived in Pakistan, however, their place of origin remains a crucial and an active source of reference with which close contact is maintained through regular visiting and participation in life crisis rituals (Karim and Robinson, 1986, p. 36). In fact, those wealthy enough to do so may maintain residences in both places, as many returned migrants have done. Rural patterns of social relations are thus likely to continue to inform urban living however modified they may become in their new setting (Gardezi, 1966, pp. 73–6). For many residents city life is thus characterised by a 'double-rootedness' and this is true not only of those in Pakistani cities, but also of those who have gone abroad.

However, it is not only the ethnic composition of cities that has altered; other urban interest groups have emerged which may cross-cut or reinforce ethnic divisions (cf. Gardezi and Rashid, 1988). Increasing affluence and better access to education has facilitated social mobility, resulting in a much greater diversity of socio–economic groups inhabiting Pakistan's urban areas than those of even a decade ago (see LaPorte, 1985). Some of the greatest changes in the urban class structure have occurred within the middle class whose ranks have been enlarged by returning migrants enriched by labour overseas. New wealth thus often sits uneasily alongside old, and those who feel they are of more established position are often forced to rethink long-accepted forms of precedence. Certainly, the geography of cities like Karachi and Lahore is marked as much by class as by ethnicity and there is good reason to suppose that class, as well as ethnicity, will shape antagonisms in the future. Yet other urban interest groups may cut across class lines; the increased political participation of women during the Zia regime, for example, forced all kinds of women to reflect on their place in Pakistani society, even though it was mainly women from the élite who were most actively involved in protest.

It is this range of different urban interest groups, coupled with the sheer size of cities like Karachi (approximately 8 million) and the concomitant pressure on public services, that has led some observers to predict the imminent collapse of city life (Ahmed, 1987; Duncan, 1989, pp. 165–86). Karachi especially is held to show signs of disintegration and even of 'approaching anarchy', evidence for this being found in the tensions which occasionally erupt into the lanes of

squatter settlements like Orangi (see Selier, Chapter 2 this volume).
Yet despite the existence of a relatively large body of literature on
the demographic and economic consequences of Pakistan's rapid
urbanisation, rather less is known about the cultural dimensions of
this process. Apart from a survey carried out in Karachi on student
attitudes towards family, marriage and dowry (see Korson, 1965,
1967, 1968, 1969) and a study of a community of Christian sweepers
in the same city (Streefland, 1979), there is very little else on urban
culture. In this regard our understanding of Pakistan lags far behind
that for India for which we have a number of such studies (Fox, 1970;
Saberwal, 1976; Vatuk, 1972). While the available literature thus
provides statistics on urban growth, levels of literacy, and standards
of health, it does not offer any view of the inter-personal relations in
urban neighbourhoods, nor of the practical and conceptual adjustments made by those who move to urban areas.

Nor have studies of migration moved much beyond economic and
demographic considerations, despite the fact that large numbers of
returning migrants are beginning to raise new issues for Pakistani
society. By the mid 1980s the Middle Eastern oil boom had reached a
peak and many migrants were beginning to return to Pakistan (despite predicted difficulties about reversing the flow of migration; see
Birks and Sinclair, 1982; Weiner, 1982). Moreover, many of those
who had gone to Britain were also beginning to return as they
reached retirement age or were made redundant. While there are no
official estimates, a survey carried out by ARTEP in 1985 suggests
that on average over 11 500 migrants were returning to Pakistan each
month (Amjad, 1986), and one study estimated that by the mid 1980s
some 400 000 migrants had already returned from the Middle East
alone (Arnold and Shah, 1984). Problems of reintegration clearly
involve not only the economic absorption of such large numbers of
workers who are now accustomed to high wages, but also social and
cultural readjustment. Although the picture may not be quite as
bleak as some think (Gilani, 1985), some returning migrants clearly
do lack the necessary experience to set up their own business or to
find alternative forms of productive investment for their hard-earned
savings. Exposure to societies with higher standards of living also
means that migrants return with raised expectations about non-
pecuniary objectives such as access to health and education (see
Birks and Sinclair, 1982). Not least returning migrants must reinte-
grate themselves into the social structure they left behind and in
which their income may have leap-frogged those of families who did

not migrate; social relationships are thus likely to suffer under the strain of renegotiation as when traditional authority is challenged by new leaders whose position is based on migrant wealth (see Ahmed, 1981; Pastner, S., 1984b). In some cases, this social and cultural dislocation has reportedly manifest itself as a psychological disorder known as 'Dubai Syndrome', a term used to refer to a range of sexual, guilt and depressive symptoms which can afflict migrants and members of their families throughout the cycle of migration (see Ahmed, 1984; Arnold and Shah, 1984).

The Significance of Migratory Movements

In Pakistan, people are thus continually having to adjust as they move from one arena to another: from village to town or city, from home to abroad, and increasingly as returning migrants. The question remains: how is this complex set of movements to be understood theoretically?

Most political economic analyses of migration have tended to construe labour migrants as fundamentally passive, 'pushed' and 'pulled' by forces well beyond their control. Yet if there is a theoretical challenge in the study of migration, it lies in comprehending the complex social processes and cultural movements migratory movements set in motion, and the moral dimensions of time–space management such movements imply. Recent sociological interest in the relation between time, space and locality, as basic parameters of social analysis (see Mellor, 1989, pp. 244–5), makes the study of migration of particular significance: in migration the people themselves must manage moral relations spanning great distances and disjunctions of both space and time.

Early anthropological studies of circulatory labour migration evolved as a critique of simplistic one-way acculturation theories. They stressed situational change as individual migrants moved back and forth between town and countryside (see Gluckman, 1961; Mitchell, 1966). Town and country were regarded as fundamentally different social systems, and individuals' behaviour was determined by the system they found themselves in: they were townsmen in town, tribesmen in the countryside. Migration, according to this view, was not regarded as entirely negative since it supported the reproduction and perpetuation of tribal structures (see Eades, 1987). Subsequent Marxist political–economic models of migration posited a dual economy based on a fundamental disjunction between capitalist and peasant modes of production (Amin, 1974; Meillassoux, 1981). The articulation between the two modes of production was seen to be fundamentally exploitative, and migratory movements were regarded as determined, indeed overdetermined, by capitalist interests and especially the demand for cheap labour. Peasant or domestic modes of production allowed for the reproduction of this cheap reserve labour force at little cost to capitalist enterprises. Recent analyses of the world system and international division of labour further document the movement of both capital and worker on a global scale, a movement mainly orchestrated from a limited number of global cities.

The dual economy model has been challenged for failing to take account of a burgeoning small-scale informal economy, underpinned by familial and ethnic networks and credit relations, and relying heavily on household labour (see for example Eades, 1987; Escobar, Gonzalez and Roberts, 1987; Gregory, 1982; Hart, 1973; Nadvi, 1989). There is now a growing recognition of the key economic role fulfilled by the so-called 'informal' economy. Its enterprises absorb a large proportion of the apparently surplus incoming labour in the Third World's expanding urban centres. Thus Roberts, while basically endorsing a dual economic model (Roberts, 1978, p. 110), nevertheless recognises the central significance of the urban 'bazaar' economy (ibid, p. 130). Nadvi, in a recent paper, documents the rapid expansion of both rural and urban informal enterprises in Pakistan, and particularly in the Punjab, underpinned by caste, regional and ethnic moral bonds:

> The importance of such *biradari* or ethnicity based information networks is underlined in an urban environment where informal sector service (retail, transport etc), construction and manufacturing activities are expanding rapidly. According to one estimate, 69% of Pakistan's urban labour force was to be found in the informal sector in 1972–3. More recent data for the manufacturing sector shows that 66% of the labour force engaged in manufacturing in Punjab and 44% in Sindh were employed by informal household and small manufacturing enterprises in 1983–4. (Nadvi, 1989, p. 17)

A more far-reaching and fundamental criticism can also be levelled against dual economic models. Such a critique goes beyond a recognition of the role of the 'informal economy' in mediating between the extremes of capitalist and precapitalist modes of production and affecting urban labour markets. The informal economy, it can be argued, is only part of a whole series of 'informal' economic strategies pursued by migrants with far-reaching consequences. The critique rests on two basic assumptions:

(a) that the 'economic activism' of the poor (Roberts, 1978, p. 130) has a major impact on localised capitalist markets and their historical development;
(b) that economic strategy is culturally constituted and precipitates religio–cultural, as well as economic, changes, which in turn impact on the local–national economy.

Labour migration is very often a disorganised social movement in which scores of thousands of individuals face similar predicaments, and make similar economic choices based on similar moral premises and values. It is the collective impact of this individual decision-making multiplied on an enormous scale which redirects the course of development of a local, historically specific capitalist economy (see Selier, 1988, on the 'individual-structural' debate). Chapters 2, 3 and 4 of this book all deal with different aspects of such collective decision-making and its effect on both the local and national economies.

Nowhere is the impact of migrant collective decision-making more evident than in the invasion and appropriation of urban space – with its consequent effect on urban housing markets. Apparently worthless and temporarily occupied tracts of land are transformed through the frugality, hard work, investment strategies and political activism of the poor into highly valuable, commercial real estate.

Selier (Chapter 2) analyses the movement into and investment in housing of refugees and labour migrants in Karachi's squatter settlements (*katchi abadis*). He argues against simplistic models of urban spatial settlement, and suggests instead that specific social and situational circumstances of migrants and refugees determine levels of investment, place of settlement, rapidity of house acquisition, and so on. With its enormous refugee *muhajir* population, Karachi is a city whose lower classes regard house ownership, even with illegal tenure, as of the highest priority. It is also a city in which both internal labour migrants and refugees settle (or are settled) in relation to pre-existing social networks of kin and coethnics. These provide the necessary information for obtaining jobs and permanent housing.

Van Der Linden (Chapter 3) argues that squatter dwellers regard their houses as constituting a major source of economic security in emergencies. They thus invest heavily in the improvement of their dwellings as the legality of their tenure is gradually established. This belief in housing as security becomes an ideology endorsing continuing investment, with long-term effect on the housing market.

Noman (Chapter 4), analysing the impact of international migration from Pakistan to the Middle East, argues that 'There is, perhaps, no historical parallel of remittances having resulted in such a rapid and wide distribution of benefits among the poorer sectors of society' (p. 83). This, he says, is remarkable especially in the light of the fact that asset distribution in Pakistan remains greatly askew. The sudden – and temporary – increase in wealth is not invested by individual migrants haphazardly: it follows a predictable and hence collective pattern, and thus has a major (mainly beneficial) impact on the local economy, starting with the construction industry which in turn affects the whole manufacturing sector:

Aware of the temporary nature of his increase in income, the migrant worker has tended to use most of his income to acquire assets for his family. Not surprisingly, the main emphasis has been on a house, acquiring consumer durables and accumulating surplus for setting up small-scale business enterprises upon eventual return. (p. 83)

Seen together, the three chapters have several implications. One has to do with the impact of *where* migrants decide to migrate to. At one extreme is short-term international 'target' migration and long-term refugee movements. Each is associated with specific patterns of economic investment. A less extreme form of migration is long-distance, long-term circulatory migration, such as that of millions of Pathans to Karachi. This type of migration has created a primate city divorced from its hinterland (Nadvi, 1989). In contrast to this form of migration is the more localised urban migration in the Punjab where there are seven ranked major industrial centres, and a large urban informal sector linked to its rural counterpart and centred around construction and agricultural mechanisation (ibid., p. 13). In the Punjab, as against Karachi, town and country are 'organically' linked within a single, integrated economic and social system.

Squatter settlement also exposes the inadequacy of the local state and its inability to provide proper public services (on this as a general feature of cities see Castells, 1983). The inadequate provision of urban services is evident in all fields, and particularly so in the medical field. In Pakistan, this has led to the emergence of a thriving *medical* informal economy, as Lyon shows (Chapter 7). Medicine in Pakistan is highly stratified. A small élite has access to the best in modern medicine (much of it private and entrepreneurial), while the lower classes have access to a wide variety of (private) traditional and eclectic medical practitioners (cf. Weiss, 1985). The question of how the poor deal with affliction in cities is, however, as Lyon argues, not simply a matter of service provision. It is also a moral and cultural question. The afflicted seek a personalised service and they wish to be treated with respect according to local cultural views about prestigious and highly valued forms of medical treatment. Patients thus determine medical practice, as well as suffering the consequences of inadequate provision.

Labour migrants are thus not mere puppets, entirely subordinated to a capitalist system. It is, of course, undoubtedly true that the vast movement of people from their natal villages in search of work is precipitated by class and capitalist strategies within a world economic system. Once set in motion, however, the movement develops its own, localised trajectory. It becomes part of an interlinked totality of related processes (see Selier, 1988, p. 12). The case of Karachi illustrates this interlinkage all too graphically. Migrants and refugees have invaded and been settled in different quarters of the city and have come to monopolise different economic niches. Urban territory has been appropriated and territorialised. Its value in the housing market has risen as both services and properties have improved and as the city has expanded. The ethnic and regional basis of this territoriality has, as Alavi shows (Chapter 8), led to ethnic violence on a vast scale in conflicts that draw ideologically on regional tensions and resentments in the nation at large. While localised and reflecting the special problems of Karachi, the conflicts feed into other social movements. At their root, they reflect competition over scarce resources: in the urban context over urban territory and ethnic economic monopolies; in the national context over allocations and resources provided by the state.

In the urban context the role of the state has also been undermined as it increasingly loses control of the management of housing allocations or the provision of services to urban dwellers. Illegal subdividers, with state collusion, control the 'informal' housing market (on a similar process in Africa see Amis, 1987). As the rule of law is publicly challenged and state authority undermined, the state loses the ability to control local conflicts and illegal practices. Thus a further complex process, precipitated by refugee and migrant movements, is established.

In general, then, we may say that migrants *create* value as active participants within a capitalist economy, despite their poverty, because they act collectively, first, in terms of commonly held cultural and moral priorities and second, through valued pre-existing social networks. Understanding and predicting the course of collective investment patterns hinges on a close, more anthropological, analysis of the priorities, aspirations and social networking of different categories of migrants/refugees. It is in this sense that Selier's subtle distinctions between four categories of migrants – commuters, circulatory migrants, working-life migrants and lifetime migrants (1988, p. 70) is important, for each refers to a different – and on a large-scale, collective – relationship to the economy, different modes of investment, territorial claims, and so on. So too the notion of the 'expanded household', a household composed of spatially separated units acting jointly for productive, reproductive and consumption purposes (ibid, pp. 25–8) should be central to any political–economic analysis of migration and urbanisation.

It is also in this sense that the study of urbanism – the experience, cultural practice and economic rationality of town dwellers – becomes crucial to an understanding of broader political–economic processes. Urban ethnographies of Pakistan are, as mentioned, almost non-existent, and most qualitative data is based on the personal experience or casual observations of Pakistani political economists, or gleaned from interview material. Paradoxically, perhaps, the study of overseas Pakistanis, particularly in Britain, is much richer, with early work by Dahya and Saifullah Khan followed by major ethnographies by Jeffery (1976), Anwar (1979), Shaw (1988) and Werbner (1989a). Much of this ethnography focuses on settlement and investment patterns in housing and petty entrepreneurship (see Dahya, 1974; Werbner, 1984, 1987), and on the meaning of *zat*, *biradari* and interhousehold networks in town. More recently, there has been a move to study the public arena of communal politics and religiosity, and in this volume Werbner (Chapter 9) analyses the political culture and factionalist tendencies evident in British Pakistani communal politics. Werbner shows that factional formation is based on fundamental cultural premises commonly also found in South Asian urban and regional politics. She raises the question of why political violence appears to be so endemic to Pakistani politics in the public arena.

Fischer (Chapter 5), in his study of rehoused refugees and migrants in Lahore, raises the general question of why traditional categories such as *zat* and *biradari* persist in town in multicaste communities, although they are no longer underpinned by occupational inter-dependency and corporate ownership. Basing his analysis on a subtle communication–information model, he argues that these cultural notions continue to be significant because they 'provide a category of social organisation that is mobile because it is distributed . . . This inbuilt relationship provides a source of mates and potential aid to the incoming migrant' (see p. 98). In theoretical terms 'change requires inherent variation, and interpretation requires inherent stability'. Traditional categories allow for a relatively fixed (and hence communicable) construction of meaning in a context in which circumstances and social practices are dynamic and changing. Based on underlying premises of control and ranking, a high proportion of intercaste marriages continue nevertheless to be understood in terms of endogamous values (cf. Holy, 1989, p. 90). Fischer's chapter thus makes a contribution to the continuing debate on the nature of Muslim caste in general and urban caste in particular, initiated by Barth (1960) and Dumont (1972 (1966)), carried forward by Ahmad (1978) and developed most recently in a series of articles in *Contributions to Indian Sociology* (see, for example, Lindholm, 1986a; Werbner, 1989b) and elsewhere (Donnan, 1988). Evident also from the Indian urban anthropological literature is the expansion and reconstruction of caste categories in town (for a review, see Fuller, 1986).

Fischer studied a multicaste community not unlike the one studied by Vatuk (1972). Caste-based *mohallas*, especially of artisan or merchant castes, have been studied in India (see Mines, 1972; Kumar, 1988; Searle-Chatterjee, 1981). These neighbourhoods often form encapsulated, highly organised communities. Yet the persistence of caste and supercastism in mixed localities as a specifically urban phenomenon is the more prevalent phenomenon throughout South Asia.

The extent to which urbanism in Pakistan has been 'ruralised' is a question which needs, perhaps, to be addressed. In a brilliant essay on the status of women and the rise of the women's movement in Pakistan, Mumtaz and Shaheed remind us that 'much of Pakistan's urban population in the large cities consists of newcomers to city life who have little to do with the pre-existing subculture of the city's elite' (1987, p. 131). Pakistani cities are marked by a 'cultural gap . . . between urban upper and upper middle classes and the rest of urban society'. This gap between the upper classes, highly influenced by western liberal ideas, and the rising conservative–religious middle class and lower classes is at times, they say, a 'veritable chasm' (ibid.). The women's movement was in part a response to the growing influence of this conservative middle class, and was in many respects an urban phenomenon.

Religiosity and ethnicity have been the two major forces, apart from migration, which have shaped Pakistani political realities since independence. Although not specifically urban, they are manifested in their most 'intensified' form in the large cities (thus Fuller argues that 'if the city is the locus of "intensification" then . . . comparative urban anthropology could be precisely the cross-cultural study of the form, process and causes of that intensification, including the impact on it of the formal characteristics of cities' (Fuller, 1986, p. 6). The women's movement, formed to contest the Islamisation policies of the state and especially the erosion of women's legal rights, was an urban based movement. Alavi (Chapter 6) analyses both the impact of this movement and the significance of female labour in Pakistani cities today. He argues that paradoxically, female labour, because of its home-based nature, has been associated with increased conservatism expressed in more extreme *purdah* and female subordination (although Fischer, Chapter 5, presents a somewhat different picture of urban *purdah*).

In an important synthesising account of the link between political and religious establishments in Pakistan, Sherani (Chapter 10) argues against modernisation theories which regard urbanisation and the rise of capitalism as associated with increasing rational secularism. Echoing Benedict Anderson's analysis of the rise of print capitalism (1983), he argues that the increase in literacy and print capitalism in Pakistan, itself associated with processes of urbanisation and industrialisation, has generated *intensified* religiosity, as hagiographies of saints are disseminated through books and the popular press. So too, he argues, both secular–democratic and military regimes have consistently sought the support of key religious figures and parties in the complex factional politics of Pakistani society, thus strengthening their broader national influence. In Britain, urban mosques have become the focus of élite competition and communal politics and form an important base for the religious establishment as Werbner shows (Chapter 9). One may surmise that the same could well be true in cities in Pakistan itself.

Islamic revivalism or fundamentalism has historically been urban based (Metcalf, 1982), and the current fundamentalist revival is often related to the alienation and confusion generated by too rapid social change. Thus Hiro argues that with the rise in Middle East oil prices

> cities have attracted vast numbers of migrants from villages. They feel lost and rootless in the new environment. This reservoir of alienated masses packed into the poor quarters of urban centres provide a ready audience and recruiting ground for radical and revolutionary groups, secular and religious. Muslim fundamentalists try to rally the alienated and underprivileged on the basis of Islam. (Hiro, 1988, p. 274)

Despite its apparent persuasiveness, such an analysis needs to be treated with some caution. Cities may well be the centres of Islamic revival but not necessarily because their inhabitants are alienated: as we have seen, they tend to be embedded in networks of kin and friends and to construct their current experiences and practices in terms of culturally familiar ideas and categories. More important is the fact that religious gatherings and mosques often become in cities a focus of communal public activities and status achievement, as well as focal meeting places. As such, the power of mosque-based religious scholars and leaders, politically organised, is enhanced and religious ideology often comes to dominate the public domain. The endemic corruption of state officials and the state's evident inability to provide adequate urban services or to uphold law and order in its large cities is explained in terms of a deteriorating social and moral order. Hence an almost millenarian vision of Islam is evoked, of a perfect Islamic state in which control (see Chapter 5) is orderly and absolute. Ahmed's case study (Chapter 11) which concludes the book discusses an instance of such millenarianism as it impacts on changing rural society, a society in which a prior order is undermined by returning migrants from the Middle East and the wealth they bring with them.

As traditional divisions of class are challenged by urbanisation and migrant wealth, people all over Pakistan are becoming more conscious of wider ideologies and world views. They are evolving new urban life-styles, novel work and consumption patterns, and different cultural ways of spanning space. This complex transformation is not, as the contributors to this volume stress, simply towards 'modernisation', 'acculturation', 'alienation', 'impoverishment' or 'westernisation'. Instead, complex cultural forms embracing traditional images and new practices are evolving within an enormously expanding 'informal' self-initiated economy. This book tries to capture some of these key processes.

References

Addleton, J. (1981), 'The Role of Migration in Development: Pakistan and the Gulf', *The Fletcher Forum*, 5 (2), pp. 319–32.
Addleton, J. (1984), 'The Impact of International Migration on Economic Development in Pakistan', *Asian Survey*, 24 (5), pp. 574–96.
Afzal, M. (1974), *The Population of Pakistan* (Islamabad: Pakistan Institute of Development Economics).
Ahmad, I. (ed.) (1978), *Caste and Social Stratification among Muslims in India* (Delhi: Manohar Book Service).
Ahmad, S. (1971), 'Islam and Pakistani Peasants', in A. Ahmed (ed.), 'Religion and Society in Pakistan', *Contributions to Asian Studies*, 2, pp. 93–104.
Ahmad, S. (1974), 'A Village in Pakistani Punjab: Jalpana', in C. Maloney (ed.), *South Asia: Seven Community Profiles* (New York: Holt, Rinehart & Winston), pp. 131–72.
Ahmad, S. (1977), *Class and Power in a Punjabi Village* (Lahore: Punjab Adbi Markaz).
Ahmed, A. S. (1976), *Millennium and Charisma among Pathans: A Critical Essay in Social Anthropology* (London: Routledge & Kegan Paul).
Ahmed, A. S. (1980), *Pukhtun Economy and Society: Traditional Structure and Economic Development in a Tribal Society* (London: Routledge & Kegan Paul).
Ahmed, A. S. (1981), 'The Arab Connection: Emergent Models of Social Structure among Pakistani Tribesmen', *Asian Affairs*, 62 (2), pp. 167–72.
Ahmed, A. S. (1982), 'Lineage Politics and Economic Development: A Case Study from the Northwest Frontier Province, Pakistan', in S. Pastner and L. Flam (eds), *Anthropology in Pakistan: Recent Socio–Cultural and Archaeological Perspectives* (Ithaca, NY: Cornell University South Asia Program, South Asia Occasional Papers and Theses No. 8), pp. 40–50.
Ahmed, A. S. (1983a), 'Islam and the District Paradigm: Emergent Trends in Contemporary Muslim Society', *Contributions to Indian Sociology*, 17 (2), pp. 155–83.
Ahmed, A. S. (1983b), *Religion and Politics in Muslim Society: Order and Conflict in Pakistan* (Cambridge: Cambridge University Press).
Ahmed, A. S. (1984), '"Dubai Chalo": Problems in the Ethnic Encounter between Middle Eastern and South Asian Muslim Societies', *Asian Affairs*, 15, pp. 262–76.

Ahmed, A. S. (1986), *Pakistan Society: Islam, Ethnicity and Leadership in South Asia* (Karachi: Oxford University Press).

Ahmed, A. S. (1987), 'The Approach of Anarchy', *Far Eastern Economic Review*, 19 February, pp. 40–1.

Ahmed, A. S. (1988), 'Faith and Fire in Baluchistan: Trial by Ordeal among the Bugtis', *Newsletter of Baluchistan Studies*, 5, pp. 3–26.

Ahmed, A. S. (forthcoming), *Stress and Structure in Pakistan Society: The Politics of Ethnicity in the Post-Colonial State*, paper presented to the East–West Center, Honolulu.

Ahmed, A. S. and Z. Ahmed (1981), 'Mor and Tor: Binary and Opposing Models of Pukhtun Femalehood', in T. S. Epstein and R. Watts (eds), *The Endless Day: Some Case Material on Asian Rural Women* (Oxford: Pergamon Press), pp. 31–46.

Ahmed, A. S. and D. M. Hart (eds) (1984), *Islam in Tribal Societies: From the Atlas to the Indus* (London: Routledge & Kegan Paul).

Ahmed, F. (1976), 'Pakistan: The New Dependence', *Race and Class* XVIII (1).

Alavi, H. (1971), 'The Politics of Dependence: A Village in West Punjab', *South Asian Review*, 4 (2), pp. 111–28.

Alavi, H. (1972), 'Kinship in West Punjab Villages', *Contributions to Indian Sociology*, 6, pp. 1–27.

Alavi, H. (1973), 'Peasant Classes and Primordial Loyalties', *Journal of Peasant Studies*, 1 (1).

Alavi, H. (1988), 'Pakistan and Islam: Ethnicity and Ideology', in H. Alavi and F. Halliday (eds), *State and Ideology in the Middle East and Pakistan* (London: Macmillan), pp. 64–111.

Alavi, H. (1989), 'Politics of Ethnicity in India and Pakistan', in H. Alavi and J. Harriss (eds), *Sociology of Developing Societies: South Asia* (London: Macmillan), pp. 222–46.

Amin, S. (ed.) (1974), *Modern Migrations in West Africa* (London: Oxford University Press).

Amis, P. (1987), 'Migration, Urban Poverty, and the Housing Market: the Nairobi Case', in J. Eades (ed.), *Migrants, Workers, and the Social Order* (London: Tavistock), pp. 249–68.

Amjad, R. (1986), 'Impact of Workers Remittances from the Middle East on Pakistan's Economy', *Pakistan Development Review* 25, pp. 757–82.

Anderson, B. (1983), *Imagined Communities: Reflections on the Origin and Spread of Nationalism* (London: Verso).

Anwar, M. (1979), *The Myth of Return: Pakistanis in Britain* (London: Heinemann).

Arnold, F. and N. Shah (1984), 'Asian Labour Migration to the Middle East', *International Migration Review*, 18 (2), 294–318.

Asad, T. (1972), 'Market Model, Class Structure and Consent: A Reconsideration of Swat Political Organization', *Man*, 7, pp. 74–94.

Aschenbrenner, J. C. (1967), *Endogamy and Social Status in a West Punjabi Village* (University of Minnesota: mimeograph of Ph.d. dissertation).

Ballard, R. (1987), 'The Political Economy of Migration: Pakistan, Britain, and the Middle East', in J. Eades (ed.) *Migrants, Workers and the Social Order* (London: Tavistock), pp. 17–41.

Ballard, R. (1989), 'Effects of Labour Migration from Pakistan', in H. Alavi and J. Harriss (eds), *Sociology of Developing Societies: South Asia* (London: Macmillan), pp. 112–22.

Barth, F. (1958), 'Ecological Relationships of Ethnic Groups in Swat, North Pakistan', *American Anthropologist*, 60, pp. 1079–88.

Barth, F. (1959a), *Political Leadership among Swat Pathans* (London: Athlone Press).

Barth, F. (1959b), 'Segmentary Opposition and the Theory of Games: A Study of Pathan Organization', *Journal of the Royal Anthropological Institute*, 89, pp. 5–21.

Barth, F. (1960), 'The System of Social Stratification in Swat, North Pakistan', in E. Leach (ed.), *Aspects of Caste in South India, Ceylon and Northwest Pakistan* (Cambridge: Cambridge University Press), pp. 113–48.

Barth, F. (1969), 'Pathan Identity and Its Maintenance', in F. Barth (ed.), *Ethnic Groups and Boundaries* (London: George Allen & Unwin), pp. 117–34.

Belokrenitsky, V. (1974), 'The Urbanization Process and the Social Structure of the Urban Population in Pakistan', *Asian Survey*, 14 (3), 244–57.

Berland, J. (1982), *No Five Fingers Are Alike: Cognitive Amplifiers in Social Context* (Cambridge, Mass.: Harvard University Press).

Berland, J. (1983), 'Peripatetic Strategies in South Asia: Skills as Capital among Nomadic Artisans and Entertainers', *Nomadic Peoples*, 13, pp. 17–34.

Bilquees, F. and S. Hamid (1981), *Impact of International Migration on Women and Children Left Behind*, Research Report Series No. 115 (Islamabad: Pakistan Institute of Development Economics).

Birks, J. S. and C. A. Sinclair (1982), 'The Socio–Economic Determinants of Intra-Regional Migration', in United Nations Economic Commission for Western Asia, *International Migration in the Arab World*, proceedings of an ECWA Population Conference 1981 Vol. 2. (Beirut), pp. 733–52.

Burki, S. J. (1974), 'Development of Towns: The Pakistan Experience', *Asian Survey*, 14 (8), pp. 751–62.

Burki, S. J. (1980), 'What Migration to the Middle East May Mean for Pakistan', *Journal of South Asian and Middle East Studies*, III, 3, pp. 47–66.

Caroe, O. (1958), *The Pathans* (London: Macmillan).

Castells, M. (1983), *The City and the Grassroots: A Cross-Cultural Theory of Urban Social Movements* (London: Edward Arnold).

Dahya, B. (1974), 'The Nature of Pakistani Ethnicity in Industrial Cities in Britain', in A. Cohen (ed.), *Urban Ethnicity* (London: Tavistock), pp. 77–118.

Demographic Yearbook (1988), *Demographic Yearbook 1986, 38th Issue* (New York: United Nations).

Donnan, H. (1985), 'The Rules and Rhetoric of Marriage Negotiations among the Dhund Abbasi of Northeast Pakistan', *Ethnology*, 24, pp. 183–96.

Donnan, H. (1988), *Marriage among Muslims: Preference and Choice in Northern Pakistan* (Leiden: E. J. Brill).

28 *Introduction*

28   *Introduction*

Duncan, E. (1987), 'Living on the Edge: A Survey of Pakistan', *The Economist*, 17 January.

Duncan, E. (1989) *Breaking the Curfew: A Political Journey Through Pakistan* (London: Michael Joseph).

Dumont, L. (1972), *Homo Hierarchicus* (London: Paladin).

Dupree, L. (1984), 'Tribal Warfare in Afghanistan and Pakistan: A Reflection of the Segmentary Lineage System', in A. S. Ahmed and D. M. Hart (eds), *Islam in Tribal Societies: From the Atlas to the Indus* (London: Routledge & Kegan Paul), pp. 266–86.

Eades, J. (ed.) (1987), 'Anthropologists and Migrants: Changing Models and Realities', in J. Eades (ed.) *Migrants, Workers and the Social Order* (London: Tavistock), pp. 1–16.

ECWA (1982) 'Socio–Economic Characteristics of International Migrants in the Gulf States', in United Nations Economic Commission for Western Asia, *International Migration in the Arab World*, proceedings of an ECWA Population Conference 1981, Vol. 2 (Beirut), pp. 685–731.

Eglar, Z. (1957), 'Punjabi Village Life', in S. Maron (ed.), *Pakistan: Society and Culture* (New Haven: Human Relations Area Files), pp. 62–80.

Eglar, Z. (1960), *A Punjabi Village in Pakistan* (New York: Columbia University Press).

Escobar, A., M. Gonzalez and B. Roberts (1987), 'Migration, Labour Markets and the International Economy: Jalisco, Mexico and the United States', in J. Eades (ed.), *Migrants, Workers and the Social Order* (London: Tavistock), pp. 42–64.

Ewing, K. (1982), 'Sufis and Adepts: The Islamic and Hindu Sources of Spiritual Power among Punjabi Muslims and Christian Sweepers', in S. Pastner and L. Flam (eds), *Anthropology in Pakistan*, South Asia Occasional Papers and Theses No. 8 (Ithaca, NY: Cornell University), pp. 74–88.

Ewing, K. (1983), 'The Politics of Sufism: Redefining the Saints of Pakistan', *Journal of Asian Studies*, 42, pp. 251–68.

Ewing, K. (1984a), 'The Sufi as Saint, Curer, and Exorcist in Modern Pakistan', *Contributions to Asian Studies*, 18, pp. 106–14.

Ewing, K. (1984b), 'Malangs of the Punjab: Intoxication or Adab as the Path to God?', in B. Metcalf (ed.), *Moral Conduct and Authority: The Place of Adab in South Asian Islam* (Berkeley: University of California Press), pp. 357–71.

Fox, R. G. (1970), *Urban India: Society, Space and Image*, Comparative Studies of Asia, Monograph Occasional Paper Series No. 10 (Durham: Duke University Press).

Fuller, C. J. (1986), 'A Selective Review of Urban Anthropology in India', paper presented to the South Asian Anthropologists Annual Meeting.

Gardezi, H. (1966), 'Urbanization in Pakistan', in H. Gardezi (ed.), *Sociology in Pakistan* (Lahore: Department of Sociology, University of Punjab), pp. 63–76.

Gardezi, H. (1968), 'The Marri: A Case Study of Tribal Life in Baluchistan', in H. Chaudhari, M. Fayyaz, M. Raza, A. Rizwani and M. Akhtar (eds), *Pakistan Sociological Perspectives* (Lahore: Pakistan Sociological Association).

Gardezi, H. N. and J. Rashid (eds) (1988), 'Pakistan at the Crossroads: The Contradictions of Class, Ethnicity, and Gender', *South Asia Bulletin*, 8 (1 & 2), special double issue.

Gilani, I. (1983), *Left Behind or Left Out: A Study of the Left Behind Families of Overseas Pakistanis*, Pakistan Institute of Public Opinion, Migration Report No. 1.

Gilani, I. (1985), *Citizens, Slaves, Guest-Workers: The Dynamics of Labour Migration from South Asia* (Islamabad: Institute of Policy Studies).

Gilani, I., M. F. Khan and M. Iqbal (1981), *Labour Migration from Pakistan to the Middle East and Its Impact on the Domestic Economy*, Research Report Series No. 126 (Islamabad: Pakistan Institute of Development Economics).

Gluckman, M. (1961), 'Anthropological Problems Arising from the African Industrial Revolution', in A. Southall (ed.), *Social Change in Modern Africa* (London: Oxford University Press).

Gregory, C. A. (1982), *Gifts and Commodities* (London: Academic Press).

Guisinger, S. E. (1986), 'The Impact of Temporary Worker Migration on Pakistan', in S. J. Burki and R. Laporte (eds), *Pakistan's Development Priorities* (Karachi: Oxford University Press), pp. 201–23.

Hafeez-ur-Rehman (1984), 'Urs of Golra Sharif', *The Muslim* (Islamabad), 30 November.

Halliday, F. (1977), 'Migration and the Labour Force in Oil-Producing States of the Middle East', *Development and Change*, 8, pp. 263–91.

Hart, D. M. (1985), *Guardians of the Khaibar Pass: The Social Organisation and History of the Afridis of Pakistan* (Lahore: Vanguard Books).

Hart, K. (1973) 'Informal Income Opportunities and Urban Employment in Ghana', *Journal of Modern African Studies*, 11, pp. 61–89.

Hiro, D. (1988), *Islamic Fundamentalism* (London: Paladin).

Holy, L. (1989), *Kinship, Honour and Solidarity: Cousin Marriage in the Middle East* (Manchester: Manchester University Press).

Honigmann, J. J. (1958), *Three Pakistan Villages* (Chapel Hill: University of North Carolina, Institute for Research in Social Science).

Inayatullah (1958), 'Caste, Patti and Faction in the Life of a Punjab Village', *Sociologus*, 8, pp. 170–86.

Inayatullah (1959), 'Democracy in Rural Communities in Pakistan', *Sociologus*, 9, pp. 36–47.

Jeffery, P. (1976), *Migrants and Refugees: Muslim and Christian Pakistani Families in Bristol* (Cambridge: Cambridge University Press).

Jettmar, K. (1986), *The Religions of the Hindu Kush: Vol. 1, The Religion of the Kafirs*. (Warminster: Aris & Phillips).

Karim, M. S. and W. C. Robinson (1986), 'The Migration Situation in Pakistan: An Analytical Review', in F. Selier and M. S. Karim (eds), *Migration in Pakistan: Theories and Facts* (Lahore: Vanguard Books), pp. 21–39.

Keiser, R. L. (1986), 'Death Enmity in Thull: Organized Vengeance and Social Change in a Kohistani Community', *American Ethnologist*, 13 (3), pp. 489–505.

Kennedy, M. J. (1957), 'Punjabi Urban Society', in S. Maron (ed.), *Pakistan: Society and Culture* (New Haven: Human Relations Area Files), pp. 81–103.

Korson, J. H. (1965), 'Age and Social Status at Marriage: Karachi, 1961–64', *Pakistan Development Review*, 5 (4), pp. 586–600.

Korson, J. H. (1967), 'Dower and Social Class in an Urban Muslim Community', *Journal of Marriage and the Family*, 29, pp. 527–33.

Korson, J. H. (1968), 'Residential Propinquity as a Factor in Mate Selection in an Urban Muslim Society', *Journal of Marriage and the Family*, 30, pp. 518–27.

Korson, J. H. (1969), 'Student Attitudes Towards Mate Selection in a Muslim Society', *Journal of Marriage and the Family*, 31, pp. 153–65.

Kumar, N. (1988), *The Artisans of Banaras* (Princeton: Princeton University Press).

Kurin, R. (1983a), 'Modernisation and Traditionalisation: Hot and Cold Agriculture in Punjab, Pakistan', *South Asian Anthropology*, 4 (2), pp. 65–75.

Kurin, R. (1983b), 'Indigenous Agronomics and Agricultural Development in the Indus Basin', *Human Organisation*, 42 (4), pp. 283–94.

Kurin, R. (1983c), 'The Structure of Blessedness at a Muslim Shrine in Pakistan', *Journal of Middle Eastern Studies*.

Kurin, R. (1984), 'Morality, Personhood and the Exemplary Life: Popular Conceptions of Muslims in Paradise', in B. Metcalf (ed.), *Moral Conduct and Authority: The Place of Adab in South Asian Islam* (Berkeley: University of California Press).

Kurin, R. (1988), 'The Culture of Ethnicity in Pakistan', in K. Ewing (ed.), *Shari'at and Ambiguity in South Asian Islam* (Berkeley: University of California Press), pp. 220–47.

Kurin, R. and C. Morrow (1985), 'Patterns of Solidarity in a Punjabi Muslim Village', *Contributions to Indian Sociology*, 19 (2), pp. 235–49.

LaPorte, R. (1985), 'Urban Groups and the Zia Regime', in C. Baxter (ed.), *Zia's Pakistan: Politics and Stability in a Frontline State* (Boulder: Westview Press), pp. 7–22.

Lefebvre, A. (1986), *International Labour Migration from Two Pakistani Villages with Different Forms of Agriculture*, Project Paper A.86.6 (Copenhagen: Centre for Development Research).

Lewis, P. (1985), *Pirs, Shrines and Pakistani Islam* (Rawalpindi: Christian Study Centre Series No. 20).

Lindholm, C. (1977), 'The Segmentary Lineage System: Its Applicability to Pakistan's Political Structure', in A. Embree (ed.), *Pakistan's Western Borderlands* (Durham, NC: Carolina Academic Press), pp. 41–66.

Lindholm, C. (1979), 'Contemporary Politics in a Tribal Society: An Example from Swat District, NWFP, Pakistan', *Asian Survey*, 19, pp. 485–505.

Lindholm, C. (1981), 'The Structure of Violence among The Swat Pakhtun', *Ethnology*, 20 (2), pp. 147–56.

Lindholm, C. (1982a), *Generosity and Jealousy: The Swat Pakhtun of Northern Pakistan* (New York: Columbia University Press).

Lindholm, C. (1982b), 'Models of Segmentary Political Action: The Examples of Swat and Dir, NWFP, Pakistan', in S. Pastner and L. Flam (eds), *Anthropology in Pakistan: Recent Socio–Cultural and Archaeological Perspectives*, South Asia Occasional Papers and Theses No. 8 (Ithaca, NY: Cornell University South Asia Program), pp. 21–39.

Lindholm, C. (1986a), 'Caste in Islam and the Problem of Deviant Systems: A Critique of Recent Theory', *Contributions to Indian Sociology*, 20 (1), pp. 61–73.

Lindholm, C. (1986b), 'Leadership Categories and Social Processes in Islam: The Cases of Dir and Swat', *Journal of Anthropological Research*, 42 (1), pp. 1–13.

Maloney, C. (1974), *Peoples of South Asia* (New York: Holt, Rinehart & Winston).

Mayer, A. C. (1967), 'Pir and Murshid: An Aspect of Religious Leadership in West Pakistan', *Middle Eastern Studies*, 3 (2), pp. 160–9.

Meillassoux, C. (1981), *Maidens, Meal and Money: Capitalism and the Domestic Economy*. (Cambridge: Cambridge University Press).

Mellor, R. (1989), 'Urban Sociology: A Trend Report', *Sociology*, 23, pp. 241–60.

Metcalf, B. D. (1982), *Islamic Revival in British India: Deoband, 1860–1900* (Princeton: Princeton University Press).

Mines, M. (1972), *Muslim Merchants: The Economic Behaviour of an Indian Muslim Community* (New Delhi: Shri Sharma).

Mitchell, J. C. (1966), 'Theoretical Orientations in African Urban Studies', in M. Banton (ed.), *The Social Anthropology of Complex Societies* (London: Tavistock).

Mumtaz, K. and F. Shaheed (eds) (1987), *Women of Pakistan: Two Steps Forward, One Step Back?* (London: Zed Books).

Nadvi, K. (1989), 'Pakistan: Rural Change and Structural Adjustments of Town and Country Relationships', paper presented to conference on *Muslims, Migrants, Metropolis* (Berlin), June.

Naveed-i-Rahat (1981), 'The Role of Women in Reciprocal Relations in a Punjab Village', in T. S. Epstein and R. Watts (eds), *The Endless Day: Some Case Material on Asian Rural Women* (Oxford: Pergamon Press), pp. 47–81.

Naveed-i-Rahat (1986), 'Meharabad, a Punjabi Village: Male Outmigration and Women's Changing Role', in F. Selier and M. S. Karim (eds), *Migration in Pakistan: Theories and Facts* (Lahore: Vanguard Books), pp. 139–60.

Owen, R. (1985), 'Migrant Workers in the Gulf', London: *Minority Rights Group*, Report No. 68.

Parkes, P. (1987), 'Livestock Symbolism and Pastoral Ideology among the Kafirs of the Hindu Kush', *Man*, 22 (4), pp. 637–60.

Parkes, P. (in press), *Kalasha Society* (Oxford: Oxford University Press).

Pastner, C. (1974), 'Accommodations to Purdah: The Female Perspective', *Journal of Marriage and the Family*, 36, pp. 408–14.

Pastner, C. (1978), 'The Status of Women and Property on a Baluchistan Oasis', in L. Beck and N. Keddie (eds), *Women in the Muslim World* (Cambridge: Harvard University Press), pp. 434–50.

Pastner, C. (1979), 'Cousin Marriage among the Zikri Baluch of Coastal Pakistan', *Ethnology*, 18 (1), pp. 31–47.

Pastner, C. (1981), 'The Negotiation of Bilateral Endogamy in the Middle East: The Zikri Baluch Example', *Journal of Anthropological Research*, 37 (4), pp. 305–18.

Pastner, C. (1988), 'A Case of Honor among the Oasis Baluch of Makran:

32   *Introduction*

Controversy and Accommodation', in K. Ewing (ed.), *Shari'at and Ambiguity in South Asian Islam* (Berkeley: University of California Press), pp. 248–58.

Pastner, S. (1978a), 'Power and Pirs among the Pakistani Baluch', *Journal of Asian and African Studies*, XIII (3–4), pp. 231–43.

Pastner, S. (1978b), 'A Nudge from the Hand of God', *Natural History*, 87 (3), pp. 32–3, 36.

Pastner, S. (1978c), 'Baluch Fishermen in Pakistan', *Asian Affairs*, 9 (2), pp. 161–6.

Pastner, S. (1980), 'The Competitive Saints of the Baluch', *Asian Affairs*, 67 (1), pp. 37–42.

Pastner, S. (1984a), 'Feuding with the Spirit among the Zikri Baluch: The Saint as Champion of the Despised', in A. S. Ahmed and D. M. Hart (eds), *Islam in Tribal Societies: From the Atlas to the Indus* (London: Routledge & Kegan Paul), pp. 302–9.

Pastner, S. (1984b), 'Emigration, Islamisation and Social Change', *South Asian Anthropology*, 5 (2), pp. 95–102.

Pastner, S. (1988), 'Sardar, Hakom, Pir: Leadership Patterns among the Pakistani Baluch', in K. Ewing (ed.), *Shari'at and Ambiguity in South Asian Islam* (Berkeley: University of California Press), pp. 164–79.

Pastner, S. and C. Pastner (1972a), 'Agriculture, Kinship and Politics in Southern Baluchistan', *Man*, 7 (1), pp. 128–36.

Pastner, S. and C. Pastner (1972b), 'Aspects of Religion in Southern Baluchistan', *Anthropologica*, 14 (2), pp. 231–41.

Pastner, S. and C. Pastner (1977), 'Adaptations to State-Level Polities by the Southern Baluch', in L. Ziring, R. Braibanti and W. H. Wriggins (eds), *Pakistan: The Long View* (Durham: Duke University Press).

Pastner, S. and C. Pastner (1982), 'Clients, Camps and Crews: Adaptational Variation in Baluch Social Organisation', in S. Pastner and L. Flam (eds), *Anthropology in Pakistan: Recent Socio–Cultural and Archaeological Perspectives*, South Asia Occasional Papers and Theses No. 8 (Ithaca, NY: Cornell University South Asia Program), pp. 61–73.

Pehrson, R. N. (1966), *The Social Organization of the Marri Baluch* (edited from the author's notes by F. Barth) (Chicago: Aldine Press).

Qureshi, M. R. (1986), 'Migration for Development: A Study of Migrants from Rural Hazara to Karachi', in F. Selier and M. S. Karim (eds), *Migration in Pakistan: Theories and Facts* (Lahore: Vanguard Books), pp. 21–39.

Rabinow, P. (1975), *Symbolic Domination: Cultural Change and Historical Form in Morocco* (Chicago: University of Chicago Press).

Rauf, M. A. (1982), 'Labour Emigration and the Changing Trend of Family Life in a Pakistani Village', in S. Pastner and L. Flam (eds), *Anthropology in Pakistan: Recent Socio–Cultural and Archaeological Perspectives*, South Asia Occasional Papers and Theses No. 8 (Ithaca, NY.: Cornell University South Asia Program), pp. 114–20.

Roberts, B. (1978), *Cities of Peasants: The Political Economy of Urbanisation in the Third World* (London: Edward Arnold).

Rouse, S. J. (1983), 'Systemic Injustices and Inequalities: Maliki and Raiya in A Punjab Village', in H. Gardezi and J. Rashid (eds), *Pakistan: The Roots of Dictatorship*, (London: Zed Press), pp. 311–27.

Hastings Donnan and Pnina Werbner 33

Saberwal, S. (1976), *Mobile Men: Limits to Social Change in Urban Punjab* (New Delhi: Vikas).
Scholz, F. (1974), 'The Modern Change of the Baluch and Brahui Nomadic Tribes', *Sociologus*, 24 (2), pp. 117–37.
Searle-Chatterjee, M. (1981), *Reversible Sex Roles: The Special Case of Benares Sweepers* (Oxford: Pergamon).
Selier, F. (1988), *Rural–Urban Migration in Pakistan* (Lahore: Vanguard Books).
Selier, F. and M. S. Karim (eds) (1986), *Migration in Pakistan: Theories and Facts* (Lahore: Vanguard Books).
Shah, N. M. (1982), 'Pakistan', in J. A. Ross (ed.), *International Encyclopedia of Population Vol. 2* (New York: The Free Press), pp. 507–12.
Shaw, A. (1988), *A Pakistani Community in Britain* (Oxford: Blackwell).
Smith, M. W. (1952), 'The Misal: A Structural Village Group of India and Pakistan', *American Anthropologist*, 54, pp. 41–56.
Spain, J. W. (1962), *The Way of the Pathans* (London: Robert Hale).
Spain, J. W. (1963), *The Pathan Borderland* (The Hague: Mouton).
Streefland, P. (1979), *The Sweepers of Slaughterhouse: Conflict and Survival in a Karachi Neighbourhood* (Assen: Van Gorcum).
Swidler, N. (1977), 'Brahui Political Organisation and the National State', in A. Embree (ed.), *Pakistan's Western Borderlands* (Durham NC: Carolina Academic Press), pp. 109–25.
Swidler, W. (1977), 'Economic Change in Baluchistan: Processes of Integration in the Larger Economy of Pakistan', in A. Embree (ed.), *Pakistan's Western Borderlands* (Durham, NC: Carolina Academic Press), pp. 85–108.
Tsakok, I. (1986), 'The Export of Manpower from Pakistan to the Middle East, 1975–85', in S. J. Burki and R. Laporte (eds), *Pakistan's Development Priorities* (Karachi: Oxford University Press), pp. 224–36.
Vatuk, S. (1972), *Kinship and Urbanization: White Collar Migrants in North India* (Berkeley: University of California Press).
Wakil, P. A. (1970), 'Explorations into the Kin Networks of the Punjabi Society: A Preliminary Statement', *Journal of Marriage and the Family*, 32 (4), pp. 700–7.
Wakil, P. A. (1972), 'Zat and Qaum in Punjabi Society: A Contribution to the Problem of Caste', *Sociologus*, 22, pp. 38–48.
Weiner, M. (1982), 'Migration and Development in the Gulf', *Population and Development Review*, 8, pp. 1–35.
Weiss, A. M. (1985), 'Medicine for the Masses: Development of the Pharmaceutical Industry in Punjab', *Journal of South Asian and Middle Eastern Studies*, IX (1).
Weiss, A. M. (ed.) (1986), *Islamic Reassertion in Pakistan: The Application of Islamic Laws in a Modern State* (Syracuse: Syracuse University Press).
Werbner, P. (1984), 'Business on Trust: Pakistani Entrepreneurship in the Manchester Garment Trade', in R. Ward and R. Jenkins (eds), *Ethnic Communities in Business: Strategies for Economic Survival* (Cambridge: Cambridge University Press).
Werbner, P. (1987), 'Enclave Economies and Family Firms: Pakistani Traders in a British City', in J. Eades (ed.), *Migrants, Workers and the Social Order* (London: Tavistock), pp. 213–33.

Werbner, P. (1989a), *The Migration Process: Capital, Gifts and Offerings among British Pakistanis*, Explorations in Anthropology Series (Oxford: Berg).

Werbner, P. (1989b), 'The Ranking of Brotherhoods: The Dialectics of Muslim Caste among Overseas Pakistanis', *Contributions to Indian Sociology*, (NS), 23 (2).

Wilber, D. N. (1964), *Pakistan: Its People, its Society, its Culture* (New Haven: Human Relations Area Files).

2 Family and Low-income Housing in Karachi
Frits Selier

According to the national 1981 census Pakistan's rural population has tripled since 1931. Its urban population has, however, increased eightfold during the same period. This phenomenal rate of growth is particularly remarkable in the case of Karachi, Pakistan's primate city, which today contains approximately 8 million inhabitants. The current population of the city is the outcome of annual growth rates of roughly 6 per cent, partly due to natural increase, and partly (about 30 to 50 per cent) to a vast influx of refugees and labour migrants. It is estimated that of the approximately 550 000 new inhabitants in Karachi each year at least 250 000 are migrants or refugees. Of those born in the city, the majority are descendants of prior migrants or refugees.

The pattern of migration to Karachi is complex since it involves different categories of economic migrants (cf. Selier, 1986) as well as several kinds of political refugees. The latter, the *muhajirs*, include those who fled India immediately after Partition and more recent refugees who emigrated from Bangladesh during the 1970s (mainly Biharis and Bengalis), and, most recently, during the 1980s an estimated 100 000 Afghan refugees fleeing the war in Afghanistan.

Fifty to 70 per cent of these migrants are low-income families who cannot afford housing on the official free market and whose opportunities of finding accommodation are consequently limited (Van der Linden, 1986a and 1986b; Nientied, 1987). In fact, for those unassisted by official institutions (the majority) and for those who choose to consolidate as owners, the only option open is to buy a small plot from an illegal subdivider. Spontaneous squatting is difficult today since plots are rarely without legal and illegal claims. Once a plot is obtained and sufficient capital saved, the owner, often assisted by relatives, usually begins the gradual process of constructing a simple house, the completion of which can take many years.

To determine whether it is more difficult for new migrants to obtain and build their own property than for those who arrived earlier, research was carried out in Orangi, a large and illegally subdivided squatter settlement in Karachi.[1]

I THEORIES OF INTRA-URBAN MIGRATION

One of the most influential theories of intra-urban mobility has been that of John Turner (1968, 1978). Turner's theory distinguishes three types of house occupancy: renting, de facto occupation and legal ownership. He assumes that it is generally more desirable for city dwellers to reside beside their work, to have security of tenure and to possess basic facilities. He also argues that migration within a city moves from its centre to its periphery. These assumptions are clearly connected in space and time (cf. Jansen, 1978, p. 65). The general model suggests that because rural–urban migrants are motivated mainly by a desire to find employment and to keep living costs to a minimum, they will seek shelter as spontaneous squatters or tenants in slum areas as soon as possible after their arrival in the city. Once some degree of integration into city life has been reached and once they feel reasonably assured of a regular income, they will begin to seek their own property. Only then do they move towards the periphery in order to obtain a plot and start the gradual process of building a house. Turner uses three terms to describe the types of urban dwellers in each phase of this process: *bridgeheaders*, *consolidators* and *status seekers* (the latter referring to those able to seek housing in well-off areas). He subsequently refined his theory by distinguishing several stages in urban development. The model outlined here would be typical of his mid-transitional phase. In the late transitional phase there are several variants of the model.

Of course, urban reality is more complex than a typology based upon a hypothetically concentric city suggests. Many Third World cities have more than one centre offering employment. But in general Turner's argument assumes that the migratory process focuses initially on *employment* opportunities and then on *owner-occupant* opportunities. Hence, the presence of already consolidated relatives may entice new migrants in search of work to peripheral areas directly after arrival. This can lead to a higher percentage of tenants in these peripheral areas than Turner's model could account for. The model has thus been adapted to recognise the fact that access to jobs, nowadays, is less a matter of residing in a particular location than of having access to informal job-recruitment networks.

Yet in addition to these modifications there are more serious criticisms of Turner's model. For many tenants the force driving them to the city's periphery is not a wish to consolidate, but merely the urge to escape continuously rising rents. Other migrants end up in the periphery as owners rather than tenants immediately upon their arrival, simply because their relatives already own plots there. Correspondingly, some potential consolidators stay behind in central stagnating squatments because, for example, of the advantages of remaining within a familiar environment (cf. Selier, 1987). But probably most important in the case of Karachi is the fact that spontaneous squatting has become less viable as the number of vacant plots has decreased. Illegal subdividers now charge for plots situated at the very edge of the city and this means that more and more Karachi residents are likely to find themselves remaining as perpetually *stagnating bridgeheaders* (Van der Linden, 1982).

This chapter attempts to determine whether it now takes bridge-headers longer to consolidate than before and if so, to establish the reasons for this. A number of economic factors such as the complete commercialisation of land in Karachi could, arguably, raise the consolidation threshold. Or the inflation of land prices caused by illegal subdividing could be a significant factor in delaying consolidation. The same could be true for increased building prices and the rising costs of basic facilities (gas, water and electricity), as well as transport costs from peripheral residential areas to central work-places. In addition to these economic factors several personal considerations could influence the time needed to become an owner. For example, those who migrated by themselves may be more inclined to remain in rented accommodation or to wait before consolidating than those arriving with their families. Family migration status is dependent on various cultural or religious considerations, and ethnic background or historical circumstances may affect the likelihood of leaving wives and children at home.

If Turner's argument is correct, economic factors such as prices, income and work opportunities are the primary parameters affecting the consolidation process. To establish if this is so, our study examined the time interval between settlers' arrival in Karachi and their consolidation of ownership. This interval, it was presumed, would depend on the *period* in which settlers arrived in the city. Later arrival cohorts, it was presumed, would show *longer* time intervals between arrival and consolidation because of the dramatic property and land price increases which had occurred in the city. Our hypothesis was thus linked to a view of different periods in Karachi's history characterised by distinct economic conditions; these relate to the structure of the illegal land market, inflation in plot prices, building prices, basic facilities, and living costs. The question to be examined in the study was whether social variables such as migrant family status and other personal factors also affect the process of consolidation.

II   ILLEGAL SUBDIVISIONS OF KARACHI

It is estimated that of Karachi's approximately 8 million inhabitants about 2 million are squatters living in roughly 360 *katchi abadis* or *bastis* (although some estimates are as high as 40 per cent; see Karim, 1987). Most of these 360 *katchi abadis* are now illegally subdivided and are the usual destination of about two-thirds of new migrants to Karachi (ibid.). The first migrants had the opportunity of occupying land near the city centre or renting rooms, but within the city itself it is now almost impossible to squat or find cheap accommodation. Those who wish to buy a plot must either pay high prices in the centre or move to the outskirts of the city.

In the outskirts, during the 1960s, a lively illegal market developed selling these peripheral plots. So called 'illegal subdivisions' arose and 'illegal subdividers' provided some basic facilities. The predominantly arid land around Karachi is state owned and generally too far from the city's main activities to be of interest to legal private enterprises. Although subdividing the area and selling the plots is illegal, authorities accept the practice as a partial solution to the immense problem of providing sufficient low cost housing (cf. Nientied, 1987).

Orangi Township

The most extensive illegal division of Karachi and probably one of the largest squatter areas of South Asia is called Orangi Township. Orangi is situated on the north-western edge of Karachi, some 15 kilometres from its centre, and is a near desert with broad valleys between rows of hillocks. The area comprises about 8000 acres (5000 official) and shelters some 1 million (officially 700 000) inhabitants (half a million in 1977). Although originally developed for low-income groups by the city authorities, Orangi quickly became subject to illegal subdivision and since 1970 an estimated 3000 families have lived there unofficially (Bos, 1970).

In the early 1970s, several hundred thousand people of Bihari origin fled from Bangladesh to Pakistan as refugees. The Biharis were not welcome as they constituted serious rivals on the labour market both in terms of their numbers and their educational level. Although officially approved immigrants, the government supported the local opinion that Karachi had had its share of refugees and that the present wave would be better accommodated elsewhere in Pakistan. In this situation the problem of absorbing these immigrants was left to the initiative of private individuals and organisations, and the system of illegal subdivision received an important impetus. Several colonies were established ostensibly 'for the rehabilitation of Bihari refugees', each of them housing a limited number of families but with the greater part of these colonies remaining uninhabited. Cases are known of a subdivider founding more than one refugee colony simultaneously. Orangi thus expanded dramatically after 1971, mainly through illegal subdivision (see Van der Linden, 1985a; see also Nientied, 1987, p. 131).

In 1980, Orangi was transferred from the Karachi Development Authority's (KDA) jurisdiction to that of the Karachi Metropolitan Corporation (KMC).[2] It is now one of the squatter settlements due to be regularised, a process, however, yet to begin. Although Orangi is illegally subdivided for the most part, it is reasonably well laid out and has a satisfactory infrastructure of main and side streets. Public services, however, are poor. In most parts of Orangi there is no sewerage system, except for areas where people have developed it themselves with the aid of the Orangi Pilot Project (OPP), a non-governmental, local self-help organisation.

Several socio–economic reports on Orangi already exist, mostly referring to one or other of its constituent colonies (KMC, 1984; Hasan, 1984; Hasan *et al.*, 1986). The report of the Orangi Pilot Project (Hasan *et al.*, 1986) provides data on the participants of this project, and while we must be cautious of generalising about the whole of Orangi from the characteristics of these participants (who belong mainly to the planned areas), they do provide some idea of the general population.

According to the OPP report, the population of Orangi is mixed, consisting of migrants from the Punjab, the North West Frontier Province (NWFP), and Sindh. The majority, however, are from outside Pakistan; these are the *muhajirs* who entered the country after Partition, as well as the more recent *muhajirs* from Bangladesh. The latter are now quite numerous (estimated at about 200 000), especially in the newer areas of Orangi.

In general, most of the heads of household participating in the Orangi Pilot Project are labourers, many self-employed and only a few with highly paid occupations, while the unemployment rate is relatively low.[3] Incomes appear to resemble or to be slightly lower than the city average. (According to the OPP report, fewer people in Orangi have a monthly income exceeding Rs 1500 than in Karachi as a whole, although the Nespak socio–economic survey (KMC, 1984) conducted in the planned area of Orangi found the opposite to be the case.[4])

III   LOCATION AND CHARACTERISTICS OF THE SAMPLE

In order to find migrants of several arrival cohorts, including long-standing settlers, it was decided to interview residents in one of the oldest areas of Orangi. To improve the chances of finding recently arrived migrants, a relatively young *mohalla* (neighbourhood) was also selected. For the sake of comparison a neighbourhood of inter-mediate age was included.

Bukhari Colony was established in the early 1950s. According to social workers active in the area, this colony was founded on a KDA rubbish dump. Of all *mohallas* in Orangi, Bukhari Colony is located nearest to the city centre (see Figure 2.1). The neighbourhood lacks any kind of sanitation and is characterised by narrow streets often partly filled with rubbish. The residents are mainly *muhajirs* who arrived soon after Partition. A sample of thirty respondents was drawn from this area.

The second *mohalla*, Hussainabad, was established at the beginning of the 1960s. The area is well planned and has a sanitation system constructed with the help of OPP. Most people in this neighbourhood came from India much later than the *muhajirs* who arrived directly after Partition. These *muhajirs* are generally Shi'as.[5] Many of them went initially to the same town of Khaipur in Sindh, where the closure of a large factory seems to have provided them with the final incentive to leave for Karachi. In this neighbourhood nineteen people were interviewed.

Figure 2.1   Orangi Township

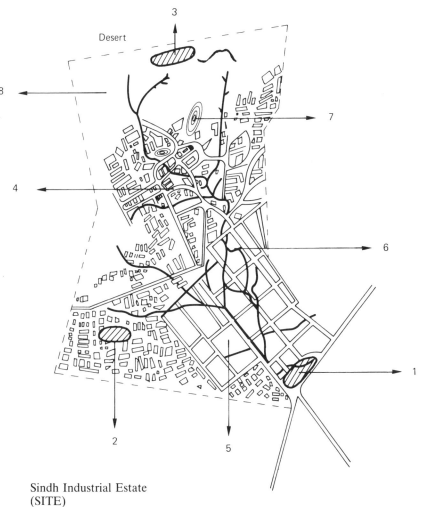

Sindh Industrial Estate
(SITE)

1. Bukhari Colony	4. Unplanned area	7. Hills
2. Hussainabad	5. Planned area	8. Undocumented
3. Gulshan-e-Zia	6. Natural creeks	inhabited
		area

The final sample of fifteen respondents was taken from Gulshan-e-Zia, an area founded at the end of the 1970s and still in the process of expansion into the desert. These respondents were mainly political refugees from Bangladesh who were more or less directed to this area by the government. The neighbourhood consists of empty plots, huts and completely finished houses. It is the most remote area of Orangi.

While recognising the limitation of the sample size, I have used the study to draw some tentative conclusions based on the covariations between place of residence and personal characteristics. Table 2.1 summarises these characteristics. It is perhaps worth noting that compared to data given by the OPP, those born outside Pakistan are slightly over-represented in the sample, while those who arrived after 1970 are rather under-represented, since Bukhari Colony, the old *mohalla*, supplied most respondents.

It is also clear from Table 2.1 that Gulshan-e-Zia is a rather special neighbourhood where mainly *muhajirs*, who fled from Bangladesh, are living. They arrived relatively recently and as political refugees have not had the opportunity of maintaining an effective relationship with their place of origin. In general, they are relatively young and only beginning to make a living; thus their incomes are still comparatively low. In this *mohalla* we did not record any highly qualified occupation.

The current sample has a similar employment profile to that of Orangi's OPP participants. In Gulshan-e-Zia, where many people are recently arrived settlers, most are labourers. The relatively high proportion of highly qualified occupations in the Hussainabad sample is interesting, although it could be a statistical artefact generated by the small number of respondents. At the same time, the remaining respondents in this subsample have a remarkably low income, a comparatively low percentage of them earning more than Rs 1000 monthly. The mean monthly income of the heads of household of this sample (i.e. those without second jobs or other extras) is Rs 934, the total household income when extras (such as rents or a second salary) are included being Rs 1588. This is comparable to the Rs 1667 mentioned by Nespak for the planned area a few years earlier (Nientied, 1987, p. 350).[6] The neighbourhood would thus appear to be highly differentiated in occupational terms.

Differences between the respondents of Bukhari Colony and Hussainabad are not very striking; in fact, many of the characteristics of the Hussainabad respondents lie somewhere between those of the other two areas. Both respondents from Gulshan-e-Zia and Hussain-

Table 2.1 Characteristics of the respondents (values are given as percentages)

Characteristics	Bukhari Col.	Hussainabad	Gulshan-e-Zia	Total
Origin				
Pakistan	19	5		11
India	81	95	27	73
Bangladesh			73	17
Arrived after 1970	14	58	93	46
Older than 40 years of age	86	74	47	73
Migrated with own family	35	63	71	53
Reason for Migration				
Political motives	4		73	20
Never visits village	50	63	100	66
Monthly income of head of household more than Rs 1000*	50	20	11	31
Employment				
Labourers	25	41	64	40
Self employed; servants	71	24	38	47
Highly qualified occupations	4	35		13
Unemployed				
Total no. of respondents	32	19	15	66

* Many missing values

abad migrated with their families, while those of Bukhari Colony arrived alone in most cases. Most striking is the high percentage of heads of household in Bukhari Colony who have a monthly income of more than Rs 1000.

In addition to the limited amount of quantitative data collected in the study some qualitative observations were also made: these consisted mainly of extensive talks with social workers, brokers and concrete blockmakers. In addition, information was gathered on transportation costs, building prices and on the costs of basic facilities such as water and gas.

IV   PLOT PRICE AND THE CONSOLIDATION THRESHOLD

Of the sample, eight respondents (12 per cent) did not own a plot or house; they were renting, living with a family, or in a *dara* (cheap lodging for males, cf. Van Pinxteren, 1974). In this respect the *mohallas* we examined did not differ significantly from one another. It appears that of the owners 60 per cent were 30 years of age or older when they acquired their property. When the decision to buy a house has been taken in principle, three options are then open: to buy a vacant plot on which to build a house gradually; to buy a plot with a small hut from which a more *pakka* house can be constructed; to buy a plot with a complete house. Buying a plot with a hut was common during the settlement of the oldest *mohalla*, but today in the most recent *mohalla* only plots are bought.

In the 1970s, the government's attitude towards illegal housing began to change. In 1978, they announced that all *katchi abadis* established before January 1978 would be regularised provided, for example, they were not situated on private land.[7] Although the regularisation has still to be realised, the official statement was perceived as *de facto* acceptance of *katchi abadis*. In accord with this perceived improved security of tenure, price rises of land and building materials are said to have accelerated. This fact might have served to make the access to secure housing very selective (Van der Linden, Meijer and Nientied, 1985).

Plots for low-income groups measure between 45 to 200 square yards according to official standards. In practice, plots even smaller than 45 square yards are in demand. A small plot in 1984 provided by the KDA cost Rs 3000 (i.e. several months income). In case of an illegal transaction by a subdivider an amount of Rs 15 per square yard for official leasing is generally levied when the area has become legalised (Nientied, 1987). According to respondents as well as brokers, new plots in the destitute corners of Orangi can still easily be found for about Rs 1500. However, as soon as such an area is more or less developed, prices rapidly rise to as much as Rs 5000 within a year. It is said that some Biharis buy several plots of land in order to accommodate in the future kin still in Bangladesh.

As indicated on Table 2.2, the majority (67 per cent – 31 plus 36) of the respondents paid up to four times their monthly income (exclusive of income of other members of the family and other 'extras') for their property. We observed that in the cohort of the earliest arrivals

Table 2.2   Development of the plot price–earnings ratio (values are given as percentages)

Price of the plot divided by monthly income* of h.o.h.	Year of obtaining property			
	<1970	1970–75	>1975	Row Total
1.0 × monthly income or less	43	42	14	31 (N=17)
1.1 – 4.0 × monthly income	21	42	41	36 (N=20)
4.1 × monthly income or more	36	16	46	33 (N=18)
Total	26 N=14	35 N=19	40 N=22	100 N=55**

*   at the moment of buying
** 11 missing observations, of which 8 were tenants.
gamma = 0.32 (This measure of association goes from −1 to +1 and indicates how much more probable a like order (positive association) will be than an unlike order (negative association). If the value is close to 1, there is a high positive association; if it is close to −1, there is a high negative association.)

more (43 per cent) found very cheap plots, equivalent to their monthly income or less. It is obvious that the most recently arrived respondents (all the inhabitants of Gulshan-e-Zia belong to this category) had to pay more for their plots. The majority of them (87 per cent – 41 plus 46) had to pay at least four times the monthly income of the head of the household to purchase a plot only.

It emerged that in Bukhari Colony some people (22 per cent) had been able to obtain a plot without any payment. In Hussainabad 5 per cent had done so, but in Gulshan-e-Zia this appeared impossible. A substantial proportion (36 per cent) of the early arrivals also paid at least four times their monthly income. This was probably because the plot included an acceptable house.

It is difficult to establish the development of plot prices more accurately, since land values are extremely hard to reconstruct and assess. The stage of development of an area, the location of a plot, and expectations about tenure security all determine its value to some extent. Subdividers initially attract clients with very low prices and may even offer free plots. But once a number of people have settled, the purchase price rapidly increases, while the plots at the outskirts of the area may remain relatively cheap. Van der Linden (1985a, p. 12) reports a plot price ranging from Rs 50 to Rs 500 for the initial settlers of a part of North Orangi in 1974 and resale prices of plots in 1984 ranging from Rs 6000 to Rs 12 000 depending on location. On average, this would be an increase of some 60 per cent per year (compound interest) which, when compared to the starting prices of a newly subdivided area, would give enormous increase rates. Another difficulty is to separate the price for the land, the building or for a plot with a house. Residents of Bukhari Colony very often found a *jhuggi* (hut) on the plots they bought for which they hardly had to pay extra. As in older *mohallas*, vacant plots become more and more rare, and prices very often refer to the house, land included. Despite the difficulty of assessing changes in plot and building prices, it is nevertheless clear that the overall trend has been of increasing plot and building prices, well beyond the rate of inflation.

Hasan (1984) presents the following classification of the contemporary housing stock in Manur Nagar, Orangi. Some of the buildings are huts (5 to 7 per cent), built by the people themselves. Prices range between Rs 3000 and Rs 4000. Most of the houses (55 to 60 per cent) are constructed with the help of skilled masons. Building materials are precast concrete blocks for the walls and usually galvanised iron sheets for the roof. The cost of a three-room house is about Rs 35 000 to Rs 40 000. However, most of the houses have only one or two rooms. Contractors are used by 15 to 20 per cent of owners to manage the construction. This increases the price of a three room house by 25 per cent. About 5 per cent of the houses have a reinforced concrete roof which makes a total cost of about Rs 70 000 (Nientied, 1987, pp. 353–4).

In older neighbourhoods such as Bukhari Colony, and to a less extent in Hussainabad, there is an assortment of accommodation ranging from nearly vacant plots (very rare) to plots with buildings of varying quality. This mixture of accommodation is reflected in the respondents' answers, as well as in the fluctuating market potential of

Table 2.3 Increased income and plot prices (source and location are given in brackets)

Year	Monthly income head of household	% yearly income increase	% consumer price increase (8)	Average plot price	Plot price/ monthly income
1970	230 (1)	6.2		794 (1)*	3.4 (1)
1973	271 (2)	16.7			12.0 (3)**
1974			30.0	500 (9)*	
1975	360 (4)				
	378 (1)		26.6	2952 (1)***	4.4 (1)
1978		15.0	8.3		
1979	589 (5)				
	542 (1)		10.4	4755 (1)***	8.7 (1)
1980		16.0	13.9		
1981	740 (5)		11.5		
1982		3.0	5.2		
1983	805 (6)			2562 (1)*	3.6 (1)
	700 (1)		8.0		42.0 (3)**
1984	1204 (7)	8.3			
1986	934 (1)				

   * Plot price only.
  ** Plot with house.
*** Average of plots only and plots with house.
(1) This research Orangi.
(2) JRP-IV, 1975, p. 38 Usmania.
(3) Nientied, 1984b, p. 24 Baldia.
(4) Weijs, 1975, p. 24 Jacob Lines.
(5) Nientied *et al.*, 1982, p. 53 Baldia.
(6) Nientied, 1984b, p. 15 Baldia.
(7) Selier, 1986 Kauser Niasi Colony; Hijrat Colony; Wahid Colony; Isa Nagri.
(8) Nientied, 1987, p. 348 Baldia; Cheema and Malik, 1986, p. 77.
(9) Van der Linden, 1985a, p. 12 Orangi.

these areas over time. In Gulshan-e-Zia, in the very destitute out-skirts of Orangi, only vacant plots are sold.

The price of these vacant plots has increased over time compared to household income (see Table 2.3). Plot prices have increased from about Rs 600 in 1970–4 to about Rs 2562 in 1983 (i.e. more than quadrupling in price, an increase of 27 per cent annually). At the same time, the head of the household income had risen from Rs 271 to Rs 750, or by about 17 per cent per year. The situation is exacerbated by the fact that vacant plots are no longer freely or cheaply available. Although plots are still cheap compared to the price of houses, they are much more expensive than before, especially relative to income.

Thus to sum up, it is clear that the threshold to consolidation of ownership has increased a good deal in relation to plot prices. Nevertheless, plots do remain cheaper than houses and more readily available, if only in the destitute outskirts of Orangi. The few undeveloped plots in the more established *mohallas* are far more expensive, and consolidation thresholds there correspondingly higher. In these *mohallas*, in any case, only plots with houses are usually available, and this too is costly as we will see in the following section.

V   BUILDING PRICES AND BASIC FACILITIES

In Bukhari Colony and Hussainabad it took an average of three years to complete a house. Some claimed that they were still building even after ten years, although, of course, since many people will never be satisfied with the condition of their dwelling they will always claim to be building. As expected, in Gulshan-e-Zia everyone still appeared to be building. As much as Rs 25 000 was reportedly spent on a house, with most of the capital coming from savings (52 per cent) and/or from family loans (25 per cent). Sometimes money is loaned by the concete blockmaker. Official institutions or informal savings associations known as *bisi* are seldom involved.[8]

Building materials constitute a substantial proportion of the construction costs of a modest house (Van der Harst, 1974a, p. 89ff), and because the blockmaker is sometimes a source of credit, he can exercise substantial control over the inhabitants and the building process. In 1986, the price of 100 blocks was Rs 120. In 1980, the price had been Rs 80 and in 1970 Rs 30 for the same amount and type of blocks. The price had quadrupled in sixteen years indicating a yearly increase of some 19 per cent between 1970 and 1986 (10 per cent on compound interest). This increase is caused both by increased concrete prices, and by the requirement since 1977 that blockmakers pay both income and business tax.

Not surprisingly, as construction costs have escalated there has been a corresponding rise in house prices. A plot with a house now costs from Rs 10 000 up to Rs 20 500 according to the respondents.

Table 2.3 presents price increases for undeveloped plots from Rs 600 in 1970–4 to an average price in 1979 for both plots and houses of Rs 4755, an increase of nearly 100 per cent per year. This is the reality of the situation for those who want to find accommodation in an area already well developed and where most plots have already been built upon. Nientied (1987, pp. 68–9) reports that according to property owners themselves, the cost of an average property (a plot with house only) rose by 28 per cent during the period 1980–1 to 1983–4 and by 43 per cent according to the informal brokers who mediate between sellers and buyers.

This in itself surely suggests a relative devaluation of the household income, so that buying a house today is more costly than before. But there is also other evidence. According to Nientied (1984a, p. 24), the cost of a plot with a house in Usmania Muhajir Colony in 1973 was on average twelve times the income of the head of household, while in 1983 the ratio was forty-two to one. Nientied (1986, p. 26) also notes that owners themselves estimated an 8 per cent rise in the cost of a plot and house between 1983 and 1984. A rise of 25 per cent (!) occurred in the same year in Ghousia Colony. This was due to the higher degree of informal security of tenure promised by the earlier announcement that the colony was to be regularised. Thus all kinds of circumstances peculiar to a particular area can influence price increases. The overall trend is, however, clearly upward.

If consumer prices, as well as prices for land and houses, have risen more rapidly than incomes in Karachi, this decrease in purchasing power could arguably cause a delay in purchasing a property. Of the consumption expenditures of the poorest households in urban areas, nearly half of their expenditure goes on food, and 10 per cent on clothing (Cheema and Malik, 1986, p. 78), while 22 per cent goes on housing. For a number of years, however, the household head income in Orangi has increased at the same rate, and sometimes even faster than consumer prices (see Table 2.3). It is thus the housing component of the budget which appears to have escalated most dramatically in relation to income.

Some support for this argument can be found in the literature (cf. Cheema and Malik, 1986). For instance, Nientied *et al.* (1982, p. 54) state that for the period 1979–81 consumer prices increased by approximately 29 per cent. They warn, however, that this estimate may fall short of actual price increases. In the same period, the increase in total household income was 40 per cent (i.e. 11 per cent more than the rise of the price-index figure). According to Nientied's survey, the mean head of household income increased by 25 per cent between 1979 and 1981. The 40 per cent increase of the household income was due to an increased number of additional income-earners per household. People who had had the same job for the previous two years and unchanged family circumstances did not perceive any significant change in their economic situation. After 1980 the situation probably deteriorated, explaining the references to inflation made by the OPP participants (Hasan *et al.*, 1986, p. 28).

With respect to other basic facilities household heads have several options which allow for different economic strategies. Piped water came to Orangi only in 1982 and today over 60 per cent of households in the planned area of Orangi are privately connected to it. From a survey in Gulshan-e-Zia carried out in 1985 (Nientied, 1987, p. 36), it appears that households unconnected to piped water could obtain water in a variety of ways: free of charge from the nearest public tap (0.5 to 1 mile away); from a big underground tank at a cost of from 25 paisa to one rupee per 4 gallons in the dry season; by order from a donkey cart water supplier; and by order from a truck. In the latter two cases home storage facilities are necessary. The costs of these options vary between Rs 75 and Rs 150 per month per household.

In Orangi, expenditure on fuel can be substantial. Wood is scarce, partly because of the arid nature of the surroundings, and to spend Rs 150 per month per household for a cooking fire is not exceptional. Another possibility is to use kerosene oil which is slightly cheaper than wood. In the planned area of Orangi a gas connection can be obtained at a cost of Rs 1500 plus the monthly charge for gas consumption which can vary between Rs 25 and Rs 40. In the planned area 20 per cent of the houses had gas but none of the houses in the unplanned area had it.

Approximately 50 per cent of the area of Orangi has no electricity; almost all houses in the planned area have electricity but only about one-third of those in the unauthorised area. The cost of connection and installation is approximately Rs 1000 to Rs 1200, with an additional monthly charge for electricity consumption ranging from Rs 25 to Rs 50 (Nientied, 1987, p. 361). For those without electricity two alternatives are available: use of kerosene for lamps, and perhaps battery cells for a radio; or electricity obtained from a so-called 'generator-wala'(Rs 3 per tubelight per day).

Households must also budget for the cost of public transport. As illegal subdivisions are usually rather remote, especially in the first stages of their development, they are not serviced by large bus companies until there is sufficient demand. Orangi was provided with a bus service only after lobbying by residents and although small minibuses extended their routes, these were more expensive than government buses. Today regular buses connect Orangi to the centre of Karachi, taking from thirty to seventy minutes and costing one or two rupees, depending upon the point of embarkation within Orangi. For a family of three working in the city centre it could thus cost as much as Rs 12 a day to reach their place of work, a not inconsiderable expense.

Yet there is evidence that transportation cost is not a much larger proportion (5 per cent) of household expenditure in Orangi than it is for Karachi households in general. Perhaps this is because Orangi is located near the Sindh Industrial and Trading Estate where many find work (see Figure 2.1), or because many have a job in Orangi itself as craftsmen, weavers and street vendors.

What this discussion shows is that while both incomes and costs have risen, there is a measure of flexibility in the planning of a household budget. Squatters may choose to have a three bedroom concrete house with a concrete roof, piped water, electricity, ample wood supplies, or high transportation costs. Or they may settle for a modest home in a peripheral, undeveloped area, obtain free water at some physical effort, cook on kerosene and work nearby, cutting transportation costs. It is this flexibility and potential for strategic economic decision-making which affects the consolidation process most critically.

VI TIME NEEDED FOR CONSOLIDATION OF OWNERSHIP

When we consider the conditions which could lead to a higher threshold for consolidation, the key factor appears to be the rise in the prices of plots, building materials and the buildings themselves relative to income. Because earnings have risen substantially as well, at least in the period from 1970 to 1980, we cannot simply speak of 'inflation', if we mean by this a decrease in household income relative to the official consumer prices index. Yet while it is possible that not all the conditions required to raise the threshold of consolidation are present, a fair number are represented. Given this, we can now

Table 2.4   Number of moves before arriving at present residence (values
given as percentages)

No. of moves	<1959	1960–69	>1970	Row total
0		23	43	25 (N = 15)
1	78	54	57	63 (N = 37)
2 or more	22	23		12 (N = 7)
Total	31 N = 18	22 N = 13	46 N = 28	100 N = 59

Missing values: 11, of which 8 are tenants.
gamma = 0.70

establish whether a threshold is operating; that is, whether given the
rising costs recently arrived migrants need more time to consolidate
ownership than earlier arrival cohorts did.

In the present study 25 per cent of respondents purchased a plot
immediately after their arrival in Karachi. As Table 2.4 indicates, a
differentiated process of consolidation, including several changes
from bridgeheader (tenant) to status-seeker as defined by Turner, is
characteristic only of respondents in the oldest arrival cohort. All
these respondents moved at least once before arriving in Orangi,
compared to only about half of the most recent arrivals.

Table 2.5 provides additional evidence that the threshold of consolidation has not increased over time. The study showed that it took
about half of the most recent arrivals less than a year to acquire a plot
of land, compared to a fifth of those who arrived between 1960 and
1970, and only 5 per cent of those who arrived earlier. The oldest and
middle arrival categories consist entirely of *muhajirs* from India.

It appears then that Turner's theory is not readily applicable to the
economic behaviour of refugees – and consequently to an understanding of the spatial development of cities such as Karachi, in
which refugees have historically predominated both as incoming
settlers and as squatters. Karachi, with its vast refugee population,
needs, we argue, to be analysed from a different theoretical perspective.

Table 2.5 Time interval and respondents' year of arrival (values given as percentages)

Time interval* (years)	Year of arrival				Total
	<1959 From India	1960–69 India	>1970 India–Bangladesh		
< 1	5	20	53	40	27 (N = 15)
1–7	21	50	40	30	35 (N = 19)
> 7	74	30	7	30	38 (N = 21)
Total	35 N = 19	18 N = 10	27 N = 15	20 N = 11	100 N = 55

* Time interval between arrival in Karachi and obtaining the property.
Missing values: 11, of which 8 are tenants.
gamma = 0.71

VII CONSOLIDATION TIME AND FAMILY

The respondents of the latest arrival cohort show several striking characteristics, some of them interconnected. The most recently arrived were concentrated in Gulshan-e-Zia, were of Bangladeshi origin, young, and belonged to the lowest income category. Furthermore, they appeared to have migrated later in life, being already married and accompanied by their family.

Table 2.6 suggests *a close correspondence between family migration status* (i.e. migrating alone or with family) *and the time needed to obtain a plot.* Of those who came to Pakistan with their family already established, 41 per cent needed the least time (under one year) to consolidate, compared to 8 per cent of those who established a family after their arrival. The former includes all the recently arrived refugees from Bangladesh. Furthermore, half of those who arrived without a family (which was established at a later stage) needed the longest time to consolidate, compared to 28 per cent of those who arrived with their family.

Table 2.6   Time needed to consolidate and family migration status (values are given as percentages)

| Time interval (years) | Family migration status | | Total |
| | Family established | | |
	Before migration	After migration	
< 1	41	8	26 (N = 14)
1–7	31	42	36 (N = 19)
> 7	28	50	38 (N = 20)
Total	54 N = 29	46 N = 24	100 N = 53

Missing values: 13, of which 8 are tenants.
gamma = 0.399

Having a family at the moment of migration thus appears to be a factor related to both the time of arrival and the time needed to consolidate. This could explain why more recent arrivals consolidate their house ownership more quickly than earlier arrivals, contrary to our earlier hypothesis. As mentioned earlier, Bangladeshis are among the most recently arrived migrants, having fled their country together with their families. That the respondents of the second arrival cohort also needed a relatively short period to consolidate, might also be a consequence of the fact that many of them arrived together with their families. Family migration status might thus, we suggest, be the most important variable influencing consolidation time, rather than time of arrival (i.e. the supposed economic threshold).

Yet there are problems with this hypothesis too. Table 2.7 shows that of nineteen respondents belonging to the oldest arrival group, only 5 per cent were able to consolidate ownership in a relatively short time, as against 46 per cent of those who arrived more recently (see Table 2.5). Of the early arrivals, 74 per cent needed a relatively long time to consolidate, against only 15 per cent of the respondents who arrived comparatively recently. This distributional picture of the

Table 2.7   Time needed to consolidate, year of arrival and family
migration status*

Year of arrival/ time interval	Family migration status		
	Family established		
	Before migration	After migration	Total
Before 1959			
< 1	17 (1)	0 (0)	5 (1)
1–7	17 (1)	23 (3)	21 (4)
> 7	67 (4)	77 (10)	74 (14)
Subtotal	21 (6)	54 (13)	36 (19)
1960–69			
< 1	25 (1)	0 (0)	13 (1)
1–7	75 (3)	50 (2)	63 (5)
> 7	0 (0)	50 (2)	25 (2)
Subtotal	13 (4)	17 (4)	15 (8)
After 1970			
< 1	53 (10)	33 (2)	46 (12)
1–7	26 (5)	71 (5)	39 (10)
> 7	21 (4)	0 (0)	15 (4)
Subtotal	66 (19)	29 (7)	49 (26)
Total	55 (29)	45 (24)	100

* Values are given as percentages; N = 53.
  No. of respondents is given in parentheses.
  gamma = 0.714

time interval only partially disappears if we control for family migration status. Even for those who established their family after
migration, we still see much the same correlation between time
interval and arrival cohort as that already noted. In this case the most
dominant factor determining the consolidation time seems to be the
arrival period.

However, in the case of those who arrived with their family, this
fact seems to influence the consolidation time independently of
period of arrival. Even those who arrived long ago but with their
families consolidated ownership more quickly than those who migrated by themselves (17 per cent and none respectively). Of the
middle arrival cohort, a quarter of those who migrated with their

families had a short consolidation time, while all of those who arrived alone took longer to consolidate. This finding is not fortuitous. Many respondents mentioned that they began looking for their own house because their family was with them and because they were unable to afford high rents. The motivation behind buying land or a house in nearly all cases was the difficulty of being a tenant. Renting for a whole family involved high rents and uncertain prospects. It seems that in many cases renting is a relatively expensive solution, feasible only as long as you are alone and willing to accept accommodation of very poor quality (cf. Wahab, 1984). If having a family makes this impossible, then this 'push factor' seems to be stronger than economic constraints. Economic constraints are apparently not insurmountable in many cases and seem to be most important when the push factor is absent. In all arrival categories more respondents without their families wait a comparatively long time (one year or longer) to settle themselves more permanently. Of the most recently arrived without families, 71 per cent took a relatively long consolidation time (one year or more), compared to 47 per cent (26 plus 21) of those recently arrived with families.

Elsewhere (Selier, 1986) we found a correlation between what has been called *family expansion* or *expanded family*, and a number of attitudes and behavioural traits of migrants in the city.[9] It became obvious that those who were part of an expanded family distributed in geographically separate locations attached a lower value to urban needs (such as shelter), than those with their whole family in the city; many of the former turned out to be tenants. This conclusion is reconfirmed by this study, despite its small scale.

Family expansion (i.e. having parents and/or wife and children at the place of origin) has been measured in this research by frequency of visits to the place of origin. Considering their refugee status, it seems clear that only a small number of the respondents had such expanded families. Of those with little or no contact with their place of origin, 26 per cent consolidated immediately or within a year, while of those maintaining contact with their place of origin none consolidated within this period. All those who visit their place of origin at least once a year (Table 2.8) took longer to settle more permanently in the city.

Table 2.8   Time needed to consolidate and expanded family (values given as percentages)

Time interval (years)	Visits to place of origin		
	Never/Seldom	*At least once a year*	*Total*
< 1	26		22 (N = 11)
> 1	74	100	78 (N = 38)
Total	88 N = 43	12 N = 6	100 N = 49

Missing values: 17 of which 8 are tenants.

VIII   CONCLUSION

Although many of the economic conditions likely to increase the threshold for consolidation are present in Karachi's Orangi squatter settlement, the present study has shown that, contrary to our original expectations, there are few indications that buying a plot and building a house in the settlement have become more difficult or take longer. On the contrary, it was found that the most recently arrived settlers needed *less* time to consolidate than those from the oldest arrival cohort.

Orangi's residents are nearly all refugees, *muhajirs*, the most recently arrived of them being refugees who were more or less directed to settle in the area. *Muhajirs* have long been numerically dominant among the migrants in Karachi, and they still form a substantial part of the settler population of the city. This special condition limits the applicability of Turner's general theory and, indeed, it questions the very assumptions on which the theory rests.

Most *muhajirs* came to Karachi with their families, and this, we have argued, significantly influenced their consolidation process. Although the study showed that the period in Karachi's history in which settlers arrived affected the length of time it took them to consolidate, in all cases families consolidated more rapidly than individual settlers or migrants. This points to the fact that social needs affect economic strategies and, in the long run, they also affect the value of properties and whole neighbourhoods, as consolidation tendencies encourage the establishment of permanent settlements. Economic constraints are never, we showed, absolute. They are subject to choice. In the case of Karachi, its vast refugee population – the majority of which arrived *with* families – has determined the general trends towards rapid consolidation in the city, the pressures to legalise squatter settlements, and the settlement of newly arrived migrants or refugees at the *periphery* of the city. Karachi's spatial development and urban landscape are, in many senses, determined by its status as a city of refugees and their descendants.

Notes

1. The data in this chapter were collected with the assistance of Yvo Klare, for whose contribution to the following section I am also most grateful. Information was gathered by interviewing heads of household (all males) with the aid of an interpreter. In addition to the respondents, thanks are due to Dr Nici Nelson of Goldsmiths College, London and to Dr Jan van der Linden of Free University, Amsterdam for their comments and suggestions. The chapter is a much revised version of Urban Research Working Paper No. 14, Free University, Amsterdam.
2. KDA, the Karachi Development Authority is the non-elected, policy-making body for Karachi's development. It is responsible for urban development schemes, town planning, traffic engineering and environmental control. It is also responsible for sites and services development, and redevelopment of *katchi abadis*. KMC, the Karachi Metropolitan Corporation is an elected body responsible for civic amenities and facilities such as primary education, public health, water supply, social welfare, upgrading of *katchi abadis*. KDA is involved in development, while KMC is in charge of management and maintenance.
3. A relatively low unemployment rate is apparent in nearly all *katchi abadi* studies. However, according to Karim (1987), there exist KDA estimates of about 15 per cent unemployment for the whole of Karachi and 20 per cent in low-income areas. A recent fast-growing unemployment rate in Karachi's *katchi abadis* is also mentioned by Hasan (1987). According to Karim, 25 per cent of Karachi's labour force is self-employed and another 27 per cent consists of unskilled labourers.
4. According to Karim (1987), about half the families in *katchi abadis* have an average income of Rs 1500 per month. The average household income for Pakistan is Rs 2500. See Selier (1986, p. 10) for an overview of personal socio–economic characteristics of other migrants in Karachi.

5. About 20 per cent of Pakistan's population are Shi'a, the remainder are Sunnis.
6. Cf: Old Golimar, Rs 1933 (Nientied, 1987, p. 350); Rs 1496 (Van der Linden, 1985b, p. 12); and Rs 1875 (Selier, 1986, p. 11). All averages relate to the year 1984.
7. Cf. Nientied, 1987. Since then the date has been changed several times by the government and in October 1986 they announced that all settlements originating before March 1986 would be legalised.
8. This research shows that only 7 per cent of people made use of *bisi* (Nientied mentions 8 per cent, 1987, p. 66). At least one *bisi* committee is found in most *mohallas*. In general, they have fifteen to twenty members (Hasan *et al.*, 1986, p. 25). The objective is to create an informal banking system which periodically makes a large lump sum in cash available to its members. The organiser, who is nominated by consensus, collects Rs 50 to Rs 200 per month from the members. Each member gets the total amount, which can be as large as Rs 8000, every month in rotation. The rotation order is sometimes changed to meet special needs such as the building of a house or the marriage of a daughter.
9. Expanded family is a term originally used by anthropologists to refer to extended families which had lost their geographical but not their functional unity (see Fortes, 1958; see also Bartle, 1980; Kaufmann and Lindauer, 1980 and Selier, 1987). The Majumdars (1978) have published a study which shows the functioning of expanded families. Banerjee (1981) speaks of multicentred families with reference to India.

References

Banerjee, B. (1981), 'Rural–Urban Migration and Family Ties: An Analysis of Family Considerations in Migration Behaviour in India', *Oxford Bulletin of Economics and Statistics*, 43(4), pp. 321–55.
Bartle, Philip (1980), 'Cyclical Migration and the Extended Community: A West African Example' (Leiden: Afrika Studiecentrum), unpublished manuscript.
Bos, A. (1970), 'Some Information About the KDA Plot Townships in Karachi: Baldia, Aurangi and Qasba', *JRP IV* (Karachi).
Cheema, A. A. and M. H. Malik (1986), 'Income-specific Inflation Rates in Pakistan', *The Pakistan Development Review*, 25(1), pp. 73–84.
Fortes, M. (1958), 'Introduction', in Goody, J. (ed.), *The Developmental Cycle in Domestic Groups* (Cambridge: Cambridge University Press).
Gilbert, A. (1982), 'The Tenants of Self-help Housing: Choice and Constraint in the Housing Markets of Less Developed Countries', *Development and Change*, 14, pp. 449–77.
Hasan, A. (1984), 'The Housing Project of Orangi Pilot Project: Initial Thinking' (Karachi, OPP), *mimeo*.
Hasan, A. (1987), 'Karachi's Godfathers', *Herald*, annual 1987, January, pp. 9–14.
Hasan, A., Rehman, P. and Shaista Sultan (1986), 'The Low Cost Sanitation

Programme of the Orangi Pilot Project' (Karachi: *NGO Habitat Project*, UN Year for the Shelterless 1987).

Jansen, R. (1978), *Wij hebben zelfs geen Recht op de Stad: vogelvrij wonen in Bogota* (Amsterdam: Ekologische uitgeverij).

JRP-IV (1975), 'Usmania Mahajir Colony' (Karachi).

Karim, M. S. (1987), 'Karachi's Demographic Dilemma', *Dawn Magazine*, 27 February.

Kaufmann, D. and D. Lindauer (1980), 'Basic Needs, Inter-Household Transaction and the Extended Family', *Urban and Regional Report No. 80–15* (Washington: World Bank).

KMC (1984), 'Katchi abadis of Karachi (special development 1984 programmes)', report prepared by NESPAK (Karachi).

Majumdar, P. S. and I. Majumdar (1978), *Rural Migrants in an Urban Setting* (New Brunswick, NJ: Transaction Books).

Nientied, P. (1984a), 'Usmania Mahajir Colony in 1973 and 1983. Research in a Centrally Located Katchi Abadi in Karachi', *Urban Research Working Papers*, no. 1 (Amsterdam: Free University).

Nientied, P. (1984b), 'Karachi Squatter Settlement Upgrading: The Third Baldi Upgrading Evaluation Survey', *Urban Research Working Papers*, no. 2 (Amsterdam: Free University, Department of Development Sociology).

Nientied, P. (1986), 'The Short-term Impact of Housing Upgrading on Housing Values', *Third World Planning Review*, 8(1), pp. 19–30.

Nientied, P. (1987), *Practice and Theory of Urban Policy in the Third World: Low-income Housing in Karachi* (Amsterdam: Free University), unpublished dissertation.

Nientied, P. M., E. N. Meijer and J. J. van der Linden (1982), *Karachi Squatter Settlement Upgrading: Improvement and Displacement?* Bijdrage tot de Sociale Geografie en Planologie nr. 5 (Amsterdam: Free University, Institute of Geography and Urban and Regional Planning).

Selier, F. (1986), 'Family and Rural–Urban Migration in Pakistan: The Case of Karachi', *Urban Research Working Papers*, no. 12 (Amsterdam: Free University, Institute of Cultural Anthropology/Sociology of Development).

Selier, F. (1987), 'Expanded Family and Expanded Community: Migrants in Karachi' (Amsterdam: Free University), unpublished manuscript.

Turner, J. (1968), 'Housing Priorities, Settlement Patterns, and Urban Development in Modernising Countries', *JAFP*, vol. 34 (b).

Turner, J. (1978), *Housing by People: Towards Autonomy in Building Environments* (London: Marion Boyars).

Van der Harst, J. (1974a), 'Low-income Housing', *JRP-IV* (Karachi).

Van der Harst, J. (1974b), 'The Cost of Residing of Low-income Groups', *JRP-IV* (Karachi).

Van der Linden, J. J. (1982), 'Squatting by Organised Invasion in Karachi: A New Reply to a Failing Housing Policy?' *Third World Planning Review*, 4(4), pp. 400–12.

Van der Linden, J. J. (1985a), 'Dalalabad: An Inquiry into Illegal Subdivision in Karachi', (Amsterdam: Free University) unpublished manuscript.

Van der Linden, J. J. (1985b), 'Ghousia Colony: The Upgrading of a

Stagnating Basti', *Urban Research Working Papers*, no. 4 (Amsterdam: Free University).

Van der Linden, J. J. (1986a), 'Squatting Is No Longer What It Used To Be', in J. J. Van der Linden, *Sites and Services Approaches Reviewed: Solution or Stopgap* (Aldershot: Gower).

Van der Linden (1986b), 'Turner's Model of Intra-city Migration and Developments in Karachi', in Frits Selier and Mehtab S. Karim (eds), *Migration in Pakistan: Theories and facts* (Lahore: Vanguard Press).

Van der Linden, J. J., E. Meijer and P. Nientied (1985), 'Informal Housing in Karachi', *Habitat International*, 9(3/4), pp. 289–97.

Van Pinxteren, T. E. L. (1974), 'The Dara: A Housing Facility for the Male Migrant', *Joint Research Project IV* (Karachi).

Wahab, E. A. (1984), 'The Tenant Market of Baldia Township: Towards a More General Understanding of Tenancy in Squatter Settlements' *Urban Research Working Papers*, no. 3 (Amsterdam: Free University).

Weijs, M. H. (1975), 'Study on Jacob Lines', *Joint Research Project IV* (Amsterdam: Free University).

3 Security and Value: Squatter Dwellings in Karachi*

Jan van der Linden

The urban landscape of Karachi's low-income neighbourhoods presents the observer with an apparent dilemma: the quality of housing in the city's squatter settlements, the *bastis* or *katchi abadis*, and in its urbanised villages, the *goths*, is characterised by remarkable disparities in the standard of housing. Yet these visible differences do not fully correspond, as might be expected, to obvious factors such as legality or illegality of tenure, length of residence in the city, or income differentials. At the same time, marked differences between neighbourhoods point to underlying common, even, one might say, collective, strategies of housing investment on the part of residents. Collective, because common investment strategies appear to reflect, as we shall argue, common perceptions about current circumstances and future needs among squatters.

More than 2 million of Karachi's 8 million residents live in squatter settlements. In order to understand the investment choices of low-income residents a profile of housing conditions in the *katchi abadis* and *goths* of the city was constructed (for details, cf. Van der Linden, 1977, pp. 84, 109).[1] The research focused on house owners' perceptions of their home and its value in relation to broader economic strategies. The chapter elucidates the underlying social and economic conditions determining individual and collective housing investment strategies, in relation to security of tenure and local 'rootedness' in the city. At the centre of the analysis here is a contrast between the strategies of *katchi abadi* and *goth* dwellers, a contrast which highlights the collective dimensions of individual housing investment choices.

By definition, inhabitants of squatments lack formal security of tenure. However, although in official thinking only two options can exist with regard to tenure – legal or illegal – the *de facto* degree of security of tenure in different squatter settlements varies widely. Earlier research in Karachi has demonstrated that the squatters in the *katchi abadis* of the city build and improve their houses in accordance with the perceived degree of tenure security currently prevalent in a settlement. For instance, it was found that the relation between investments in a house and income is much weaker than the relation between such investments and the *hope* the dweller has that he will be allowed to keep living in his present squatter house (JRP-IV, 1975, pp. 50–1).

Hence, the moral-cum-legal claims squatter residents make to own their property are apparent in the very appearance of their houses, and their investments in them. Legal ownership is not simply a clear-cut, unambiguous status, but a matter of a gradual, incremental accumulation of rights. Such rights are tangibly underpinned by levels of investment.

The quality of the housing stock in *katchi abadis* (i.e. squatments) varies along with perceived security of tenure. Initial tentative squatter neighbourhoods consist mostly of mere reed huts. In the next stage, when, for instance, deals with the local police have been negotiated, these huts are replaced by simple houses of temporary material such as wooden planks, tin sheets, mud or stones. When the dwellers manage to convince the authorities to provide certain facilities in their neighbourhood, such as piped water, electricity and other amenities, they perceive this as a sign of further recognition of the settlement on the part of the authorities who, they conclude, are not likely to demolish the settlement. Upon each such sign of growing recognition, the dwellers react by improving – or rebuilding – their houses. Walls of concrete blocks replace walls of inferior materials; roofs are raised; in a further stage, house walls are plastered with cement, and so on. When finally the threat of eviction is totally removed, the better off among the squatters will have a reinforced concrete roof constructed on which they can eventually build rooms, thus adding a storey to their house.

Squatments in which negotiations with the authorities for improved facilities or other symbols and signs of recognition fail, do not show this evolutionary development. They stagnate in the early stages for long periods of time.

Since *perceived* security of tenure is the main determinant of the developments described above, the housing stock of any single squatment tends to be of a rather uniform quality. A majority of houses in a neighbourhood conform to a current standard; a few houses may lag behind the norm by a single stage of development, while others may have been improved a stage further than the majority. But overall, the general condition of housing reflects the degree of public legitimacy a squatter settlement has achieved at any particular historical moment. The response to collective negotiations with the state or its representatives is thus a *collective response*, as each squatter objectifies his individual symbolic ownership through improvements in his home. In general, then, investment makes a claim to legal ownership at the same time as it reflects the current negotiated order.

In sharp contrast to this are the houses in Karachi's urbanised villages, known as *goths*. Here, practically always, a few houses of very high quality dominate the neighbourhood, reflecting the high degree of tenure security *goth* dwellers have. Indeed, although dwellers of most of the *goths* do not enjoy codified legal tenure rights, their *de facto* security of tenure is very high. Since the *goths* have been in existence for at least two generations, customary law opposes any attempt to deny the *goth* dwellers' rights to the land they live on.

Oddly enough, it seems as though many of the *goth* dwellers are not able or willing to translate this high level of security into investment in their houses, as the squatters tend progressively to do. In the *goths*, one finds the most primitive type of huts beside houses of very good quality. Thus, contrary to what is common in the squatments, the housing profiles of the *goths* show a very wide spread, ranging from simple shacks to sophisticated bungalows. Quite often, the range of housing types between the two extremes is virtually absent. While the profiles of houses in squatter neighbourhoods seem to reflect a collective process of steady improvement, the profiles of the *goths* suggest that improvements take place more individually, and in sudden bursts.

How are we to explain this remarkable difference between the housing investment strategies in the squatments and urbanised villages of Karachi? In order to analyse these differences, the research focused on the economic motives behind dwellers' investment decisions.

I ECONOMIC RATIONALITY AND HOUSING INVESTMENT STRATEGIES

An obvious explanation for the difference between *goth* and squatter housing strategies could be economic: that *goth* dwellers who live in relatively poor housing conditions are also the most deprived economically. Indeed, the *goth* dwellers themselves, when asked to explain the occurrence of primitive huts alongside modern well-constructed houses, invariably argued that this is due to differences in income. In fact, however, investigation showed that while such differences were significant within the *goths*, the income of the *goth* hut dwellers did not differ, in absolute terms, from those of squatters, and thus did not, in itself, prohibit investment in house improvements. Many squatters with equally low, or even lower, incomes made much higher investments in their houses, even under less favourable tenure circumstances. Thus, rather than an absolute shortage of financial resources on the part of some *goth* dwellers, it seems that their economic and social priorities are different.

The differential economic rationality governing the investment choices of squatter and *goth* dwellers goes some way towards explaining the occasional bursts of improvements in the *goths*. If investment in housing does not have a high priority, it is only the comparatively 'rich' who do decide to improve their houses. They are in a position to make substantial improvements all at once. The squatters, on the other hand – both 'rich' and poor – appear to invest constantly every little bit they can save in their houses, continually improving them. This pattern of squatter housing investment appears to be quite common and is reported from elsewhere, as well as from Karachi itself (see, for example, Eyre, 1973; Turner, 1976a; Mangin, 1967; regarding Karachi, cf. Van Huyck, 1972; MPD, 1974 p. 24; Van der Linden, 1977, chapters VII, IX and XI). Given its wide occurrence, the need is to ask what it is about residence in settlements officially defined as illegal which generates this collective form of housing strategy.

In view, moreover, of the *different* behaviour of the *goth* dwellers, the squatters' behaviour may not be as self-evident as is sometimes suggested (e.g. Fathy, 1973). Discussions in the literature have suggested several reasons why it is especially squatters who take so much interest in their houses (Turner and Goetze, 1967; Mangin, 1967; Peattie, 1969; Vernez, 1976). To the squatter, the house serves as 'a substitute for the loss of the traditional security of the local kinship network . . . and the inaccessibility of institutionalised insurance, enjoyed only by the relatively wealthy' (Caminos *et al.*, 1969, p. vii).

It is also sometimes suggested that for squatters, lacking other visible symbols of status, such as cattle or agricultural implements, as well as invisible symbols like a recognised local ancestry, their house becomes a primary symbol of status and/or achievement (Alcock *et al.*, 1963; Alonso, 1964; Turner, 1976b).

If these arguments are valid, migrant squatters in Karachi attach a higher priority to their houses than the autochthonous people do because the house enhances their socio–economic security, and because it is an important symbol of status and achievement. For *goth* dwellers whose roots are in the city, by contrast, housing is not the primary determinant of status.

While this proposition may have some merit it is, as stated, inadequate: the need is to analyse the complex relationship between achieved legality, investment in housing, embeddedness in long-term networks of kin or friends, and value; this complex combination of factors is a unique feature of squatter settlement.

II THE SURVEY

I will describe here the findings from a survey based on a small sample of twenty-five migrant squatters and an equal number of *goth* dwellers. It is of interest to note here that the sample of migrant squatters consisted of three different ethnic groups (eight Punjabis, eight Pathans and nine *Muhajirs*), living in six different colonies of Karachi; the sample of *goth* dwellers comprises ten Sindhis and fifteen Baluchis, living in five different *goths*. Interestingly, hardly any differences between ethnic groups were found within the two categories – 'migrant-squatters' and '*goth* dwellers' – studied here.

It is also of importance to note here that only slight differences exist between *goth* dwellers and migrant squatters with respect to their occupations: in both categories, a majority work as labourers, servants or petty salesmen. In the *goths*, only 7 per cent of the heads of households are engaged in agricultural professions (mostly cattle keeping for dairy production; Van der Linden, 1977, App. V, 4 and 18).

In order to find evidence of the different priority which *goth* dwellers and migrant squatters attach to their houses, I asked the interviewees the following question: some people live in a *katcha* house or hut although they can afford to build a *pakka* house. They find other things more important. Are there – in your opinion – such people in this area? If yes, what then is the more important thing in their opinion? (*katcha*: clay-built, half-done, without use of cement;

Table 3.1 Frequency of replies regarding alternative ways of spending money by 'rich' people living in 'inferior' houses

Category	Reply	Frequency of the reply by:	
		Goth *dwellers*	*Squatters*
Negative	Miserliness	1	5
or	Spends on women		1
unable to	Is illiterate	1	
imagine	No idea		7
Total		2	13
Neutral	Matter of custom		2
	No lease	7	2
	Not planning to live permanently		5
Total		7	9
Real	Save for hard times	5	1
alternative	Business	4	
spending	Wedding	4	
	Education of children	1	
	Cattle	1	
	Gold	1	
	Send home		2
Total		16	3

pakka: solid, lasting, permanent). Both categories – *goth* dwellers and squatters – agreed that such people were living in their areas, although, of course, the standard used in interpreting the meaning of 'can afford to' may have differed widely between respondents.

Replies to the second half of the question, regarding alternative ways of spending money, revealed the different priorities respondents attached to their houses, as Table 3.1 shows.

The figures in Table 3.1 convincingly support the expectation that squatters find it 'natural' to attach a high priority to investing in their houses. They have a low regard for those who could, but do not, invest in home improvements. In many cases, when they admit that the phenomenon occurs, it seems as though they cannot imagine why anybody should behave in that way. In the *goths*, with a few exceptions, not investing in houses seems to be regarded as a wholly legitimate option. Other costly priorities – education, the marriage of children, business demands, the need for cattle or gold – were regarded as equally valid targets for financial investment. The absence of a lease was cited as a further deterrent to investment in housing. For squatters, by contrast, not investing in housing was a sign of moral decadence (miserliness, philandering) or was simply inconceivable as a rational strategy.

My investigations did not lead to unambiguous results regarding the different conceptions of 'status' and 'achievement' *goth* and squatter dwellers held, although the answers point towards the direction hypothesised. A possible shortcoming of this part of the research was terminological: it was extremely difficult to find ways of defining complex concepts such as 'status' or 'position'. Respondents often referred to *religious* behaviour as the main determinant of status and even position. Only one informant thought that '*Izzat* (respect) is a matter of money alone; all the rest is nonsense'. Most others were more inclined to agree with one of the interviewees who said that '*izzat* cannot be seen; it is in your heart'. When I substituted the word '*martabah*' (lit.: degree, dignity, class, order) for '*izzat*', the result was hardly better: almost half the respondents maintained that '*martabah*' cannot be seen. The survey pointed to the limitation of this technique for studying complex social phenomena which are not easily defined in economic terms. 'Status', whether translated as '*izzat*' or '*martabah*', is clearly regarded by such low-income groups as an *individual* and fundamentally *moral* achievement rather than – as among higher income groups or in the West – as chiefly a matter of occupation or income.

The three questions pertaining to economic security, however, elicited a more significant pattern of replies. One question addressed the possibility of obtaining loans, and the source of such loans. Replies to this question are recorded in Table 3.2.

Contrary to my original expectation, it appeared that squatters can obtain loans as easily as *goth* dwellers. However, if we examine the sources of loans, we see that *goth* dwellers can get loans more often from established kinship sources: their expectation of doing so is two and a half times higher than that of squatters. Squatters, in their turn, expect to rely more frequently on non-kinship sources. In such cases, it is likely that loans will require some form of security or at least an assurance of continued residence, although only in four cases was housing cited explicitly as a basis for securing a loan.

It is of interest to note here that the 'non-kinship' sources of loans

Table 3.2 Possibility of obtaining loans and sources of loans

Possibility	Source	Frequency of the reply by:	
		Goth *dwellers*	*Squatters*
No		8	8
Yes	Relatives	5	5
	Biradari (= Community of relatives)	8	1
	Qaum (= Tribe)	2	
Total relatives/*biradari*/*qaum*		15	6
	Neighbours/friends	1	4
	Employer		3
	On basis of house	1	4
Total neighbours/employer/house		2	11

are still very informal. Squatters cannot mortgage their houses since they are illegal occupants. The expression 'on basis of the house' indicates that the house serves as a security against which others are *willing* to give a loan. Sometimes it is not easy to distinguish between borrowing from neighbours and borrowing 'on the basis of a house', as a quotation from an interview on the subject may illustrate: 'Everybody around knows that I have spent Rs. 3000 on this house. So my neighbours know that I would not run away, and when my wife had to be admitted into hospital, I could borrow from my neighbours.' Investment in housing implies a commitment and hence also residential stability. A man who invests in his house is a known person whose movements and future are predictable. Such a man is likely to return a loan.

The second question regarding the house as a source of security had to do with the safest way for low-income people to protect their savings. Table 3.3 gives a review of the respondents' first choices.

Although the differences between squatters and *goth* dwellers are not very decisive, it can be seen that squatters have a higher preference than *goth* dwellers to use investment in housing as a way of safeguarding their savings. *Goth* dwellers also invest readily in business and other objectives. It should be remembered here that occupational characteristics cannot explain this difference, apart from the

Table 3.3   Opinions on the safest way to keep money (first choices only)

Ways of keeping money	Frequency of the reply by:	
	Goth *dwellers*	*Squatters*
Build a house	13	19
Invest in business	9	3
Keep in a bank	2	3
Buy animals	1	

case of the one *goth* dweller who considered the purchase of animals to be a secure form of investment.

Perhaps the clearest indication of the house's function as a source of social, as well as economic, security can be found in the replies to a third question on this matter, namely, the question of how a family would deal with a crisis. Hence, I asked the respondents what their families would do if the respondent fell seriously ill (for obvious reasons, I could not ask the more extreme question as to how a family would cope in case of the death of the head of the household). Table 3.4 shows the result.

The response to this question makes clear that the squatters expect to rely on self-help in an emergency much more than the *goth* dwellers do. *Goth* dwellers appeared to feel that they could get help more often from informal sources than the squatters did. Very clearly, in a great majority of cases, squatters expected to rely on their *houses* as their primary asset. This reliance was almost entirely absent among the *goth* dwellers.

Investment in houses, it should be noted, even in squatter settlements, is inflation proof. In fact, house prices in Karachi have increased much faster than incomes and the general cost of living. Thus, investment in their housing has proved to be, for squatters, a highly profitable economic strategy.

In 1987, I recorded a very clear example of the way housing is used, in practice, as a source of security. The example concerns an elderly couple who had three adult sons, all of whom lived independently and did not support the parents. For several decades, the old father had invested what he could in his house which had, over the years, become a double-storeyed well-plastered and decorated structure of reinforced concrete. When the father, who was an unskilled factory worker, was no longer able to continue working in the factory, he sold the house for Rs 150 000 and bought instead a much smaller,

Table 3.4   Frequency of replies to the question: what would your family
do if you fell seriously ill?

Category	Reply	Frequency of the reply by:	
		Goth *dwellers*	*Squatters*
Self-help	sell house	1	17
	mortgage house	1	
	Total relying on house	2	17
	use savings	3	4
	wife will work		3
	Total self-help	5	24
Help	loan/help from relatives	19	4
	loan/help from neighbours	3	1
	loan/help from friends	1	1
	Total informal loan/help	23	6
	loan/help from employer	1	2
	loan, not specified		2
	Total help from others	24	10

single-storeyed house, located along one of the main streets in the
same neighbourhood. This house cost only Rs 85 000. With the
balance, the father paid off all his outstanding debts and deposited
Rs 50 000 in the bank. Because of the location of the new house, the
father was able to open a small sweet shop in it, the earnings from
which cover a major part of the old couple's daily expenses.

III   CONCLUSION: VALUE AND INCORPORATION INTO THE HOUSING MARKET

Although the research described here was limited in scope and the
sample was very small, it yielded sufficient evidence to show that for
migrant squatters, their house is much more than a mere shelter. In
many cases, despite its apparently illegal, and thus insecure, tenure,
the house in fact serves as a source of socio–economic security to the
squatter. From this conclusion, a number of tentative implications
are worth considering.

First, the fact that, contrary to expectations, squatting provides economic security goes some way towards explaining the failure of so many officially launched, 'low-cost housing schemes', based on long-term loan repayments. As long as the dweller cannot call his abode – however modest it may be – his own, and, especially, as long as he remains under long-term financial obligations – however 'soft' these may be – he lacks the security he could derive from the outright ownership of his own house, even if that house is located in a squatter area. This was underlined in an interview with a squatter who had attempted to move into a housing scheme (see also Turner, 1976b; Sudra, 1976): 'We were given a quarter in New Karachi [official low-cost housing scheme] on rent, but after some time I fell ill and we had no savings; so after a few months we had to leave that house and now we are back again in an illegal settlement.'

Secondly, the squatter's eagerness to save and invest his savings in his house would seem to constitute a good reason why the authorities should encourage and support existing informal systems, associated with squatting, rather than opposing them as they so often do. This is not to deny that there are many injustices associated with the existing informal systems, such as, for instance, in the allocation and distribution of scarce resources. Here, the government could take a regulatory role without destroying the system which, at the very least, performs some basic functions that cannot be easily replaced.

In the third place, there are good reasons to doubt the effectiveness of building loan schemes. Van der Harst has shown that about 50 per cent of Karachi's squatters take informal loans when building their houses (1974, p. 57). More recently, it was found that around 25 per cent of them also take loans for home improvement. Practically all these loans derive from informal sources, even when tenure has been legalised, so that house owners qualify for official mortgages or loans from the House Building Finance Corporation (Kool *et al.*, 1988, p. 95). It should be stressed that such informal loans tend to be rather small. Given the informal nature of the loans and the small amounts involved, it is very doubtful if squatters – and especially the most needy among them – would take much interest in formal loans which, instead of helping the borrower, could result ultimately in diminishing his security. This accords with my findings here that housing is a major source of security for squatters rather than an additional liability. Since it appears that most squatters obtain the kind of loans which they can manage without much difficulty, official loan schemes are likely to be taken up only by the better off, who are able to afford the risk involved in repaying them. Consequently, only the relatively wealthy sections of the population are likely to benefit from the subsidised interest rates which are a common feature of such loan schemes.

There is a further point, however, which shows the complex relation between migration, squatting and collective housing strategies. *Katchi abadi* residents in Karachi, like squatter dwellers elsewhere, *create* their own housing market. They do so by establishing, negotiating, and consolidating their settlement, both through pressure on the authorities or local politicians and through continuous improvement of their houses. As a housing market, initially informal and unofficial, develops, the incentive to negotiate for further facilities and to improve housing further gathers momentum. Individual choice is here subject to a collective drive towards enhancing the value of a settlement's housing stock within the broader housing market. This collective drive is represented in respondents' answers as a taken-for-granted ideology regarding the priority of housing investment and the future security it is likely to afford.

Individual perceptions of increasing tenure security thus converge with, and are articulated through, a collective ideology which both expresses the level of security achieved tangibly – in bricks and mortar – and also, *ipso facto*, raises the value of a neighbourhood and the houses within it – and hence the incentive to future investment.

Unlike migrant-squatters, *goth* dwellers not only do not *create* a housing market, in some ways they remain detached from it and actively ignore it. The value of their property cannot be measured entirely in terms of its market value, despite the facts that security of tenure is high and that their land and property can be legally bought and sold on the open market. For *goth* dwellers, rooted in their communities within the city, their land and property is a patrimonial trust, embedded in kinship and long-term neighbourly relations. As such, it is not lightly sold on the open market, and thus investment in housing becomes a matter of personal preference rather than collective strategy. Collective pressures on *goth* dwellers, it seems, are towards expenditure on communal consumption – on weddings, gold and other such items which secure the long-term reproduction of the community as a social group.

Hence, the very permanence of residence and long-term attachment to their homes detaches *goth* dwellers from the open housing market. By contrast, migrant-squatters who migrate to the city to earn money, and who lack a long-term attachment to their homes, invest more in their houses in order to ensure their continued and increasing value within the broader housing market. Both for *goth* and *katchi abadi* residents, therefore, the relationship between collective premises and individual perceptions and choices is crucial for an understanding of urban housing investment strategies. This argument is sharpened if we examine the overall development of the Karachi housing market, and the incorporation of *katchi abadis* into it.

Hence, recent research has shown that access to ownership of even illegal housing has become much more difficult in Karachi than it used to be. One evident cause of this has been the Karachi Development Authority's failure to supply land for housing the poor (Van der Linden, 1982, p. 403; 1986, pp. 2–7; Nientied, 1987, pp. 120–75). As a result, around half of Karachi's 8 million strong population has no option, in seeking housing, but to buy a plot in an illegal subdivision. Today, however, the newly established illegal subdivisions are located ever farther from the city and its centres of work than they were in the past, rendering it increasingly difficult for the poor to settle there. To top all this, the system of illegal subdivision has become so institutionalised that prices in squatter settlements now approach those in the legal housing market, thus further excluding the poor. In one illegal subdivision, for instance, it was noted that land and house prices had doubled between 1981 and 1987 in relation to the average household income (Kool *et al.*, 1988, pp. 78 ff and 113 ff). Alongside this inflation in house prices, the shortage of houses has resulted in an increase in the proportion of tenants in illegal settlements, and in high levels of subdivision, so that the cost of renting has at least doubled over the past twelve years (Van der Linden, 1988, p. 55). Hence, in line with the general inflationary trend, rents too have risen and squatter housing is now a profitable form of investment property which can draw large incomes. For tenants, non-ownership of even a squatter house means that they lack the type of substitute squatters have for other forms of socio–economic security. One wonders how tenants, lacking the minimal security squatting provides, will be able to cope with the continually increasing rents, or with personal crises, especially in view of increasing unemployment rates. Certainly, recent organised land invasions can be explained by the sort of processes referred to here, and be better understood in the light of the important function of house ownership, however tenuously and unofficially secure, as a component of the survival strategies of the poor.

Notes

* This is a much revised, extended and updated version of Jan van der Linden, 'The Squatter's House as a Source of Security in Pakistan', *Ekistics*, vol. 48 (1981), pp. 44–8.
1. In connection with a survey of low-income settlements in Karachi, a typology of houses was developed based on the quality of building materials used. Samples were taken from most squatter settlements – or 'squatments' for short – and (passively) urbanised villages in Karachi, so that a profile of the house conditions in each of these settlements could be constructed on the basis of the distribution of the various house types (for details see Van der Linden, 1977, pp. 84–109).

References

Alcock, A. E., K. N. Misra, J. L. McGairl and G. B. Patel (1963), 'Self-help Housing: Methods and Practices', *Ekistics*, 16, pp. 81–7.
Alonso, W. (1964), 'The Form of Cities in Developing Countries', *Regional Science Association Papers*, 13, pp. 165–73.
Caminos, H., J. F. C. Turner and I. A. Steffian (1969), *Urban Dwelling Environments* (Cambridge: MIT (MIT Report no. 16)).
Eyre, L. A. (1973), 'The Shantytowns of Montego Bay, Jamaica', *Ekistics*, 36, pp. 132–8.
Fathy, H. (1973), *Architecture for the Poor* (Chicago: University of Chicago Press).
JRP-IV (Joint Research Project IV) (1975), *Usmania Mahajir Colony* (Karachi: JRP-IV).
Kool, M., D. Verboom and J. van der Linden (1988), *Squatter Settlements in Pakistan* (Lahore: Vanguard).
Mangin, W. (1967), 'Squatter Settlements' *Scientific American*, 217, pp. 21–9.
MPD (Master Plan Department of Karachi Development Authority) (1974), *Karachi Development Plan 1974–1985* (Karachi: MPD).
Nientied, P. (1987), *Practice and Theory of Urban Policy in the Third World* (Amsterdam: Free University), Ph.D thesis.
Peattie, L. R. (1969), 'Social Issues in Housing', in B. J. Frieden and W. W. Nash (eds), *Shaping an Urban Future* (Cambridge: MIT Press).
Sudra, T. L. (1976), *Low-income Housing System in Mexico City* (Cambridge: MIT Press).
Turner, J. F. C. (1976a), *Housing by People* (London: Marion Boyars).
Turner, J. F. C. (1976b), 'Housing as a Support System', *Architectural Design*, 4, pp. 222–6.
Turner, J. F. C. and R. Goetze (1967), 'Environmental Security and Housing Input', *Ekistics*, 23, pp. 123–8.
Van der Harst, J. (1974), *Low Income Housing* (Karachi: JRP-IV).
Van der Linden, J. (1977), *The Bastis of Karachi; Types and Dynamics* (Amsterdam: Free University) Ph.D. thesis.

Van der Linden, J. (1982), 'Squatting by Organized Invasion: A New Reply to Failing Housing Policy?' *Third World Planning Review*, 4, pp. 400–11.

Van der Linden, J. (1986), *The Sites and Services Approach Reviewed* (Aldershot: Gower).

Van der Linden, J. (1988), 'Low-income Housing Markets in Karachi'. (Consultant's report on low-income housing in Karachi) (Washington/ Karachi: Padco).

Van Huyck, A. P. (1972), 'Towards a Housing Policy for Karachi', *Morning News* (Karachi), 18 March.

Vernez, G. (1976), 'A Housing Services Policy for Low-income Urban Families in Developing Countries', *Ekistics*, 41, pp. 8–14.

4 The Impact of Migration on Pakistan's Economy and Society
Omar Noman

I INTRODUCTION: MIGRATION AND THE PAKISTAN ECONOMY

Perhaps the most significant economic development in Pakistan over the past decade has been the dramatic growth of remittances from the Middle East (see Figure 4.1). Manpower export to the Middle East began on a large scale in 1975. None the less, as one can see from Figure 4.1 a sudden jump in remittances coincided with the first year of the Zia government as the first influx of migrants began to remit their incomes. The rupee value of remittances also registered a sharp rise between 1982 and 1985, on account of the delinking of the rupee from the dollar. During this three-year period, the rupee declined by 52 per cent. This led to a substantial increase in the rupee value of remittances, since the same dollar amount remitted could be exchanged for more rupees. By 1984 remittances constituted the largest single source of foreign exchange earnings; they were four times greater than net aid inflow to Pakistan. Not only did they provide 40 per cent of total foreign exchange earnings, but they also financed 86 per cent of the trade deficit (Pakistan Economic Survey, 1983–4). Their volume, 3.2 billion dollars annually at their peak, was substantial in relation to the size of the economy. The value of remittances has been approximately equal to 8 per cent of GNP.

Although we have referred to some official figures above, it is extremely difficult to be precise about the magnitude of migration and remittances. Government data underestimate these flows for two reasons. First, a substantial proportion of remittances come through 'informal' financial intermediaries. Migrants quite often rely on these mechanisms since they are more efficient than banking channels and at the same time offer an exchange rate premium. The 'hundi' system in the frontier is perhaps the most well known alternative financial market. The second reason for underestimation is the frequency of

77

Figure 4.1   Remittances by Pakistani migrants

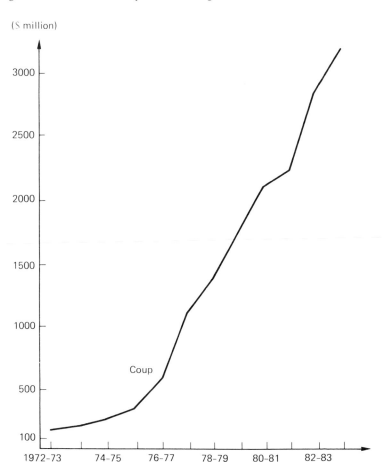

Source: State Bank of Pakistan

travel by migrants to the Gulf. They visit Pakistan at fairly regular
intervals which enables them to bring part of their incomes in kind
and in cash, without these being registered in the official figures. The
discrepancy between recorded and actual flows appears to be quite
substantial; according to one ILO estimate, remittances through
official channels account for only 57 per cent of total remittances

Table 4.1   Remittances from the Middle East

	Official Channels		Official and Unofficial Channels	
	Million US$	Percentage of GNP	Million US$	Percentage of GNP
1972–73	24.9	0.4	43.7	0.7
1973–74	39.6	0.5	69.5	0.8
1974–75	75.7	0.8	132.8	1.2
1975–76	203.0	1.5	356.1	2.7
1976–77	434.3	2.9	761.9	5.0
1977–78	932.9	5.2	1686.7	9.2
1978–79	1095.7	5.6	1922.3	9.8
1979–80	1362.6	5.8	2390.5	10.1
1980–81	1667.4	5.9	2925.3	10.4
1981–82	1835.7	6.0	3220.5	10.6
1982–83	2402.9	8.4	4215.6	14.8
1983–84	2344.3	7.6	4112.8	13.3
1984–85	2069.3	6.7	3630.4	11.7
1985–86	2021.5	6.2	3546.5	10.8

Source: Pakistan Economic Survey, various issues; ILO/ARTEP, 1987.

(ILO/ARTEP, 1987). Perhaps a more accurate impression of the total amount remitted can be obtained from Table 4.1 which shows both the official figures as well as data adjusted for unofficial flows. The latter suggest that at their peak remittances were nearly 15 per cent of GNP. This remittance/GNP ratio is one of the highest in the world.[1]

The escalation of migration to the Middle East coincided with a period of rapid growth in the Pakistani economy. Some of the GNP growth was accounted for by remittances. A study has attempted an assessment of this contribution (see Burney, 1987). Disaggregating the analysis into four time periods, this study suggests that the contribution of remittances to GNP growth could have been as high as 24 per cent in the mid 1970s. In other words, nearly a quarter of growth in the economy was due to remittances. Such high influence on GNP growth was partly due to the sluggish performance of other sectors of the economy during the 1975–6 period. During the late 1970s and early 1980s there was an acceleration in the rate of growth of the economy. As other sectors picked up, the contribution of remittances to GNP growth fell to 19 per cent and then to 11 per cent. However, these figures should be treated with some caution, since consumption expenditure accounted for a large part of the economic expansion (Burney, 1987, pp. 6–9 for detailed discussion of these issues). Consumption in turn was affected by remittances. In brief, remittances had a substantial influence on GNP growth between the mid 1970s and early 1980s. Since 1983–4 remittances have begun to decline quite substantially and this has been reflected in slower growth of the economy. Present trends in the Middle East suggest that remittances are unlikely to play a major role in Pakistan's growth process in the future.

II EFFECTS OF REMITTANCES ON PATTERNS OF CONSUMPTION AND PRODUCTION

Migration has had an impact on both the composition of demand and the choice of technology. The pattern of demand unleashed by remittances has moulded the growth of certain sectors in the economy. The sectors most favourably affected appear to be construction, transport and communication and consumer goods' industries (see Amjad, 1986; Burney, 1987). There has been a corresponding increase in the small-scale manufacturing sector.[2] Trading activities have also been encouraged by increasing demand for imported consumer goods; there has been a sustained expansion of the retail and wholesale trade.

The manner in which these multiplier effects have spread through the economy can be illustrated by the example of the construction sector. As indicated in Table 4.2, nearly 22 per cent of an average remittance was spent on real estate. Most of the families affected by the Gulf did not own their houses prior to migration. Naturally enough, their first priority has usually been to build a house. This led to a substantial construction boom.

The labour market effects of the boom were largely positive since there was an increase in both real wages and employment (World Bank, 1982). However, severe strains were put on the infrastructure. The construction industry required an adequate provision of public utilities, such as electricity. Table 4.3 documents the effects of the growth in the construction sector on electricity consumption. The share of domestic consumption of electricity rose from 10 per cent of the total in 1970 to 30 per cent in 1984. However, while the demands were growing, constraints on supply were imposed by resource shortages in the public sector investment programme. While energy supply was increasing by 11 per cent, the rate of domestic demand expansion

Table 4.2   Remittance spending patterns (average across migrants)

	% of total expenditure
Consumption	63.09
Real estate	21.68
Savings	12.05
Residual	3.18
Total	100.00

Source: Gilani, Khan and Iqbal, 1984.

Table 4.3   Use of electricity by economic groups (% of total sales)

	1969–70	1976–77	1983–84
Agriculture	26.6	25.68	16.74
Industry	45.7	42.09	36.94
Commercial	3.4	4.5	8.24
Domestic	10.2	14.31	30.29
Public lighting	14.1	12.62	6.92
Other		0.79	0.89

Source: Pakistan Economic Survey, 1983–4.

was approximately 24 per cent per annum (Water and Power Development Authority, 1986). The effects of poor planning in the energy sector became visible irritants in the form of constant power shortages. Urban areas have been subject to regular power cuts which distribute inadequate supplies by restricting availability. More significantly, private sector investment has been hampered by insufficient provision of infrastructure, a failure publicly acknowledged by the Planning Minister (*The Herald*, 1984).

Migration has not only affected the demand side but appears also to have had a direct bearing on the supply side by determining the choice of technology. Research evidence suggests that specific skill shortages due to migration led to a bias in production processes. More capital intensive methods have been adopted by entrepreneurs dissatisfied by the skill diminution of their workforce:

The composition of expenditure of remittances in Pakistan is such that it could adversely affect the labour absorptive capacity of the economy. This could occur through the influence of such expenditure on the sectoral composition of aggregate growth on the one hand, and the choice of increasingly capital intensive techniques within particular sectors on the other. (ILO/ARTEP, 1984, p. 69)

In this context we need to mention two well-known features of the Pakistan economy. The country has one of the highest population growth rates in the world. The current population of approximately 100 million is growing at an annual rate of 3.1 per cent. The problem is particularly serious since Pakistan is the tenth largest country in terms of population. The task of productively employing this rapidly growing workforce would be formidable for any economy; in Pakistan the problem has been compounded by high capital intensity in virtually all sectors of the economy. This problem appears to have been made worse by migration. There has, for example, been a decline in the elasticity of employment with respect to value added in the tertiary sector (ILO/ARTEP, 1983). This sector, which includes construction and services, has been the fastest growing sector in recent years. Its employment generating capability per unit of value added seems to have been impaired by technological bias due to migration-related skill shortages. Employers have often adopted capital intensive techniques to compensate for shortages of skilled labour as well as poorer efficiency of workers who replaced migrants.

Thus, it appears to be the case that whereas migration has undoubtedly eased labour absorption problems, it has at the same time contributed towards a capital intensive bias in the domestic economy. The latter has partially mitigated the job creating capacity of remittance-induced demand. The problem may become particularly serious if employers retain this bias towards capital intensive methods as the return flow of migrants accelerates.

III THE EFFECTS OF MIGRATION ON THE DISTRIBUTION OF INCOME

The crucial aspect of the migratory flows to the Middle East lies in the class background of migrants. The majority of the migrants are unskilled or semi-skilled workers. The dominance of the urban poor among them is reflected in the prevalence of production workers as the major occupational category (see Table 4.4). As evident from Table 4.4, migration to the Gulf has not been a primarily middle-class phenomenon. Previous waves of migration from Pakistan have often

Table 4.4   Occupational composition of migrant population (% of total)

Professional and technical	4.2
Clerical and administrative	1.6
Sales	5.6
Production workers	78.9
Service sector	4.7
Agriculture	4.8

Source: Gilani, Khan and Iqbal, 1984.

involved skilled groups, such as doctors. For example, migration to the USA and Canada largely involved professional classes. In most cases, whole families have moved. This form of migration, and the physical distance, implied a very different relationship with Pakistan when compared with the migration to the Gulf. Migration to North America and Western Europe also involved a considerable and permanent loss of skilled manpower for Pakistan. In contrast, the most favourable consequence of the bias towards male, unskilled workers in the Middle East has been the decisive impact on the living standards of a large number of poor families. Approximately 10 million people or 11 per cent of the total population (a figure which includes dependants) have benefited directly from the exodus to the Middle East. The vast majority of the beneficiaries come from low-income households. On average, their salaries increased between 600 to 800 per cent.[3] The increased family incomes from remittances have had a pronounced egalitarian impact in both urban and rural areas.

There is, perhaps, no historical parallel of remittances having resulted in such a rapid and wide distribution of benefits among the poorer sections of society. This is largely because migration normally involves, as pointed out above, a move of the whole family to the labour-importing country. Since only male workers have tended to go to the Middle East, the links with the labour-sending economy have been far more substantial. Aware of the temporary nature of his increase in income, the migrant worker has tended to use most of his income to acquire assets for his family. Not surprisingly, the main emphasis has been on building a house, acquiring consumer durables and accumulating a surplus for setting up small-scale business enterprises upon eventual return.

It is true, of course, that the record on income distribution of the four fast growing Asian economies – Taiwan, Singapore, Hong Kong and South Korea – has been reasonable. Such an outcome was achieved in spite of the adoption of economic policies which did not specifically pursue distributional objectives. A reasonable income distributional outcome was the consequence of initiating a policy framework of private, export-led growth after an initial redistribution of assets; for example, the far-reaching land reforms in Taiwan. In Pakistan, the asset distribution remains greatly askew. Yet, over the last decade, the country has been able to achieve a substantial increase in the living standards of a large number of poor families. This has been achieved through manpower export, without having to undergo the politically sensitive process of asset redistribution.

Data on wages of production workers suggest that there has been a rise in real wages in the late 1970s and early 1980s. There are several reasons for this growth and the influence of remittances is only one factor. None the less, according to a recent study (ILO/ARTEP, 1987), real wages between 1978 and 1983 increased by nearly 25 per cent and this coincides with a period of substantial migration. More circumstantial evidence is provided by data on wages in the construction sector. This sector is particularly affected by the Gulf, since a large number of Pakistani workers went to work on infrastructure developing projects. The same study gives relevant data for informal sector construction workers. The real wages for masons and carpenters increased by 41 per cent and 47 per cent respectively. Unskilled workers experienced a wage rise of over 70 per cent after migration to the Gulf began in 1974. This study also reports a short-term spurt in wages immediately after the flood of outmigration began in 1974–5. This helps to confirm our impression that migration appears to have contributed to the growth of real wages among construction workers and unskilled labour in certain sectors of the economy.

So far we have emphasised the positive effect of remittances on living standards of low-income households. However, migration has not involved a unidirectional movement of income towards poor families. A caveat needs to be noted with respect to the structure of the labour migration process. A peculiar feature of this flow has been the important role played by organised recruitment agencies. A substantial number of Pakistani workers have found jobs in the Middle East through these intermediaries. Studies conducted in several labour-exporting countries suggest that recruitment agents are often able to take a significant chunk out of the earnings of migrant workers (see Farooq-e-Azam, 1986; Government of Philippines, 1984; Roongshivin, 1984). The magnitude of the income

Table 4.5   Estimates of direct income transfers due to recruitment intermediation, 1977–85

	US Dollars in millions
Pakistan	364
Philippines	647
Thailand	232

Source: Abella, 1987.

transfer may be quite substantial. An estimate for Pakistan is reproduced in Table 4.5 which suggests that approximately 40 million dollars were earned annually by recruitment agencies between 1977 and 1985. This is likely to be an underestimate since the figure refers only to migrants and does not include payments made by unsuccessful job-seekers. On the basis of this information one cannot make any definitive statements about income distributional effects. However, one can safely suggest that these transfers represent a shift of income from low-income to higher-income groups. To this extent they somewhat mitigate the positive distributional effects of migrant remittances.

IV   THE EFFECT OF REMITTANCES ON THE LABOUR MARKET

We have earlier referred to the acute unemployment and underemployment problems faced by Pakistan. Manpower export has helped to ease the difficulties of productively absorbing the rapidly growing labour force. During the fifth plan period (1978–83), approximately 33 per cent of the increase in labour force was absorbed by overseas migration.

Migration on this scale normally entails a shortage of trained manpower in the labour-sending economy. This effect has not been so relevant since the skills that were in demand in the Gulf were easily replaceable. In a number of areas the quality of work suffered because of rushed apprenticeship periods. But, by and large, specific shortages of unskilled and semi-skilled labour were overcome by internal migration and informal training schemes.

A disaggregated analysis of the impact on particular labour markets is beyond the scope of this chapter. Only the effect on certain categories will be referred to here, for example, in the case of technicians (mainly diploma holders from polytechnics) there would have been significant unemployment without migration (Government of Pakistan, 1981). Similarly, projections for 1979–83 had suggested that the domestic supply of engineers was greater than the domestic demand. Thus, in the absence of migration, there would have been a surplus of engineers. In the event, domestic shortages were felt on account of the outflow to the Gulf (ibid.). Shortages of production workers were felt in some areas but they were temporary and relieved by internal migration (ILO/ARTEP, 1983, pp. 190–205). Perhaps more difficult to replace was the fall in the quality and quantity of qualified managers and administrators (ibid., p. 210). Skill shortages were also felt in certain sectors by the late 1970s, in response to which the government launched a technical skill training programme. In brief, although the government and the private sector have had to bear certain replacement costs for skills lost to the economy (ibid., p. 212), the magnitude of this burden has been less than would normally be the case. This was due to the fact that a labour surplus economy was primarily exporting low-skilled manpower for a temporary period.

V THE EFFECT OF REMITTANCES ON THE BALANCE OF PAYMENTS

Remittances have led to obvious benefits in the external sector. They eased balance of payments problems in the wake of the second oil price rise in 1979, enabling the economy to absorb the shock far better than it would have otherwise done. Balance of payments difficulties have been compounded by the recession in the West, which has led to restrictions in export markets and a decline in the terms of trade.

The effect of remittances on the external sector can be seen in Table 4.6 which documents Pakistan's balance of payments position between 1974 and 1986. As the proportion of remittances to GNP rose from 0.7 per cent in 1974 to 5.7 per cent in 1986, there was a corresponding decline in the current account deficit as a proportion of GNP. This ratio fell from approximately 10 per cent to 3 per cent. At the peak of remittances, in 1982–3, the current account deficit was only 1.3 per cent of GNP. In this year, debt servicing was equal to

Table 4.6 Balance of payment

Year	Trade balance	Non factor services + investment income (net)	Private transfers Net	Remittances from ME	% of GNP	Current account balance Million US$	% of GNP	% of trade balance	Debt servicing Million US$	% of RME	% of receipts	% of foreign exchange earning	Foreign exchange reserves	Terms of trade
		Million US$												
1974-75	-1137	-261	229	75.7	0.7	-1169	-10.3	6.7	248	327.6	23.9	16.3	419	94.6
1975-76	-977	-334	353	203.0	1.5	-958	-7.1	20.8	250	123.2	22.0	13.8	546	100.0
1976-77	-1286	-386	590	434.3	2.8	-1082	-6.9	33.8	12	71.8	27.3	15.4	363	108.9
1977-78	-1469	-362	1226	932.9	4.9	-605	-3.2	63.5	332	35.6	25.3	11.4	969	105.3
1978-79	-2172	-438	1496	1095.7	5.2	-1114	-5.3	50.5	436	39.8	25.5	11.9	414	126.2
1979-80	-2516	-519	1895	1362.5	5.3	-1140	-4.5	54.2	584	42.9	24.7	11.9	831	111.4
1980-81	-2764	-515	2242	1667.4	5.5	-1037	-3.4	60.3	602	32.8	20.4	10.4	1080	97.0
1981-82	-3450	-496	2412	1835.7	5.6	-1534	-4.7	53.2	492	26.8	20.0	8.8	862	89.2
1982-83	-2989	-509	3081	2402.9	7.6	-417	-1.3	80.4	634	26.4	23.5	9.6	1975	89.2
1983-84	-3324	-717	3044	2344.3	5.9	-997	-2.9	70.5	727	31.0	26.3	10.9	1788	93.1
1984-85	-3552	-815	2687	2069.3	5.2	-1680	-5.0	58.3	788	38.1	31.6	12.8	585	92.0
1985-86	-2990	-963	2808	2021.5	5.7	-1145	-3.2	67.6	906	44.8	29.5	12.6	968	92.3

Source: Pakistan Economic Survey, 1985/86, Statistical Supplement

approximately a quarter of total remittances. The latter were the largest single source of foreign exchange earnings. Thus remittances eased some of the foreign exchange constraint enabling a higher growth rate of the economy and reducing debt servicing difficulties. Debt servicing amounted to 52 per cent of total export receipts in 1970; by 1982 it was equal to 9 per cent of total foreign exchange earning, on account of the growth of inflows from the Middle East (for further discussion see Burney, 1987). This ratio has risen again as remittances have begun to decline.

Migration to the Middle East has had other indirect effects on the balance of payments. The presence of such a large volume of Pakistani workers, at a time of such rapid growth in the Gulf, assisted in the expansion of exports. Between 1974 and 1983, the share of Pakistan's exports to the Middle East in its total exports rose from 16 to 34 per cent.

We have noted above the beneficial effects of migration on the balance of payments. Two features of contact with the Middle East need, however, to be noted to gain a more comprehensive picture (see Saith, 1987 for a theoretical discussion of relevant issues). First, remittance spending patterns have involved a liberalisation of consumer goods' imports. To the extent that these have been of non-essential items, they reduce the utility of remittances in easing foreign exchange constraints on economic development. Second, the very feature responsible for migration to the Gulf, the oil price rise, has in turn been responsible for a substantial squeeze on Pakistan's balance of payments as the oil import bill rose dramatically in 1974 and 1979. Thus migrant remittances should partly be seen as a mitigating factor for the balance of payment problems caused by developments in the Middle East, rather than as windfall gains in the external sector.

VI THE POLITICAL AND SOCIAL IMPACT OF MIGRATION: CLASS FORMATION AND THE EFFECT ON OPPOSITION MOVEMENTS

The effect of large-scale manpower export has naturally extended to the political sphere. The urban bias in emigration is of particular relevance since urban areas constitute the nerve centres of the political system. A total of 9.3 per cent of rural households and nearly 16 per cent of urban households have at least one migrant member (Pakistan Institute of Public Opinion, 1979). The movements to topple both Ayub and Bhutto were based in the cities. Consequently, the political parties which opposed Zia's military regime relied critically on mobilising these organised groups in urban regions. Ironically, it was precisely from this category that a large proportion of emigrants came. The classes which the Movement for the Restoration of Democracy (MRD) was relying on to be in the vanguard of a national movement against the military were to become the primary beneficiaries of the Middle East. The damage which this process inflicted on the ability of the political parties to mobilise a mass movement was acknowledged by MRD leaders in interviews with the author.

Indeed, even those who were left behind were reluctant to spoil their chances of migrating by engaging in political activity. Since the Gulf countries adopted a policy of giving short-term contracts to hired workers, there was rapid turnover in the labour market. The rotation and mobility in the job market extended the network of opportunities to a larger number of aspirants than would have been the case otherwise. This led to the formation of expectations, among the working class who remained in Pakistan, that opportunities might yet occur to raise living standards dramatically. This effect on working-class psychology was noted by an ILO study: 'with such large scale migration of workers, people feel that with a little bit of luck, it is possible to be among the next batch of emigrants . . . the working class has come to believe that it is upwardly mobile' (ILO/ ARTEP, 1984, p. 10).

Further evidence for this process of class formation is provided by data on activities engaged in by migrants after they return to Pakistan. A survey carried out by the Overseas Pakistanis' Foundation (1984) suggests that few migrants wish to go back to their previous low-paid occupations. Many returning migrants wish to set up some kind of small business. This process of class formation has two implications. First, political parties have to adjust their appeal to this class to take account of changes in their material and social position. Second, the extent to which their aspirations are realised or not will determine the process of readjustment of migrants. A substantial group of frustrated returnees can exacerbate rapidly accumulating urban tensions.

Table 4.7   Provincial composition of migrant population compared with
provincial composition of national population

Province	National population (%)	Migrants (%)
Punjab	56	70
NWFP	13	12
Sindh	23	14
Baluchistan	5	4

Source: Gilani, Khan and Iqbal, 1984.

The Regional Distribution of Migrants

The provincial composition of the migrants reveals interesting variations of impact (see Table 4.7). The most widespread migration has
emanated from the Punjab. Punjab is the only province whose share
of the migrant population exceeds that of its proportion in the
national population; whereas Punjab's share in Pakistan's total
population is 56 per cent, it provides 70 per cent of the migrants.
Urban centres such as Lahore, Faisalabad, Rawalpindi, Gujranwala
and Jhelum have provided the bulk of the migrants. Similarly, a
substantial flow of unskilled labour from the North West Frontier
Province (NWFP) has gone to the Gulf. Sindh, however, has contributed a disproportionately small number of the total. Since a large
number of migrants to the Gulf from Sindh come from Karachi, the
effect on the troubled interior of Sindh has been minimal.

The Punjab's large share of overseas migration has important
implications. A tranquil and politically docile Punjab was of vital
importance to Zia's regime, and by and large this was maintained
over the last decade. The prosperity generated by migration has
played an important role in this process. Whereas it is not difficult to
extend state patronage to incorporate élite groups, it would not have
been possible for the domestic economy to increase living standards
for such a large number of people in the Punjab. It is also worth
emphasising that, as noted above, the area least affected by migration, interior Sindh, has been the most politically hostile region.
There are several reasons for this. We are not suggesting a simple
correlation with migration. However, the absence of remittances as a
source of widespread prosperity could only have aggravated a sense
of alienation and relative deprivation *vis-à-vis* other regions of the
country.

VII ISLAMIC INFLUENCE

Prior to 1975, Pakistani migrants tended to go to North America or Western Europe which increased contact with secular liberal democracies. The effect of this was largely intergenerational. Children of migrants tended naturally to incorporate social values and norms prevalent in their adopted country. By and large, these were not based on religious prescriptions.

In contrast, increased contact with the Middle East has important religious connotations. Migration is part of a much larger process of political, economic and ideological reorientation of Pakistan's position in international affairs. The country's Islamisation programme has received considerable financial and intellectual support from Saudi Arabia. The latter has become one of the major aid donors in recent years, exercising considerable influence on domestic policy with respect to the enforcement of Shari'a and on foreign policy, particularly regarding the form of support for the mujahadeen in Afghanistan.

The majority of Pakistani migrants, approximately 60 per cent, have gone to Saudi Arabia.[4] In view of that country's current influence on Pakistan and its historical significance for Muslims, it is somewhat surprising that we know so little about the social impact of the increased contact over the past decade. In the absence of research on this aspect of interaction with the Gulf, we can only suggest certain issues which are worth examining:

(1) To what extent have migrants been influenced by the more conservative flavour of Islam found in Saudi Arabia? Has the reaction been negative or positive, in the sense of being favourably or unfavourably disposed towards the interpretation of Islam in the labour-importing economies?

(2) Are there any discernible differences in attitudes between those who went to Saudi Arabia and those who migrated to other countries?

(3) Was the duration of their stay long enough to have a lasting effect on attitudes? If so, how has their behaviour been affected after returning?

(4) What has been the impact on women of male migration? What proportion have been working? Have attitudes of husbands/brothers/fathers been affected by migration?

(5) Have migrants to the Middle East approved of the Islamisation

Table 4.8   Share of countries in total Asian labour migration flow to all
destinations, 1977–85 (in percentages)

Countries	1977	1978	1979	1980	1981	1982	1983	1984	1985
South Asia	55.7	51.8	55.4	51.6	52.3	42.5	38.9	35.0	35.4
Bangladesh	4.7	5.1	3.9	3.7	5.3	5.4	4.8	5.0	7.4
India	6.9	15.5	27.4	28.7	25.7	20.8	20.4	18.1	15.6
Pakistan	42.4	29.4	20.0	15.7	15.9	12.2	10.5	8.8	8.5
Sri Lanka	1.7	1.8	4.1	3.5	5.4	4.1	3.2	3.1	3.8
East/S-E Asia	44.2	48.2	44.6	48.4	47.7	57.5	61.1	65.0	64.5
China					1.6	2.6	2.4	4.1	3.8
Indonesia	0.9	1.8	1.6	2.0	1.7	1.8	2.4	3.5	5.4
Korea	20.9	23.0	19.3	17.8	16.5	16.8	15.1	13.4	11.4
Philippines	21.2	19.9	21.9	26.0	25.2	26.9	35.4	37.4	37.2
Thailand	1.2	3.3	1.7	2.6	2.5	9.3	5.6	6.6	6.7
All Countries (in thousands)	331	443	627	824	1056	1168	1223	1136	1044

Source: Official statistical reports.

programme in Pakistan? Can they be said to have provided a constituency for this process or is it meaningless to talk of migrants as a separate category for this kind of social analysis?

Such questions need to be asked if we are to make an adequate assessment of the multidimensional impact of migration to the Middle East on Pakistani society.

VIII   RETURNING MIGRANTS AND THEIR REASSIMILATION INTO PAKISTAN'S ECONOMY

For Pakistan the period between 1976 and 1983 represented the peak of the Middle East boom. During this period remittances rose virtually every year. Since then, there has been both an absolute and a relative decline in Pakistan's presence in the Gulf. The relative decline in the labour force is illustrated in Table 4.8, Pakistani labour gradually being displaced by workers from Korea, the Philippines and India. In 1977, South Asian labour provided 55 per cent of the total labour force. This share declined to 35 per cent in 1985 as the share of Southeast Asia went up to 64 per cent. Particularly dramatic has been the fall in Pakistan's contribution. Pakistan's share in total migration in 1977 was greater than the whole of Southeast Asia put together. By 1985, however, Pakistan's position had declined to fourth, behind the Philippines, Korea and India, as Middle Eastern countries diversified their sources of labour supply. Far Eastern countries have been taking a larger share due both to their wage competitiveness and their command of a better educated manpower. A fall in relative share has been compounded by a decline in wage levels. The drop in wage rate for manual labour was over 30 per cent between 1983 and 1986. For more skilled workers, wages fell by approximately 10 per cent. Not only have wage rates declined but a large number of migrants have also been sent home. Even though the value of remittances is still quite substantial, they have been falling every year. There is also now a reverse flow of migrants. Other avenues for migration have closed: Iran has stopped importing Pakistani labour since 1979; so has Libya. With widespread unemployment in Europe and North America, the international labour market has dried up. In this situation, the Pakistani economy will be confronted with the following areas of concern for policy-makers.

First, policy-makers will be faced by the problem of employment generation. Migration has played a major part in easing problems of labour absorption over the last decade but the domestic economy must now absorb the entire annual increase in the labour force. This is likely to become a particularly intractable problem, since there are difficulties on both the supply and demand side of the labour market. As far as the supply side is concerned, efforts to control the population growth rate have been abysmal. If anything, the rate may have registered a slight increase in recent years. The ability of the government to act on the supply side has so far been severely hampered by an overall policy framework of Islamisation. The religious constraints on population planning appear to be far too difficult to overcome in the current environment.

On the demand side, Pakistan's industrial sector is plagued by excessively high capital–output and capital–labour ratios in relation to the resource endowment of surplus labour and scarce capital. Further, current import and tax policies have provided little incentive for entrepreneurs to alter these ratios for a more favourable outcome for labour absorption. Similarly, far too rapid mechanisation in agriculture has speeded up the process of rural–urban migration, as the labour absorbing ability of rural areas has been affected adversely.

The future scenario appears to be one of sharply rising unemployment and underemployment. The relief provided by migration is no longer available. Whatever room for manoeuvre exists seems to be confined to the demand side. Even here measures being undertaken to encourage employment are far too half-hearted and inadequate. A second area of concern is the reabsorption of migrants. The return of migrants requires the creation of additional employment opportunities. To some extent, they will create employment opportunities themselves, since a substantial proportion of returned migrants wish to start small enterprises. In order to encourage this development the government will have to ensure adequate credit availability. Numerous schemes have been launched to provide supplementary capital to small entrepreneurs and returned migrants, but it is far too early to assess the impact of these schemes. Apart from providing facilities to encourage the establishment of small businesses, there is little that the government can do specifically for returned migrants. The problems that migrants encounter in trying to find work are shared by a growing volume of entrants to the labour market. This may be of small comfort to the large body of young men who experienced a sharp, but temporary, rise in their incomes, but who now face unemployment. Their frustrations will be shared by those who never went to the Middle East but who continued to dream that they would be on the next plane.

Ironically, the very reason for which Middle Eastern migration was such a boon is now posing problems for the economy. *Temporary* large-scale migration meant substantial remittances to maintain families and build assets. The retention of such links, however, implied eventual return. The migrants are now coming back. Whether they can consolidate their position as an emerging *petite bourgeoisie* or become part of the accumulating discontent among the unemployed remains to be seen. Their absence had a great impact on Pakistan's economy and society. Their return is likely to prove equally significant in shaping the future course of development. The government of Pakistan has shown considerable interest in the war reparation effort in Iran and Iraq. It is too early to predict the extent to which these war torn economies will absorb Pakistani labour on reconstruction projects. The 'Gulf boom' may yet have another reincarnation.

Notes

1. Specially when one discounts for extremely small economies, where even minor remittance flows represent a substantial part of GNP.
2. The relationship between the growth of these sectors and development of small-scale manufacturing is a complex issue. The latter will be growing also because of domestic factors, entirely independent of migration. None the less, some effect of migration induced demand is apparent.
3. Estimates of precise magnitudes vary. The World Bank estimates an average increase of 650 per cent. ILO estimates are nearer 800 per cent.
4. The distribution of Pakistani labour in the Middle East is as follows:

Saudi Arabia	59%
UAE	15%
Qatar	8%
Kuwait	6%
Bahrain	3%

References

Abella, M. I. (1987), 'Asian Labour Mobility', *Pakistan Development Review*, xxv (8).

Amjad, R. (1986), 'Impact of Workers' Remittances from the Middle East on Pakistan's Economy', *Pakistan Development Review*, xxv (4).

Burney, N. A. (1987), *Workers' Remittances from the Middle East and their effect on Pakistan's Economy* (Islamabad: Pakistan Institute of Development Economics).

Farooq-e-Azam (1986), 'Working Conditions of Pakistani Workers in the Middle East', *ILO Working Paper*, MIG WP 25 (Geneva).

Gilani, I., Khan, M. and Iqbal, Z (1984), 'Labour Migration', Research Report No. 126 (Islamabad: Pakistan Institute of Development Economics).

Government of Pakistan (1981), *Demand/Supply Balances for Selected Occupational Groups* (Islamabad: Manpower Division).

Government of Philippines (1984), *Working Abroad* (Manila: Institute of Labour and Manpower Studies).

Herald, The (1984), June (Karachi).

ILO/ARTEP (1983), *Employment and Structural Change in Pakistan – Issues for the Eighties* (Bangkok: ILO/ARTEP).

ILO/ARTEP (1984), *Impact of Return Migration on Domestic Employment in Pakistan – A Preliminary Analysis* (Bangkok: ILO/ARTEP).

ILO/ARTEP (1987), *Impact of Out and Return Migration on Domestic Employment in Pakistan* (New Delhi: ILO/ARTEP).

Overseas Pakistanis' Foundation (1984), *Survey of Returning Migrants* (Islamabad).

Pakistan Economic Survey (1983–4) (Islamabad: Government of Pakistan).

Pakistan Institute of Public Opinion (1979), *Survey of Households* (Islamabad).

Roongshivin, P. (1984), *Some Socio–Economic Consequences of Thailand's Migration to the Middle East* (Bangkok: NESOB).

Saith, A. (1987), 'Macro-Economic Issues in International Labour Migration – A Review', ILO/ARTEP Working Paper No. 1 (New Delhi).

Water and Power Development Authority (1986), *Annual Report* (Lahore).

World Bank (1982), *Home Remittances in Pakistan* (Washington).

5 Marriage and Power: Tradition and Transition in an Urban Punjabi Community

Michael D. Fischer

The equality of all Muslims is a basic tenet of Islam. In Pakistan, as with other predominantly Muslim areas, equality is held as an ideal, but the social organisation and social reality of Pakistan is hierarchical. There are several levels of contrast within the hierarchy. This chapter is restricted to two, a category, *zat* and a group, *biradari*. The chapter examines the development of social hierarchy in a new urban community in Lahore called Greentown.[1] This provides a context to explore social organisation in urban Punjab, and possibly the Punjab as a whole. A model is proposed to account for these forms which presents change in the urban environment not as a process of modernisation, but as an adaptive transformation to the city where the morphology and pragmatics of the forms are altered, but much of the interpretation of these forms remains the same. Further, community formation is presented as a process of lessening ambiguity, where relations within families are seen as maximally ambiguous, and relations between families as minimally ambiguous. I conclude with a brief analysis of close agnatic marriage in this context, and a discussion of the relevance of traditional tribal–caste categories to the process of defining a social hierarchy.

Zat is a hereditary non-corporate category often translated as caste, or tribe, and literally as kind, species, genus (Platts, 1968). The importance of *zat* in Greentown is denied by residents but nevertheless *zat* appears to be correlated to marriage; 85 per cent of marriages in Greentown are contracted between families of the same *zat*. *Zat* are ranked with each other, although there is considerable variation in the specific ranking in any given locality (Marriott, 1965). In Greentown, there is little agreement on ranking except for the extremes. The *biradari* can be considered as either the corporate manifestation of a *zat* locally or as a minimal patrilineage, depending

97

on context of use. The *biradari* (minimal patrilineage) are ranked
with each other within the localised *zat/biradari*. There is ranking
within the *biradari* also. At each level of contrast, the members
within the unit ranked are usually assigned the same rank. In practice
individuals gain some of their status by these category associations.
Ranking is not static and may change. In a context such as Greentown, where a community is forming, the process of ranking is in
progress and some of the mechanisms of change are visible.

The people of Greentown had undergone great personal change in
the six to eight years that most of them had been in Greentown prior
to 1982. The Punjab as a whole has been a place of demographic and
economic change since the mid-nineteenth century when the irrigation canals opened up the land for intensive agriculture. And the
legacy of Partition on Lahore is unmistakable; 43 per cent of the
population was exchanged (Qadeer, 1983). It follows that the form of
social organisation in this context must be adaptive to changes in
personnel and circumstance. This is possibly one of the functions of
non-corporate tribe–caste categories; to provide a category of social
organisation that is mobile because it is distributed. Everywhere in
the Punjab the same *zat* may be found. This in-built relationship
provides a source of mates and potential aid to the incoming migrant.

In their new situation, Greentown residents are isolated geographically from old relations and have new relations in Greentown to
negotiate. In the process of community formation, people have
apparently applied 'traditional' categories, at least in terms of marriage. In Greentown, and the Punjab as a whole, the expressed ideal
of marriage is endogamous. Contracting a marriage is an assertion of
sameness, and marriage outside the extended family[2] further serves
the purpose of establishing a basis for comparing the two families and
indirectly the relatives (*rishtidar*) of the respective families. Those
members of a family are viewed externally as the same kind, and
equal. Internally, they are ranked. Contracting a marriage is a
powerful means of indicating status and making statements about
solidarity. Initially, marriage is far more a concern of parents than
the actual participants. Marrying one's children establishes, consoli-
dates or improves the social position of the family and other members
of their *rishtidar* and localised *biradari*.

This suggests a strategy for adapting to changing status: after
achieving the requisite standing it is necessary to arrange a marriage
with someone of the same status, and it is necessary that independent
observers agree it is an equal marriage, as a marriage must be

between equals.[3] Marriage is an expression, rather than the vehicle of status increase. Marriage is the demonstration, the currency of earned measure, not merely a device for integration into new society. Greentown residents do not simply follow traditional rules of behaviour. Nor are they 'modern' Punjabis who have changed the rules of the game. Rather, they attempt to manipulate and negotiate their social environment using the categories and meanings with which they are familiar. Their behaviour and social practices are dynamic and changing, responsive to the new set of circumstances in which they find themselves. The interpretation of this behaviour, however, the construction of meaning, is relatively fixed, extended by analogy from prior contexts.

Clearly, the people's own interpretation of their behaviour is as much a part of the ethnographer's analysis as the behaviour itself. Interpretative rules, indigenous theories of why particular instances of social behaviour occur, are applied to behaviour in interactive situations. In novel contexts, actors make sense of perceived behaviour in the light of existing categories of meaning. In the case of arranging marriages in Lahore, a regular list of conditions and preferences for marriage candidates is elicited from residents. These are posed as different options of performance available to the participant. I suggest this is possible only when there are flexible classification procedures for reducing the variation of the acts that are observed and the acts that are possible to the limited list of options elicited. It is necessarily easier to have a system with a finite set of interpretations than a system with a finite number of acts, especially as the system must be capable of change. Change requires inherent variation, and interpretation requires inherent stability.

I GREENTOWN

Greentown is the result of a plan by the Lahore Development Authority (LDA) in the early 1970s for low-cost housing and allotments for low-level civil servants. As with many plans, the development took a somewhat different course. When houses were built in 1974 there were two pressing problems, one local and one national. After the civil war with East Pakistan a number of Bihari refugees fled to Pakistan. A section near Greentown was designated as a relocation centre for these refugees. Some of these early refugees were allocated plots in Greentown, forming the area known locally as

'Bihari Mohalla'. A second problem were *katchi abadi* (squatters' communities) situated on government land, presently the sites of the Badi Building and Wapda Building. The residents of these *katchi abadi* were given plots in Greentown to clear these sites. The remaining plots were allotted to civil servants and military personnel, many of whom sold the plots to Lahore residents. The resulting composition combines three complete ex-*katchi abadi* communities, a group of refugees, and overflow civil population, and by 1982 was an integrated community. The internal and external identity of these groups based on their origin is maintained within this community framework.

II MARRIAGE CANDIDATES

The marriage pattern of all groups in Greentown is generally endogamous. There are a number of degrees of endogamy, ranging from marrying one's child to children of siblings, to intra-*zat* endogamy. In Greentown, inter-*zat* marriage among Muslims has an incidence of about 11 per cent. There is a large number of factors that lead to the evaluation of appropriate candidates for marriage. The traditional criteria are as follows.

Forbidden Marriages

Marriage is absolutely forbidden between parent and child, siblings, parent's sibling and child, parent's parent and child, parent and child's spouse, sibling's spouse (while sibling lives) and marriage between people who share the same human breast milk (*maka dudh*). The latter applies to breast milk from an unrelated wet nurse (*dai*). These are exclusions given in the Qur'an, the Islamic holy scripture. The explanations given by informants for these prohibitions varied. They were not formulae. There was a firm conviction that these were not correct marriages; they were 'bad deeds' (*kharab kam*). Reasons given included 'for the good of families, of children, and the good of culture', and 'Islam is the reason and the best culture in the world.'

Disapproved Marriages

There are two basic categories of disapproved marriages. The first is a marriage to a family that is of bad character, usually expressed in terms of the conduct of the women of the family ('their women creep'; they are not controlled with respect to enforcing proper – invisible – behaviour), and the second is marriage to a family that is of low status, often expressed in terms of low occupation. The two are often combined, and for the purposes of contracting a marriage are equivalent; a man who must take a bad job must be bad.

Preferred Marriages

In general, the preferences given by informants for marriage are based on degree of genealogical closeness. A rough order relative to the parent, the decision-maker, is:

(a) Same-sex sibling's child.
(b) Opposite-sex sibling's child.
(c) Parent's sibling's child's child.
(d) Spouse's sibling's child.
(e) Other relation (*rishtidar*).
(f) *Zat* member's child.
(g) *Sayyid's* child (not approved by most Sayyid).
(h) A good family, any *zat* of equal *izzat* (honour, status) (not universally approved).

There is considerable variation in the application of these preferential categories among the different groups of Greentown, although the above list can be consistently elicited from representatives of them. In a sample of eighty-eight marriages, the residents previously from the *katchi abadi* Beri Hata follow the list quite closely; almost 45 per cent contracted marriages between first cousins. Recent Bihari migrants to Greentown have no instances of first cousin marriage in the sample. The other groups show 20 to 33 per cent first cousin marriage. The distribution of marriage by relative and non-relative of different groups is summarised on Table 5.1.

III FINDING A CANDIDATE

Marriages are arranged by the parents in association with other members of the *rishtidar*. This practice is not under pressure to change in Greentown and is credited as a far superior method to that used in the West, love marriages. For first marriages it is also

Table 5.1   Marriage by degree of relationship for different origin groups

Origin group	N	% First cousin	% Other relative	% Non-relative
Bihari	19	0	5.3	94.7
Civil	13	23.1	0	76.9
Badi	20	20.0	0	80.0
Beri Hata	29	44.8	34.5	20.7
Christian	12	33.3	8.4	58.3

convenient, as unrelated males and females rarely interact, and it is to a potential bride's credit if she were previously invisible. It is difficult for parents to locate suitable potential candidates, even with their formidable networks of connections, much less for a relatively unconnected male.[4]

Love marriages are not unknown, especially for second marriages (polygamous or serially monogamous) which are often arranged directly by the husband-to-be. A second marriage is more likely to be the sister of a friend or another relative than strictly a love marriage, although marrying the sister of a close friend is often considered a love marriage, at least by the husband.

There is a fascination with love marriages which are a common theme in mythology, songs, poetry, and cinema, though the result of the love match in these media is usually hardship and/or death. Those love matches that occur are often between cousins. For some people the only proper meaning of love match is in the latter context. All the respectable, and hence marriageable, females known to a prospective groom are likely to be relatives. In a sample of ninety-three marriages one love match was recorded between an unrelated couple.

Marriage is a civil contract between the groom and the bride and establishes a relationship between the respective families; families marry, expressed in the contract between a bride and groom. The marriage affects the *izzat* (honour, status) of both the participating families, in their extended form. It will establish or reinforce social relationships, and the conduct of the bride and groom will continue to affect the parent families in the future.

The making of a proper match is an issue of ideology; the complementary nature of the man/woman married unit. This is expressed in terms of social and economic criteria. One of the arguments for marriage within the *zat* in agricultural communities is that specific skills are required by both members of the marriage unit. Associated with the low-status service positions (*kammi*) and the landholding groups (*zamindar*) are both male and female roles, and only people who were raised to acquire the necessary skills can successfully carry out these roles (Eglar, 1960; Gough, 1960). For example, the role of the barber (*nai*) includes services by the barber and his wife; he for the male clients and she for the female clients. There is a male and female universe, and the married unit is the synthesis of the two.

This situation is similar in Greentown, for although the wife of a bureaucrat, factory worker or construction worker does not share that work, she must have the social skills to support whatever claims to status the husband may command. If the parents hope to marry their daughter to a non-menial civil servant (one of the highest status occupations in Greentown), depending on the grade of the civil servant an educational level of eight years, matric (ten years), or even FA/FSC (twelve years) may be appropriate. This emphasis on necessary skills has led to an increase in education of women in Greentown in recent years, especially relative to Pakistan as a whole, with most women under 21 in Greentown having at least six years of education, while many advance through matric. There are relatively few women who gain educational qualifications beyond this level. There are few employment related objectives in most of these cases. Women make up less than 4.2 per cent of the workforce in Greentown, although this does not take into account work done in the home.

The practice is not isolated to Greentown. In Lahore, it is not unusual for a middle-class family wishing to marry their daughter to a lawyer, to send her to law school, or to a doctor to medical school, not to meet potential husbands but to acquire the skills necessary to be the wife of the given professional. These women will usually not practise their profession, although there are some niches brought about by the isolation of women from men. Some parents see the education of daughters as part of their dowry (*jihez*), others comment on the necessity for the wife to understand what her husband is doing. Objectively it *is* necessary, for the parents of a male doctor will often only consider marrying their son to another doctor or to a girl with some medical training (although not nursing which is a very low-status occupation in Lahore).

IV PREPARATION FOR ARRANGING A MARRIAGE

The preparations for marriage far precede that day when actual candidates will be sought, especially for daughters. It is common for a man with two or three young daughters to reflect on how he will marry them off. This is important not only because of the economic aspects, but because daughters are the primary elements for a man's ambitions to increase his status or *izzat*. The marriage of sons is important but not generally perceived as a serious problem. The marriage of daughters is seen as difficult, for if daughters are badly married this will reflect on the family. Women are the core of the family's *izzat*. They define its range and their behaviour reflects on this. After marriage the family of the husband assumes responsibility for her behaviour. If that responsibility is not taken, this reflects on the family of the girl; they take the blame, although she is not under their direct control, because it was their responsibility to find a respectable family and to provide a woman who would maintain the honour of both families. If she is married to a bad family, the only interpretation is that she was married to a family that was equal to her own. If she behaves badly, such as abandoning her husband without cause, or has sexual relations with men other than her husband (*zina*, fornication), then it is the responsibility of her family to remedy the situation, in the latter case sometimes by her death.

V FINANCING A MARRIAGE

Another consideration is the great expense of a wedding. For either sons or daughters the cost is great, on average about £650 in 1982, which is just over the median yearly household income in Greentown. Daughters require a dowry (*jihez*) which is as much as £650 and sometimes twice or three times that amount. The amount of the dowry varies with several factors, including the closeness of the relationship to the potential husband, the general status of the family, and the degree of support of the *biradari* and *rishtidar*, as well as the actual status of the family and the customs of their *zat* or *biradari*. Sons must give expensive sets of jewellery and clothing to the bride. The expense of these gifts may be equal to the amount of *jihez*. However, it is the cost of the *jihez* that fathers complain about. Possibly this is because the *jihez* will leave with the daughter, while the presents of the groom to the bride will come into the house with the bride. Certainly most couples consider the jewellery as a form of contingency funds and savings.

With a completed fertility in Greentown of between five and six children, a household's (*ghar*) total wedding expenses can be staggering. The average total cost of marrying every child to maximum benefit can amount to eight years household income. Though demographic variability will lead to different situations for different households, financing weddings is clearly a serious problem.

There are three basic methods of dealing with the financial aspects; savings, contributions from the *biradari* and *rishtidar*, and lowering the cost. Savings from the income of the household is difficult but there is a variety of methods used for savings. The most common are prize bonds from the government, and 'committees' – rotating credit associations. Prize bonds are fixed term bonds that pay no interest but enter one in a lottery (since the basic amount is never at risk, this is not considered gambling by Shari'a law). Families with seemingly very small surpluses often have large sums invested in these bonds.

Committees are used for a variety of savings purposes. The most common form of committee is organised around a community-based group where each contributes a fixed sum on a monthly basis, and each month one member collects the monthly receipts by draw. The winner is ineligible to win again but is responsible for paying the periodic sum for the life of the committee, until everyone collects. The major advantage of this form of committee is the possibility of accumulating a large sum of money at one time if one is fortunate, and, more quickly than by saving oneself. This form of rotating credit association, which has an important role in the social life of Greentown, ranges from small-scale committees among boys to larger-scale committees among shopkeepers, who regularly use it as a means of collecting money for restocking. The committee is held together by a man sometimes called the *izzatwala* who personally underwrites each member's continuing contributions to the committee, even after winning, and is responsible for finding replacements for those who drop out. The larger the committee, and the larger the funds involved, the bigger the *izzatwala* must be, for the other members of the committee depend on him for their investment; they must trust his ability to control everyone else.

Often a man will start a five-year committee for each daughter at around the age of 14, planning her engagement for the time the committee pays off. The committee may not be large enough to pay all expenses, but will usually be sizeable enough to defray much of the expense. A typical five-year committee will be 200 to 500 rupees per month yielding a payout of £450 to £1200.

Contributions from the *biradari* and the *rishtidar* are an important means of financing a wedding. At all weddings these members are obliged to contribute although amounts are regulated such that payments balance over time. To ensure this, contributions are entered into a ledger at every wedding. Reciprocity is strictly maintained. Large contributions by myself were rejected because there was no possibility of reciprocity. Objectively the system is used to gain influence within the *rishta*, for one is free to give more than it is feasible for another to return, putting these people under obligation. For the purposes of finance though, contributions can be seen as another form of savings.

There are occasions when the contributions from the *biradari* will exceed that which could ever be repaid, especially when making a *rishta*, marriage, of high status. This kind of marriage is very risky as the entire *biradari* could suffer greatly in terms of status if its side did poorly (i.e. did not present an image reflecting its *izzat*), while standing to gain much if its side does well. It also occurs when the majority of the *biradari* have done rather well socially, though the family hosting the marriage has not done as well. In order to preserve the image of the *biradari* and maintain its *izzat*, it is necessary to subsidise the marriage. This may also be necessary when a man has many daughters.

Reducing costs is the third option. There are two basic strategies in Greentown. The first is marriage between cousins. Although some marriages in this category have fairly low *jihez* and *haq mehr* amounts associated with them, others involve amounts not unlike those associated with outside marriages.[5] The second option is marriage within Greentown. All things considered, these are the cheapest marriages.

VI EXOGAMOUS MARRIAGES

There are two types of exogamous marriage in Greentown; marriages outside Greentown, and marriages within Greentown. The former creates the possibility of asserting higher status, although at some risk. The latter results in respectability and the affirmation of Greentown as an honourable community. There is an analogical similarity between intra-Greentown marriage and endogamy; marriage within Greentown is a kind of in-marriage. Residents of Greentown have more intimate relations with one another than with the world outside.

For example, in traditional terms *purdah* requires the separation of men from women. In Lahore, this is often associated with the wearing of the *burqa*, a heavy tent-like garment, somewhat like a habit, often with a face covering. In Greentown, most women do not wear the *burqa* but only a *chaddar*, a large shawl. However, if one examines the mini-buses that leave Greentown for the markets of Township and Modeltown, many of the women are wearing *burqa*. Wearing the *burqa* outside Greentown has a significance it does not have in Greentown; within Greentown only a *chaddar* or even a *dupatta* (scarf) is required to establish respectability.

Eglar (1960) reports that the *biradari* within a village is often both a social group and a group of relatives – the usage of *biradari* is extended to the immediate social group, as well as denoting those members of the patrilineage. Within the *biradari* there is not the same need for demonstrating in a symbolic (and uncomfortable) manner extreme modesty by wearing the *burqa*. Higher and lower status groups associate the wearing of *burqa* with people who are attempting to increase their position. All informants associated it with a conservative attitude, the expression of *purdah* (seclusion). The wearing of *burqa* is a sign of *izzat*. It is not required if there are sufficient other signs available. For instance, the women of the upper social groups in Lahore rarely, if ever, wear the *burqa*, apparently with little concern for losing *izzat*. Women of the lowest economic groups never wear the *burqa*, explaining that they cannot afford to do so since they must work, purchase goods at the market, and interact with the world. Women who wear the *burqa* would be defeating the purpose if they were to be seen interacting, as it is an expression of non-interaction. The rich need not make the demonstration at all as their position is secure, their control established. It would be incorrect, though, to say that the use of the *burqa* is restricted to those who are attempting to increase the standing of the family; rather, it is required of those approaching a critical point on the *izzat* scale. Without the demonstration of the secluded (and hence controlled) woman, their claim is uncertain. There is, however, little point in making demonstrations to those of equal standing – equals in identical context – especially with the real sacrifice involved in wearing such a garment in the often sweltering heat of Lahore.

Among the practical factors that must be considered in arranging a marriage are the demands or requirements of kin, the requests and requirements of neighbours, the maintenance, improvement, or consolidation of the position of the family, the *biradari*, the *rishtidar*, and the community, the finances available both within the household, and from kin and friends, the age of the prospective bride or groom, and the availability of candidates from the network of contacts. Even with a perceived status advantage to a marriage with strangers, contacts are necessary to ensure that the marriage is viable and will prosper.

VII THE CONCEPT OF *IZZAT*

Izzat is a parameter, a measure of social control. The more control one can be seen to exercise, the higher the *izzat*. This assertion is a bit glossy but it is reasonable. All instances that can cause a loss of *izzat* involve a loss of control – an elopement, women 'creeping', disobedience by sons, being abandoned by one's wife, a refusal of marriage, losing in a conflict. Likewise, all things that lead to an increase in *izzat* demonstrate control – good marriages, women in *purdah*, obedient sons, winning conflicts, operating committees, heading political groups. In the élite groups in Lahore, where social dominance and control are more explicit, people often represented their position in terms of their subordinates ('how many rifles'). The less one has to do because others do it instead, the higher the *izzat*. For example, medical doctors who practise medicine have high *izzat* relative to other residents of Greentown, but not as high as comparable professions. They complained about the lack of respect. However, doctors who do not practise but maintain a clinic with young doctors handling the practice have considerable *izzat*.

Izzat is based upon control, the ability to control key social and economic groups and persons in the society. Almost all the things that directly affect *izzat* are instances of success or failure to control these social elements. The most fundamental level of control is control of women. Without this basic level of control, opportunities in the *izzat* game are non-existent. The next level of control is over the younger males of the family. This tends to be a local role, and like control over women, is generally a maintainer rather than a facilitator of *izzat*. The next level of control is over the males in general of the extended family. Rises in *izzat* are possible but limited to the potential of the group; the present *izzat* of the group is a limiting factor.

Control over other men of the *biradari*, or even better, outside the *biradari*, is the highest form of control – the greater the sphere of control the better. This, for example, helps account for the high status that civil servants enjoy purely as a result of attaining office, for by controlling the allocation of rights and privileges they exert tremendous amounts of control (Kennedy, 1957).

The establishment of the level of *izzat* of a social unit is the establishment of the degree of control one can expect from that social unit. In marriage this is realised in the choice of degree of endogamy – the degree of *izzat* to be gained increases with the distance from ego – it is a demonstration of control, both over the external family the marriage is made with, and over the local group who theoretically would desire a close marriage. Also, by extending the number of contacts, which only an out-marriage can really accomplish, the potential level of control is increased.

There is also a corresponding risk in such out-marriage, the risk increasing with the degree of distance, for unless one is actually sure of their control, there is a risk that breakdown of control – rejection or exposure – will trigger a drop in *izzat*.

The closer the marriage, the closer to one's sphere of control, and the less ambiguous is the relationship of control. The dangers are very real, for marriage negotiation is a risky business and can appear adversarial in nature. The adversarial nature extends up to and through the marriage celebration. I attended one marriage that was notable for an almost complete lack of competition, where the father of the groom was also the guardian of the bride, and another involving parties previously unknown to each other where my case of food poisoning was met with delight on the part of the groom's family as a demonstration of the shoddy efforts of the other party. The adversarial appearance arises from the ambiguity of the situation. Although the marriage is theoretically between equals, the actual social organisation is based upon inequality, with bride takers higher than bride givers. When new social relations are formed, as in marriage to strangers, these two conflicting views must be reconciled: on the one hand, the presentation of equality between the newly contracted affines, and, on the other, the demonstration of extended control which the new alliance represents. This demonstration is underlined by the public flaunting of conventions and 'rules', for the ability to break a rule without provoking retaliation is itself a power-ful display of control.

Social control is not to be conceived of in isolation for it entails responsibility; responsibility to use one's control for the benefit of those one controls and responsibility to remain worthy of the respect required to gain control. One implication of this is that the number of external marriages can be an index to the level of *izzat*, and hence the level of control. There is a high cultural value placed on marriages representing a high degree of endogamy, but marriages representing a high degree of exogamy are also highly valued. What is the relationship between the two apparently conflicting forces?

They must both emanate from the same centre – they are different reflections of a common underlying structure. Marrying endogamously might seem to be marrying into the same level of *izzat*. To some degree this is so, but the situation is more complex. There are significant variations of *izzat* between different residential units of the joint family. Brothers do not end up on equal terms. There is in-built inequality in the relations between brothers which is expressed by formal kin names for elder brothers, and the use of honorifics when addressing them. The elder brother has the right of control over the younger brothers, and the elder brothers of the father have a right of control over the father and his sons. It would follow that these elder males have more *izzat* than the younger brothers by virtue of having a greater level of control.

There are also the fortunes of the world, especially in the dynamic period since Partition. Occupation and *izzat* are related – it is impossible for someone with a 'low' job to be considered of 'high' *izzat*. If brothers get different jobs, they may be ranked on the basis of the jobs rather than the internally assigned roles of control, that is the external control expressed by a younger brother may yield a higher *izzat* overall than the older brother with an inferior job. Of course, the elder brother may make gains over the younger brother if his occupation is at least neutral, or he is unemployed, as he still theoretically controls the younger brother. If the younger brother is a civil servant, the elder brother will definitely make gains.

A marriage between conceptually equal families, the families of two brothers, affirms this equality in practice. No one can suffer for marrying into their sibling's family, even if the marriage were impossible between unrelated families.

This fits into the pattern of responsibility that accompanies *izzat* – a responsibility to those controlled, as well as to the model of equality of siblings. Functionally, it provides a safe place to marry daughters when economic resources are insufficient for a marriage to an external family, and it tends to maintain the model of equality in practice by levelling those higher placed individuals to that of their family as a whole.

VIII MARRIAGE AND *IZZAT*

Marriage is integrally tied to *izzat*, and through *izzat* to other considerations. The minimum condition of success for a marriage is that it maintain the *izzat* of the family. Fortunately, as with most successful social games, there is a number of possible marriages that do so, and many social forces that facilitate each option. Formally, marriage is based on a system of social endogamy, where closer relationships bear more value. There are few positive formal rules – one must marry daughters within the *zat*/*biradari*, and if one marries a son out of the *biradari*, it should be to a daughter of a family equal or slightly lower in status. In terms of preference and values the choices tend within these limits, with about 26 per cent of marriages in Greentown between sibling's children, 13 per cent to *rishtidar*, and 61 per cent to non-relatives (or distant relatives who are regarded similarly) within the *zat*, including 15 per cent to non-*zat* members (based on a random sample of 93 marriages). Non-*zat* marriages are most prevalent among the Christian and Bihari residents of Greentown, but indigenous Muslims still average 11 per cent.

Marriage within the first category of preferred candidates (cousins) is considered safe and respectable, as well as desirable. The marriage to a sibling's child is favoured for several reasons. First, it is certain that all details that could affect *izzat* are known. Such a marriage is, in theory, between parties of equal (or one could say the same) *izzat*, although in practice this is not always the case. A marriage of this type reinforces the position of equality – it increases the likelihood of the interpretation of equality by outsiders – and is a demonstration of solidarity. Second, it is safe because the negotiations can be carried out with the security of an *izzat*-saving measure if it does not materialise (see also Donnan, 1985 for a village account of this aspect). It is to no one's advantage to advertise a failure, as both parties would lose *izzat*, one for being rejected, the other for refusing kin. Third, the potential bride's and groom's characters are well known, and future deportment can be estimated, a very important consideration for the long term. Also, a close marriage may be an obligation to the group. Although the father and his *biradari* have the final right of acceptance of a marriage candidate, the mother is often the person who finds the candidate. From a father's perspective there is a stated preference for marriage to his brother's child, and then his sister's child. From a mother's perspective there is a stated preference for her sister's child, and then her brother's child. In practice, for marriage to a sibling's child, the result in Greentown is a predominance of same-sex sibling's child marriage, which occurs five times more frequently than different-sex sibling's child marriage.

Marriages of the second category (*rishtidar*) are similar to the first, but less secure in terms of ensuring maintenance of *izzat*. Much is known of the candidate and his or her family, but not all. Some of the relationships will be heavily reinforced through several marriages by different families of the *rishtidar*, others not. There are gains and losses of *izzat* possible in marrying within the *rishtidar*, as some of the marriages in the past may have been between families that have recast the *izzat* differentials. A marriage which was proper in the past between families, may not be proper if there has been change since that time, although the usual interpretation would be that they were equal. I would consider marriages within Greentown to be in this second grouping, given the observations made earlier.

Marriages within the *zat*, with no closer relationship, are less secure than within the *rishtidar*. Often the only information about the family of the proposed match is that acquired through mutual contacts. Marriages to non-relatives are associated with increases in status, but also create the possibility of lowering *izzat*. There are two possible interpretations of such a marriage by the community. One interpretation is that one family is marrying down, and the other is a match between equals. In the former case, there can be a net *izzat* increase in the long term for the lower family, as they gain contacts into higher status circles, and a net increase for the higher family in the form of extension of influence, for the lower family takes on a number of obligations in the transaction. However, in the short term both families lose some *izzat* which they can regain later by more appropriate marriages.

In marriage between equals there is no theoretical increase in status, as they are equal, but the marriage serves to increase the circle of contacts of both, and to consolidate the status of the family; since they were able successfully to negotiate the marriage, this implies they consider themselves equal. There is the possibility of non-uniform interpretation of the match by the communities of the two families. There is much effort by both parties to create the proper interpretation of equality, and at the same time compete for the notional control in the relationship.

IX MARRIAGE STRATEGY

Greentown is a community undergoing rapid change, much of it in terms of the observable, and hence the interpretable, features associated in the past with a level of status that is higher than residents possessed only a few years earlier. As a consequence of government policy, residents are now holders of *pakka* land, live in *pakka* houses, have good jobs, and can send their children to school. This has given rise to a problem. Now that they possess the potential of higher status, residents must make efforts to consolidate it by being careful about the kinds of social relationships they maintain and initiate. *Izzat* can be gained, but it can also be lost much more easily. Residents are aware of this, for example, when extending social relationships through friendships.

Friendships are unranked relations. Friendship is a *lena-dena*, take and give, relationship. One must have something to offer in exchange for what is taken in equal measure. The primary commodity friends have to offer each other is loyalty and influence. A friendship in Greentown is an intensive, demanding relationship, where each side expects demands and makes them. When a promising acquaintance is made, a person will initiate a friendship by recounting who his relations are, allowing the other to evaluate what is on offer, and expecting reciprocation. Each, through his or her kinship connections, has something to offer, and, if they are well matched, friendship can develop.

Within the kin group or the *zat*, one has influence as both a patron and a client. As a patron, demands can be made of clients. As a client, requests can be made of the patron. The patron must deliver his influence in exchange for the loyalty of the client, and the services the client can deliver. In a friendship, there are two kinds of influence on offer; that which can be given as a patron, and that which can be delivered as a client. The former is more secure, but the latter is the principal role that powers society in the Punjab, as patrons are nothing without their clients.

A necessary condition of friendship is conceptual equality. Equality is an important attribute to be able to establish, and can only be established when the respective groups, and the relative position of the prospective friends within these groups, can be established. Friends do not need to be in the same relative position within their respective groups, but in the same position in 'absolute' terms. Thus a highly placed member of a lowly placed group is an acceptable friend for a lowly placed member of a highly placed group. This comparison of positioning can be done on several bases; one by comparison of the apparent levels of direct and secondary influence – gauging the respective importance and quality of contacts, by comparing the internal standing of a prospective friend within his group, examining existing friendships between the two groups, or by examining a potential friend's orientation to an existing marriage between the two groups, or with another kin group significant for both. The hierarchy between kin groups is due to the degree of political influence each can command, which is a consequence of the sum of relationships both by marriage and friendship that each group claims. If one group changes in this respect in relation to the other, then the friendship requires realignments; old friendships are transformed to patron–client relationships, and new ones are forged with those more equal under the new circumstances. The basis of hierarchy is internal to the group and is necessary to make connections outside it.

Greentown residents must consolidate their status in other ways too and among the conditions that must be fulfilled is the maintenance of the equality of the patrilineage, the proper marriage of its members' children, the acknowledgment of their *zat*, working at proper jobs, and demonstrating control over those whom they have the right to control. In marriage this is manifested in choosing a mate for their children. Reducing ambiguity appears to be the operative principle in this choice. That is, in making a good choice it appears important to make it as *publicly* interpretable as possible. In Greentown, this is realised by reducing the number of social categories marriage partners are chosen from. There appear to be only three principal categories of choice: children of same-sex siblings, distant relatives, and *zat* members. In other parts of Pakistan there is a much broader range of kin marriage, and more *inter-zat* marriage. But we cannot attribute this situation to Greentown, as the trends precede the formation of Greentown. Nor can we attribute it to ethnic origin. The only thing that most residents have in common is their exposure to change, much of it positive when interpreted in 'traditional' terms.

First parallel cousin marriage has the internal effect of fulfilling obligations, minimising expenses, and demonstrating equality between siblings. Such marriage helps to raise everyone's status when one sibling has been more fortunate in life than another. There is still competition for *izzat* within the family, but it encourages an interpretation of equality when seen from the outside.

In a situation where everyone is attempting to consolidate their status, it is important not to allow ambiguity to cloud the desired interpretations. Hence, first parallel cousin marriage, both patrilateral and matrilateral, is unambiguous, in the sense that the male and female spouses in the families contracting the marriage are in structurally equivalent positions. In father's brother's son marriage the fathers, as brothers, are regarded as sharing an identical status jointly, even if one of the brothers has been more successful economically. In mother's sister's daughter marriage, the two prospective brothers-in-law are, as wife-takers from a single conjugal pool, regarded as equivalent in status. By contrast, cross cousin marriage makes ambiguous status claims. The mother's brother, as wife-giver, is nominally inferior to his sister's husband, given the prevalent cultural view that wife-takers should be superior (or at least equal) to wife-givers. In perpetual alliances between exogamous groups, women move consistently in a single direction and this may reinforce a hypergamous system. The complexity of Muslim marriage patterns precludes, however, any such simple interpretation of the direction in which women move: exchange marriages are common, wife-givers in one generation may become wife-takers in the next, while cross cousins may also be parallel cousins. The virtual absence of first cross cousin marriages in my Greentown marriage sample is thus not easily explained. I suggest that it may perhaps be due to the more ambiguous statement about family *izzat* which such marriages make.

Marriage to a distant relative is one in which some expression of status is possible for each side. In Greentown, given its history, this category almost always entails marriage outside the township. This gives opportunities for different interpretations in each community. There is a relationship that is the basic bond between the two contracting families, but it is not so close that it precludes competition for control to some degree. Marriage outside the *rishtidar* is structurally compatible with gaining the most *izzat* of any marriage type, and is the riskiest because it makes possible clearer distinctions; a comparison of status is direct rather than assumed to some degree with *rishtidar* or cousin marriage.

These three cases represent three clear points on a possible continuum of choices centring on the immediate family. While most stable communities in Pakistan exhibit many of these other choices,

Greentown does not. For the purposes of this discussion I am assuming that they represent the three most important points in a structural configuration based on gaining and consolidating status and power in an environment of change.

The major visible association of *zat* in Greentown is to provide a boundary for marriage. Most marriages in Greentown are within the *zat*. In the village this is also an association but it is not derived in the same manner; the *biradari* is more influential, and the influential members can enforce sanctions against members who marry a child out of the *biradari*. This is effective and entails that the marriage is within the *zat*. In Greentown, the *biradari* have this power in theory but it is not as significant in practice; the withdrawal of *hooka-pani* (commensal relations) is not so grave as in a village context where it constitutes social death. The people who symbolically share *hooka-pani* in Greentown are usually not members of the same *biradari* but are friends. The influence of the *biradari* is taken seriously but it cannot exercise the same level of authority and should there be a refusal to comply, the *biradari* as a whole, and the senior members in particular, would lose *izzat*. Qadeer (1983, p. 35) notes there is a tendency in Lahore for the operative *biradari* to be smaller, but for those members to have more contacts with non-kin members. This has advantages because a wider range of social relationships is useful in the city.

Marriott (1965) suggests that castes (*zat*) do not have an absolute status but tend to be locally defined by their conduct and adherence to convention. In the village, all the localised *zat* will also be the *biradari*. In Greentown this is not the case, the *zat* is mostly composed of *opra*, strangers. In ideological terms *zat* is a kind of kin, or more specifically defines the same kind; *zat* members are the same sort of people.

As Greentown is a new community the relations between groups are in flux. Groups are seeking a position within the overall social structure of Greentown. The relatively small *biradari* are presenting their position, and the localised *zat* is a collection of these *biradari*. But these localised *biradari* come from different places where they had different local positions. Marriage provides a means of expressing and negotiating position within the *zat*, for only equals can marry. They are setting up visible comparisons for observers to use in ranking them. *Zat* is internally hierarchical – *zat* members may be of the same kind, but they are not all equals when patrilineal kinship can be reckoned; there is no ambiguity between generations as to who has influence over whom. Younger brothers must defer to older, and their children to that brother as well. The sons of the brothers are in an ambiguous situation, for unless the father can be mobilised, the son of the older brother has no authority over the son of the younger. However, by using the idiom of marriage, these segments will become aligned. When no relationship exists, there are a number of bases that can be used, by examining the active social relationships of the parties. If two men are friends, that is, show the obligations of friendship, they consider the other as equal. If the children of two men marry, this is also a demonstration of a higher order of equality. The ideal marriage is one in which the participants are of the same kind and equals.

As a community, the groups within Greentown appear to be engaging in several kinds of marriages. With the exception of the Beri Hata group, they are marrying either very close kin, first cousins, or more accurately, siblings are exchanging children, or they are marrying *opra*, non-kin. They are not, for the most part, marrying other relatives. This is not typical of the Punjab. The list of preferences would lead one to expect a range of marriages between people of various degrees of relationship, and certainly more marriages within the *rishtidar* than are found in Greentown. In village Punjab, the complete range is found, and, indeed, Das (1973) reports village groups who would tend to concentrate most (or all) marriages within the *biradari* and/or *rishtidar*.

Given this, it would appear that the Beri Hata group (Table 5.1) is following the norm and the others deviating to some degree. The marriages between *opra* are of two sorts, marriages within Greentown and marriages outside Greentown. Within the idiom described, a marriage within Greentown serves to relate two families as equal, and to align their respective segments (*biradari* and *rishtidar*) for direct comparison based on the relative standing of the two. A marriage outside Greentown serves to align the related groups within Greentown to the world outside Greentown, again by allowing direct comparison against the new assertion of equality. The two kinds of marriage work in concert to create a stable social order for Greentown. In this context, it would appear that the residents of Greentown are spreading connections through marriage, gaining as many *rishtidar* as possible rather than consolidating older *rishta* ties, as appears to be more usual. To form and participate in a larger society one needs representatives in as many places as possible, and for people to be able to have other kinds of social relationships they must be able to gauge the position of a person. I have ignored comparing the groups within Greentown because of the particular social forms I have looked at. In terms of these forms they are not very different. This is in part because I have focused on social forms rather than cultural forms. For Greentown to fit the _nagar_ (community) mould, it is necessary that there be mechanisms which are shared amongst the many diverse groups of which the community is formed. Regardless of group specific practices, there must be common themes that each group can interpret for there to be society.

This conformity within diversity is not restricted to the city, nor to Muslim South Asia. In village Punjab, there is agreement as to the economic roles of various groups that comprise the village. The _zamindar zat_ has land and an accepted method of transferring that land from father to son. The _kammi_ groups each have an economic speciality attributed to them. As a result of this division of labour, the latter enjoy a certain autonomy from the élite as Leach (1962) has noted. Both groups accept their role within this socio-economic context. When that context changes, though, so do these relationships. However, when change takes place, as it did in Taunsa (Sherani, n.d.), the society did not disintegrate – it simply changed and the different social roles were realigned. For example, a carpenter in the villages around Taunsa has a _kammi_ relationship to the _zamindar_. After moving to Taunsa, remaining a carpenter but earning a cash salary, the carpenter buys land. If the carpenter prospers, he will sometimes assume a new _zat_ or even sometimes sub-_zat_ identity. In Taunsa, as in the American South, the 'emancipated' _kammi_ often adopts the _zat_ name of one of his _zamindar_. This reflects a realignment on the part of the ex-_kammi_, but for the change to be accepted by the community at large the change requires validation (for a general discussion of such strategies see Werbner, 1989a, 1989b).

X CONCLUSION

The primary cultural parameter used by residents of Greentown to measure social status is _izzat_ (honour/prestige). _Izzat_ is, I have argued, a direct consequence of the degree of control that can be exerted by an individual or group over the other members of the community. Within a community such as Greentown a man can have direct control over the members of his household, his family and his patrilineage – his 'group', 'natural' relations by birth or marriage. Further control arises from friendships with members of other groups (who, in turn, can control their lower ranking members). For a given man, social relationships are ranked within the group, as well as with other groups. Relationships outside the group must either be interpreted as equal relationships of friendship and thus of access, or as patron–client relationships of obligation.

To increase one's level of control (and *izzat*), the images (properties) of more control must be both projected and publicly accepted. The need is thus to decrease the status ambiguities between segments within the group so that observers can establish the 'proper' interpretation; they can rank the group segments. Marriage is one means of decreasing this ambiguity.

In Greentown, many of the residents have, in recent years, acquired some of the attributes of higher status they lacked before; a house, education, and higher prestige employment. Associated with this new status cluster is an emphasis, on the one hand, on marriage to distant relatives, unrelated *zat* members, and even non-*zat* members and, on the other, on first parallel cousin marriage. The residents of Greentown are attempting in the choice of marriage partners for their children to establish either a maximum reduction of publicly stated ambiguity through marriage with unrelated families, or a sustained ambiguity, through close, 'internal' marriages between siblings' children; they thus appear to be rejecting the moderate ambiguity associated with marriage within the *rishtidar*, the consanguineous kin group.

The marriage system practised in Greentown, although not an elementary system, has marriage rules that are usually phrased positively; one must marry within the maximal patrilineage (*zat* or *biradari*) and like should marry like. In ideological terms, these statements are equivalent. In the *practice* of Punjabi social organisation, they are not equivalent. It is the presumption of equivalence which supports models that social organisation depends upon.

The highest expression of endogamous marriage rules is to marry one's children with the children of siblings. This comes closest to satisfying the rule of endogamy. While it is minimally ambiguous with respect to the rules, it is maximally ambiguous with respect to the larger social order; no new information is revealed; rather, it is an affirmation of what everyone already knows. Marriage between relatives produces more public information, and marriage between non-relatives, distant relatives and unrelated *zat* members produces even more. The lowest expression of the rules, marriage to non-group members, produces maximum public information; it provides a basis not only for ranking the immediate families of the bride and groom (and the segments superior and below them), but also for ranking and aligning the kin groups themselves.

The choice of a son's or daughter's marriage partner indicates where one thinks one is located in the social world; a proposed marriage is not likely to be attempted unless it is certain to be accepted, and it will not be accepted unless the other party considers itself equal. Because of the presumption of equality implicit in marriage, internal marriages act to deny internal ranking within the lineage. They consolidate pre-existing relationships and assert the high value in which the lineage holds itself. External marriages increase and extend the sphere of contacts a family has and demonstrate its capacity to do so.

Hence status (*izzat*) depends crucially on the interpretation and recognition of external observers. Increased status comes from being the acknowledged winner of a competition. In the Punjab only equals compete, and both competitive and non-competitive situations are defined by specific properties. As in other parts of Muslim South Asia, and indeed perhaps across the whole Middle East, it is equal collaterals who compete, and competitive units extend from the lowest levels of social segmentation to the highest (see Barth, 1981 (1959); Peters, 1959; Lindholm, 1982).

In Greentown, where the localised *biradari* is small, and a small segment of the overall political structure of the community, marriage between related kin is not strategically useful. There are so few representatives of the *biradari* living locally that most of the ranking within it is predetermined. To engage in society at large, activity in larger groups is necessary. *Zat* is therefore substituted for *biradari*. It has the advantage that as a more extensive category it is present over a wide area geographically, and thus provides a social means of integrating into a new community.

Within the *zat*, the need is to establish hierarchy. This is not simply in the interest of its high-ranking members. The localised *zat*, even though larger than the localised *biradari*, is still a small segment of a community such as Greentown. To extend social relationships, entry into friendship circles is necessary. These friendships connect, we argued, the groups into a community.

In sum, then, the present analysis has attempted to locate the generative principles underlying Pakistani marriage strategies in the context of rapid social change and occupational-cum-geographical mobility. Basic to the analysis has been the cultural view that marriage implies equality. It is thus a means of making public statements about current and achieved status, both of individuals and of the social groups they belong to.

I have argued that to understand marriage patterns and the continuing significance of 'traditional' social categories, such as *zat* and *biradari*, as articulating cultural explanations of marriage choices, the need is to deconstruct the cultural concept of *izzat* (honour/status/prestige). *Izzat*, I argued, is determined by levels of social control achieved by individuals or groups over other groups or individuals. It is either consolidated by 'internal' marriages which determine an internal ranking within a lineage, or extended through external marriages, determining ranking within progressively wider groups: the localised *zat*, the urban community, and the city. Whereas in internal marriages ambiguities are internally contained to create a public solidary image, external marriages expose family status to public scrutiny as local residents attempt to translate recent material gains into gains in status and prestige through strategically negotiated marriage alliances.

Zat and *biradari* thus remain important categories in town where socially and geographically mobile strangers create new viable relations with one another based on a locally emergent social order, while competing with one another for honour, status and prestige. Community formation is therefore the outcome of a multitude of individual actions and decisions, all nevertheless motivated by culturally shared assumptions about value and widely shared social aspirations.

Notes

1. In 1982 and 1983 I spent twenty months in research on various topics concerning Greentown, the second half in residence. Besides interviewing and participant observation, a census for the 19 000 residents was carried out with the Pakistan Medical Research Center, and a number of sample surveys were conducted to determine the range of variation of a number of issues that emerged in the interviews. All information in this chapter is from these interviews or surveys unless noted otherwise.

Marriage and Power

2. In the sense of *ghar*; two or three generations often (in Greentown) living in different households, but maintaining very close economic and political links.
3. The possibility of hypergamy was suggested by Greentown residents, but was not considered ideal. It exists in principle but the degree of status difference, which does not affect the subsequent status of the marrying parties, appears to be notional at best.
4. The male bias is appropriate, as formally the groom's family always initiates marriage negotiations. Also, for a daughter to take an active interest in a specific marriage would be quite unacceptable, even to the most progressive of Greentown. A popular conception among unmarried boys is that they can avoid marriage to a particular girl if they express a desire for that girl. They assume that their father would be distrustful of the family of a girl that could be asked for.
5. There is a significant inverse correlation between closeness of the marriage and the amount of *jihez* and *haq mehr*.

References

Barth, F. (1981), 'Segmentary Opposition and the Theory of Games' (1959). Reprinted in *Features of Person and Society in Swat: Collected Essays on Pathans* (London: Routledge & Kegan Paul), pp. 55–82.

Das, V. (1973), 'The Structure of Marriage Preferences: An Account from Pakistani Fiction', *Man*, 8 (1), pp. 30–45.

Donnan, H. (1985), 'The Rules and Rhetoric of Marriage Negotiations among the Dhund Abbasi of Northeast Pakistan', *Ethnology*, XXIV, pp. 183–96.

Eglar, Z. (1960), *A Punjabi Village in Pakistan* (New York: Columbia University Press).

Gough, K. E. (1960), 'The Hindu Jajmani System', *Economic Development and Cultural Change*, IX, pp. 83–91.

Kennedy, M. (1957), 'Punjabi Urban Society', in S. Maron (ed.), *Pakistan: Society and Culture* (New Haven: HRAF), pp. 81–103.

Leach, E. R. (1962), 'Introduction', in E. R. Leach (ed.), *Aspects of Caste in South India, Ceylon and North-West Pakistan* (Cambridge: Cambridge University Press).

Lindholm C. (1982), *Generosity and Jealousy: The Swat Pakhtun of Northern Pakistan* (New York: Columbia University Press).

Marriott, M. (1965), *Caste Ranking and Community Structure in Five Regions of India and Pakistan* (Poona: Deccan College).

Peters, E. L. (1959), 'The Proliferation of Segments in the Lineages of the Bedouin of Cyrenaica', Curl Bequest Essay, *Journal of the Royal Anthropological Institute*, 90 (1), pp. 25–53.

Platts, J. T. (1968), *A Dictionary of Urdu, Classical Hindi, and English* (London: Oxford University Press).

Qadeer, M. (1983), *Lahore: Urban Development in the Third World* (Lahore: Vanguard Books).

Sherani, S. (n.d.), 'Shi'a-Sunni Conflict in Taunsa', unpublished essay (Canterbury: University of Kent).

Werbner, P. (1989a), *The Migration Process: Capital, Gifts and Offerings among British Pakistanis*, Explorations in Anthropology Series (Oxford: Berg).

Werbner, P. (1989b), 'The Ranking of Brotherhoods: The Dialectics of Muslim Caste among Overseas Pakistanis' *Contributions to Indian Sociology*. 23 (2).

6 Pakistani Women in a Changing Society
Hamza Alavi

The decade of the 1980s has truly been a decade of the women of Pakistan. A powerful women's movement made a dramatic impact on Pakistan's political scene. The concrete achievements of the women's movement in its struggle against policies of General Zia's military regime, directed against women in the name of Islamisation, have not been inconsiderable. A number of women's organisations in the country came together in this struggle, including the Women's Action Forum (WAF), the leading and the most effective of these, the Democratic Women's Association, the Sindhiani Tehrik and the Women's Front, as well as the All-Pakistan Women's Association (APWA), the oldest of these, which has been run by wives of senior bureaucrats and politicians and has had a reformist but rather a patronising orientation.

The decade of the 1980s was also a decade of degradation of Pakistani women. The Zia regime, in its search for legitimacy, in the name of Islam, embarked upon a series of measures that were designed to undermine what little existed by way of women's legal rights, educational facilities and career opportunities – as well as the simple right for freedom of movement and protection from molestation by males. This galvanised Pakistani women into militant action in defence of their rights. The military regime's actions, rhetoric and propaganda created an atmosphere which encouraged bigoted and mischievous individuals to take the 'law' into their own hands and harass women under the pretext of enforcing 'Islamic' norms of dress or, indeed, for simply appearing in public. Such lawlessness was allowed to go on with impunity. Women had to defend themselves not only *vis-à-vis* the state but also against hostile mischief-makers in society at large. Such attacks still continue. The women have fought back.

These developments must be viewed against the background of quite far-reaching changes in Pakistan society in the four decades since independence, changes which have affected women's place in Pakistan, both in rural and urban society. It is the latter, urban society, with which we shall be most concerned here, for this is where the changes most forcefully challenge established social practices and attitudes.

It must be kept in mind, however, that everywhere, in both rural as well as urban society, Pakistan remains a rigidly patriarchal society in which women are treated as chattels, 'given' or 'acquired' through arranged marriages, to spend their lives in the service of a male-dominated social system. By and large, women are married within *biradaris* (lineages) and the *biradari* organisation provides a framework within which women's lives are ordered. In the case of corporate *biradaris* the power of the *biradari panchayat* (council) derives largely from control over decisions about whom a woman is to marry. It is not only a single patriarch, the head of a nuclear family, but the whole male-dominated kinship organisation which has a stake in the subordination of women (for an account of *biradari* organisation cf. Alavi, 1972). No woman, even one with an independent career in a city, can set up a home on her own without the *saya* (lit: shade or protection) of a male. A divorced woman or a widow must turn to her father or brother, if they will have her, unless she has a grown up son under whose protection she can live. This is a powerful factor of control over women. Furthermore, not infrequently, especially amongst the poorer sections of society in cities and amongst *kammis* or 'village servants', a daughter is 'sold' for money to a prospective husband and, likewise, husbands divorce and 'sell' their wives. A woman who is not prepared to accept such a fate has little choice. She is a valued object, a prized chattel.

Demographic statistics provide a measure of the effects of discrimination against women. Pakistan is probably unique in the world in having a lower number of women in its population than men, i.e. 906 women for every 1000 men (Census of Pakistan, 1981) as against a world average of 111 women to every 100 men. In the population segment of 15 to 40 year olds there are 75 per cent more female deaths than male. This is attributed to nutritional anaemia that affects most women in the country resulting from discrimination against them in the sharing of food. They are given less and have often to make do with left-overs. Because of the lower resistance of their underfed bodies women are more susceptible to killer diseases; malaria, gastro-enteritis and respiratory ailments, especially tuberculosis. Repeated pregnancies also take a heavy toll by lowering their resistance to disease. In the case of urban lower middle class women their condition is aggravated both physically and psychologically by their incarceration within the four walls of their appallingly confined and insanitary homes. They get little of the sun and fresh air and no recreation at all, while their men go about everywhere freely and are not affected quite so much by their poor housing conditions. When attention is drawn to the subordination and oppression of women in Pakistan and demands made for improvement in their lot, Pakistani ideologues are quick to rebut such charges by painting an idealised picture of the high status of women in Islam. But this is a *non sequitur*, a specious line of argument that is intended to obscure the real issues, those of the actual conditions to which women are subject. It is against such a background that questions about women in Pakistan society must be examined. Changes of various kinds are under way, some improving their condition, others worsening them.

In rural areas, the place of women in society and their role in the division of labour in production differs very widely from region to region and also between different classes. Indeed there have been far-reaching changes everywhere, as seen from just two instances. In the Potowar area of North West Punjab, for example, which is a region of fragmented bankrupt farms, massive numbers of men of working age have left the villages for jobs in the army, in factories all over Pakistan and, not least, as migrants, for work in Britain and Western Europe and especially in the Middle East where they are not permitted to take their families to live with them. This has brought about an extraordinary situation in the villages of this region, many of which are, as a result, inhabited mainly by old men who are past working age, young children and women. It seems that in these cases women have to carry the main burden of working the land, over and above their customary share in the farm economy and their domestic responsibilities.

By contrast, in the rich Canal Colony districts of the Punjab, in the wake of the Green Revolution, many women have been withdrawn from the farm economy and confined within *purdah*. Until these developments in recent decades (with the exception of landlord families), women have always had an active role in agricultural production in weeding, harvesting and threshing of crops, and other operations. It is their duty to cut fodder and to look after farm animals. Accordingly, these women enjoy freedom of movement and are not confined behind *purdah*. A custom that gives them a degree of economic freedom is their exclusive right to pick cotton (this is being undermined by recent changes). For this women are paid in kind. The cotton that they receive in payment is ritually sacrosanct, their privileged property which men cannot lay their hands on. After the cotton harvest it is a common sight to see women walking to town with a bundle of cotton perched on their heads, going shopping, to barter the cotton for something for themselves or, more likely, for their children, without having to ask the husband for permission. But after the Green Revolution of the 1970s many well-to-do peasants, who had prospered, withdrew their womenfolk from the labour force and confined them to *purdah*, secluded and isolated within the four walls of their homes, as a mark of their new higher social status. In the course of research in rural Punjab, my wife and I found that far from rejoicing in the partial relief from the burden of work, the women resented this change. Many of them described their new situation to my wife as the equivalent of being locked up in a prison. They had lost the small degree of economic freedom and with it their freedom of movement. When one considers the implications of such a change, one is led to a conceptual distinction between *exploitation* of a woman's labour and a woman's *oppression*. While the burden of labour on women has eased, though only slightly, their oppression has increased enormously, a change which the women themselves see as one which has left them feeling greatly deprived.

It is in the urban context that women's contribution to the family economy has changed beyond recognition, as compared to conditions forty years ago. These changes seem to be having a greater impact on lower middle class families than either working-class or upper-class families. A large component of the working class in Pakistani cities consists of migrant workers from the north of the country whose families have been left behind in their villages. We know too little about the consequences of this on the life of single male workers in the city and the consequences for their families left behind in the villages. In the case of workers whose families live with them in the cities, many of the women either do unskilled work in factories or operate in the so-called 'informal economy', or are engaged in domestic employment. They often prefer such employment over home-based work, for waged employment pays better. Despite the great increase in their burden of work and their independent contribution to the family budget, judging from evidence brought up in court cases during the last decade, it seems that the women continue, nevertheless, to be subject to patriarchal domination.

By contrast, the problems of the majority of upper-class women are different. They have servants to do their chores and do not need to (or are not allowed to) take jobs and have careers. Their worries stem from their total dependence on the husband and from their fear of being abandoned by him in favour of a second wife. In the absence of the possibility of an independent job or career, compounded by extreme difficulty for women in setting up an independent household without the *saya*, or protection, of a male head of family, their dependence on the husband is total. They are therefore virtually reduced to the status of well-fed, well-dressed and well-ornamented slaves who depend absolutely upon the whim of their husbands. Where the husband ill-treats or abuses them, they must put up with it. Because of the difficulty of setting up an independent household even women with careers share this problem.

Amongst the *nouveau riche*, in particular, a familiar pattern is one of a first 'traditional' marriage to a woman from the *biradari* (lineage), possibly not very well educated or fashionable. This is often followed later in life by a marriage to an attractive socialite, a fitting spouse for the *arriviste*, a woman well qualified to perform the duties of a sophisticated hostess who can receive and entertain his friends and associates, businessmen and bureaucrats, in style. The first wife is discarded like an old shoe. She dare not insist on a divorce for, generally, she has nowhere to go and virtually no prospects of building a new life in a society that despises a divorced woman who is invariably blamed for the failure of her marriage. She is lucky if she has grown-up sons who might make it possible for her to set up an independent home. But in general, given such prospects, upper-class women are likely to live out their lives in insecurity and anxiety. How common such situations are would be difficult to quantify.

Nor is the problem of dependence upon husbands absent in the case of women of the lower middle classes or the working class. However, in their case, as well as in that of members of upper classes to a lesser degree, pressures from *biradari* members and elders tend, to some extent, to restrain husbands from abandoning wives who are daughters of their kinsmen. In Pakistan, unlike the West, the social life of most people functions within frameworks of extended kinship, and the values and norms of kinship obligations cannot be flouted without penalty, except by the rich and the powerful or those who live in cosmopolitan circles. On the whole, one gains the impression that the risk of a woman being abandoned by her husband in favour of a more attractive woman is less common, though by no means absent, in the case of lower middle class husbands. They can less afford two wives and are in any case too ground down by the humdrum daily routine of their rather ordinary lives for such fanciful indulgence.

In the case of lower middle class families, we can identify a twofold division. On the one hand, there are families whose women are educated, sufficiently at least to hold down a 'respectable' job. On the other hand, there are more traditional families whose women have not received a good education and who therefore do not qualify for 'respectable' salaried positions. In these latter cases, women contribute to the family economy by taking in home-based work under a 'putting out system' operated by entrepreneurs who are only too happy to exploit this extremely cheap source of labour. General Zia's Islamisation policies threatened most directly the first category of lower middle class women, triggering the militant women's movement of the 1980s.

Underlying these developments is the growing crisis of the lower middle class household economy over the last forty years. At the time of independence it was the normal expectation that the man would provide for the family. Joint families were favoured because of economies of scale in the domestic economy. A patriarch and his brothers, with his sons and nephews, would all go to work and bring in the income needed to keep the family. Burdened with domestic labour, women of this class were not classified as 'economically active'. It might be said that urban lower middle class women were amongst the most oppressed of women in Pakistan, being confined to the '*purdah* and *char diwari*' or the four walls of their home. In villages, even those women who are confined behind the *purdah* nevertheless have relatively easy access to the company of other women of the village, which is very supportive for them. Likewise, in old cities the layout of the *mohalla* (wards) has provided a similar possibility of social interaction amongst women. However, with the explosive expansion of Pakistan's cities such patterns of spatial organisation of society seem to have broken down. In these circumstances urban lower middle class women became virtual prisoners in their diminutive homes, for going visiting would entail an elaborate logistic operation reserved for very special occasions.

The continuous inflation in the cost of living in Pakistan over the decades has engendered a situation where a man's wage is no longer sufficient to keep the family. There was, therefore, constant pressure to broaden the base of the family economy. Gradually and steadily, more and more women were forced to find jobs to supplement family incomes. The change is now visible and quite striking. At first, only a few occupations were thought to be respectable enough for such women, but as the pressure for jobs increased the concept of a 'respectable job' was progressively broadened to allow a wider perspective. Initially, apart from high status professional occupations, notably that of a doctor (what better), jobs in the teaching profession, especially in girls' schools and colleges, were considered to be respectable enough. About a third of the doctors and an equal proportion of school teachers were women. Gradually this changed also. The mantle of respectability then covered clerical jobs in open plan offices where women could work with men, but in public view. The role of the personal secretary was suspect to begin with, although it was much better paid, because it entailed a close relationship with the boss. But that too has altered. Today one finds women in a wide range of occupations, including laboratory assistants, ticket clerks at railway stations or clerks at post office counters and so on, as well as lawyers, architects, engineers, journalists and broadcasters. Needless to add, the numbers in the latter categories of occupation are extremely small. With more and more women taking up salaried jobs and in keeping with an increasing number of women participating in higher education, new values have emerged. Women now desire jobs and careers for their own sake so that an increasing number of wives of well-heeled professionals and women from the upper classes take jobs not out of economic necessity but for self-fulfilment.

Education is the key to acceptable, respectable jobs and careers. Lower middle class families would find it degrading to let their women take up jobs as domestic servants or to work on the factory floor (though some are driven to this out of desperation); that is, to take up jobs for which education is not a prerequisite. But families who expect their women to take up jobs as teachers or office clerks (or better) tend therefore to put a higher value on women's education than was the case before – though financing the education of sons still takes precedence. There was a time when women's education was thought to be mere indulgence and wasteful of the money spent on it. Now there is a demand for it from professional men who want to marry reasonably well-educated wives, although not too highly qualified. There is a concept of an 'overqualified' woman, that is, a woman who has better qualifications than her potential spouse. Such a woman is positively at a disadvantage. Far too many engagements have been broken when the fiancée has done too well at college or university. Where both spouses are professionals or academics, if the wife's career advances more rapidly, it becomes a threat to the false pride of the husband. Because of the heavy price a woman has to pay if her marriage breaks down, sometimes she holds back to keep her marriage safe. But some marriages do fail on this account.

Given these social changes and the high degree of functionality of women's education for middle-class and lower middle class families, the threat to women's education posed by Islamic fundamentalism and General Zia's so-called 'Islamisation' policies was a threat to the family economy and to the new values and attitudes. These families have therefore tended to subscribe rather to liberal social philosophies or 'modernist' interpretations of Islam. They tend to be sceptical of dogmatic versions of Islam propounded by 'uneducated' *mullahs*. There is thus a considerable and growing social base of secularism in Pakistan's political as well as social life, a fact that is reflected in the repeated routs of the Islamic fundamentalist Jamaat-e-Islami in three successive elections in the country, namely those of 1985, 1987 (local bodies) and, again, in 1988.

There are, however, many lower middle class households in Pakistan where women have not received an education which would equip them for 'respectable' salaried jobs. Traditionally, they were relegated to the role of housewives. But gradually and with increasing rapidity new avenues for exploiting the labour of these women have opened up. This has come about by way of an extension of the 'putting out system', mainly in the clothing trade but also in other areas of production. The labour of lower middle class women, as well as those of the upper working class, is exploited without requiring them to leave the four walls of their homes. The orders for the work to be done and the materials that are required are brought to them and the finished goods collected; for their long hours of labour, carried out in the midst of the demands of a variety of domestic chores and the clamour of a multitude of children, they are paid a mere pittance.

We can identify two patterns in such cases, although there are no data available that can allow us to quantify their relative importance. One pattern occurs when the family patriarch controls the operation. He mediates with entrepreneurs, brings home the materials and work orders, delivers the finished goods and, most important of all, pockets the money paid by the entrepreneurs. In effect, the women of his household are virtually his slaves. He guards their subordination quite as jealously as any slave owner, deploying ideological weapons against the women by a constant invocation of Islamic values, as interpreted by himself and the *mullahs*. On the other hand, he builds up images of the 'modern' ordinary working women who take up outside employment as corrupt and un-Islamic, an image which he contrasts with that of his own enslaved kinswomen who are good and pure, unsullied by the eyes of strange men. Ideologically fundamentalist interpretations of Islam reinforce the authority of the patriarch over his enslaved womenfolk.

There is also another pattern of the putting out system by which entrepreneurs employ women agents to go to houses (especially in *katchi abadis* or shanty town homes) distributing orders and materials for work and collecting the finished goods. In this way they are said to make payments directly to the female head in the household. In the absence of research one can only speculate whether the balance of power in the household is thereby shifted (even if only partially) in favour of women. An interesting study of Muslim women 'beedi' makers (cheap 'cigarettes' made of rolled tobacco leaves) in Allahabad, by Zarina Bhatty, found that as a result of contributing substantially (over 45 per cent) to the household incomes, the women acquired a 'greater importance in the household decision making process . . . (i.e.) an increased say in spending money' (Bhatty, 1981, p. 45). It would be hazardous to extend this conclusion drawn from a study of a community of Muslim rural labourers in India to urban lower middle class families in Pakistan. Clearly, there are a number of issues here which invite systematic investigation.

Home-based women workers, denied the freedom of movement and relative independence of their sisters employed in salaried jobs, rationalise their own predicament in ideological terms, through a self-image of their moral superiority. Frustrated by their increasingly straitened circumstances and lack of freedom, they are easily mobilised by their men against women who go out to work. They are even made to join public demonstrations, suitably enclosed in the *chaddar* or *burqa* (the all-enveloping women's overalls that cover them from head to foot). They parrot the complaints of their men that women's employment takes jobs away from men and undercuts their salaries, and that it is quite shameless and un-Islamic for women to go about the city and work in offices with men. In their own minds, as well as in the minds of the men who control their lives, their confinement to their homes offers a gain in respectability.

The life of a lower middle class woman in salaried employment is subject to rather different kinds of pressures. Her working day starts early, for she must feed her husband and children and send them off to school before she herself rushes off to work. Travelling to work is itself quite a battle, given the state of public transport in Pakistan's cities, especially Karachi. In order to attract women workers whom they need, many large companies maintain fleets of minibuses to pick up their women employees in the morning and take them home after work. In the case of a woman who is the first to be picked up or the last to be dropped off at home this can add an hour, or even two, to the long day spent at work. She comes home tired. Whilst her husband relaxes with a cold drink under a fan, she has to rush straight into the kitchen to prepare the family evening meal. And there are umpteen little chores to be attended to, young children to be looked after and the family fed and put to bed. Some chores, such as washing clothes and cleaning the house, are inevitably put off until the weekend which therefore is not a time for rest or for demonstrations in aid of women's rights. Given the race against time, only a very few working women are able to go to meetings and demonstrations even though they sympathise solidly with their aims. Women who happen to have particularly enlightened and helpful relatives (e.g. a mother-in-law) or a cooperative and politically committed husband (a rare commodity), who are willing to take over some of their chores during their short absence, can support meetings concerned with women's rights. Only those who are sufficiently well off to have servants to take care of the domestic front can play an active and continuing part in such activities. Mobility is another major obstacle: only those women who have their own cars or who have women friends or close male relatives who can give them a lift (going with unrelated males is unthinkable) can participate without too much difficulty.

It is because of these difficulties that the vast majority of lower middle class women in employment cannot take a regular, let alone an active and leading part in the women's movement. But this does not mean that the vast majority of working women who are not blessed with the advantages which make such activities possible 'lack consciousness', or that they are unaware of the issues that confront women in Pakistan. One has only to go and talk to some of them to get a measure of the depth of their feelings and the clarity with which they themselves see the issues. Under these circumstances the activists and the leadership inevitably comes from women of better-off families, especially those who can afford servants and cars, mainly professional women in their thirties. But it needs to be emphasised that by and large they articulate attitudes and demands that affect all working women. This relatively small number of activists is like the tip of a huge iceberg, their inarticulate sisters being submerged, for the time being, in an ocean of work.

The women's movement in Pakistan thus revolves around educated women, both professionals and those who take up salaried jobs. Official propaganda during the long years of the Zia regime tried to discredit the women's movement by caricaturing it as a movement of English-educated, Westernised, upper-class women whose heads were filled with foreign, imported, ideas and who, the propaganda claimed, had no roots amongst true Pakistani women. The fact of the matter is that the vast majority of activists in the women's movement are closer to working women of all classes than either the bureaucrats in government or much of the political leadership or the journalists who sit in judgement over them. Most of these activists are new to the tasks that they have taken upon themselves in organising and leading the movement. Nevertheless, they have demonstrated quite remarkable qualities of leadership – not only ingenuity and flexibility but also a noteworthy personal humility. This last quality is reflected in the commitment of WAF members to non-hierarchical organisation.

The Zia regime itself was instrumental in creating conditions that precipitated the women's movement and caused it to break out with such force. Problems that confront women in Pakistan today have been accumulating over several decades. The reason why the women's movement suddenly erupted in the 1980s has much to do with the outrageous attacks that were actually undertaken or were contemplated by the Zia regime in the name of 'Islamisation', a policy that was designed (unsuccessfully) to provide political legitimacy. These policies were calculated to degrade the place of women in Pakistan society and to erode such legal rights as they did possess. They were designed to put up barriers in the way of women's education and their freedom of movement and to obstruct their access to jobs and professional careers.

Among the new 'Islamic' laws that were enacted by the Zia government was a change in the law of evidence, in October 1984, purportedly to bring the existing law in line with the prescriptions of Islam. Except in the case of the *Hudood* Ordinances of 1979 (prescribing 'Islamic' punishments), which laid down their own special rules of evidence for *hadd* offences, the new law of evidence provided that two male witnesses or in the absence of two men one male and two female witnesses would be required to prove a crime. This law, as well as other proposed legislation, equated one man to two women. This was so, for example, in the proposed new laws of *Qisas* and *Diyat* which provided for financial compensation to be given to the injured party by an accused in lieu of punishment in cases of murder or bodily injury, it being held that in such cases the 'Islamic' remedy lay not in punishment of the offender but in compensation to be paid to the victim or his family. This law was proposed by the Council of Islamic Ideology and passed by the Majlis-e-Shoora (Zia's legislative institutions). The compensation in the case of women was to be fixed at half that for men. Such laws, which put the worth of women at half that of a man, were a powerfully symbolic factor that set the women's movement in action.

Besides these blatantly discriminatory laws that reduced a woman's humanity by half, there were policies undertaken or contemplated by the Zia regime that threatened the life and prospects of working women more directly. Although the militant activities and demonstrations of the women's movement were, in the first instance, directed against the new laws, there were some no less weighty and more directly felt underlying concerns, especially about the future of women's education. In general, laws and policies pursued by the Zia regime were directed towards discouraging women from taking part in activities outside the home and to limit the scope for their self-expression.

There were proposals, for example, which threatened women's access to higher education. Perhaps the most important of these was the idea of segregating women within 'Women's Universities'. As proposed by Zia's University Grants Commission, the existing three colleges of Home Economics located at Karachi, Lahore and Peshawar were to be upgraded to university status. Women were to be given the education that was thought to be appropriate for them, namely, to be trained as housewives. They were to be denied a wider education that might prepare them for professional or academic careers, or jobs in government, commerce or industry. Obstacles such as higher required grades were placed in the way of women seeking admission to science courses in universities or places in medical colleges.

There was an attack, too, on women's participation in sports. Pakistani women athletes and the women's hockey team were prevented from participating in international events. Zia's Federal Minister for Sports and Culture explained that women could participate in sporting competitions only before an exclusively female audience, or one in which only *mehram* males and no other males were present! Reporting this, the press translated the term '*mehram*' inaccurately as 'blood relatives'. That is not the case. The category of *mehram* defines relatives whom a Muslim may not marry. A woman's *mehram* comprises her siblings, ascendants and siblings of ascendants, descendants and descendants of siblings and, amongst some sects, sisters' husbands. A first cousin, such as a father's brother's son, is not *mehram* though he is a 'blood relative'. Since *mehram* defines an ego-centred kindred, which would be differently constituted for each woman, male spectators are effectively ruled out. Women could engage in sports only in *purdah*! This ridiculous and meaningless rule illustrates only too well the arbitrary and cavalier manner in which religious symbols were invoked to restrict women's activities.

The issues of higher education and sports, in a society such as that of Pakistan, affect mostly upper-class, middle-class and lower middle class families. There are other policies of the Zia government that bore down more heavily on the most vulnerable component of Pakistan society, namely, women of the poor. It must be said that degradation of women in Pakistan is nothing new and is not the result solely of the so-called 'Islamisation' policies of the Zia dictatorship, though it reached abysmally low levels in the wake of its legislation and policies.

In the name of fighting against 'obscenity' and 'pornography', the Zia government set in motion a mass campaign against women seen in public. An atmosphere was generated in the country in which attacks against women became commonplace, legitimated in the name of religion. Such campaigns were led by *mullahs*, the custodians of ignorance, and by criminals and mischief-makers in general, who all seem to derive a kind of perverted psychic pleasure from molesting women under the pretext of enforcing morality. A spate of directives was issued by the Zia regime ordering female government employees, women teachers and girls at schools and colleges to wear 'Islamic' dress and the *chaddar* or *burqa*. As a direct result of such campaigns against women who were depicted as a threat to male virtue, the morality of Pakistani males sunk to new depths. They did not seem able to resist the temptation to interfere with and manhandle women, posing as guardians of public virtue. Violence against women increased behind the cloak of 'Islamisation'. The most obscene examples of such hypocrisy are numerous, widely publicised incidents where women's noses have been cut off or they have been disrobed and paraded in the nude in public to 'teach them a lesson'.

As a result of public outrage aroused by such incidents, the Zia government announced punishments for such actions. But his so-called 'Islamic' regime did little to track down the culprits and punish them. Nor did it engage in any public campaign to denounce such actions and arouse public opinion against those who perpetrated them. Such incidents and attacks on women still continue. The Zia regime introduced *Hudood* Ordinances purportedly to lay down 'Islamic' punishments for certain crimes. There were barbaric punishments such as the cutting off of hands and stoning to death. There has been some controversy in the country as to whether these are truly Islamic prescriptions. That, as such, is not a matter that we need to pursue here, except to say that even where these were not actually carried out in all cases, they carried a symbolic charge and provided a rallying point to *mullahs* who demanded their full implementation. Public lashings, however, were carried out before vast crowds and television cameras quite savagely – members of the crowd urging the 'executioners' to hit 'the bastards' even harder. These were incredibly degrading sights to watch. The law that concerns us here most directly, however, is the *Zina* (Enforcement of *Hudood*) Ordinance of February 1979. This ordinance provided a new basis, as we shall see, for intimidation and terrorisation of women by husbands or male relatives, especially amongst the urban poor, though not amongst them alone. Ironically, the ordinance has also created a situation in which women victims of rape dare not even complain about the sexual violence done to them for fear of penalties that they themselves invite under this iniquitous law, while the culprits go scot free because of its extraordinary provisions.

The ordinance provides new weapons for men against women by virtue of making *zina*, that is, adultery and fornication, crimes against the state, cognisable offences for which the police can take action. Previously this was not the case, for adultery had been a matter of personal offence against the husband by the male party to adultery and extra-marital sex had not been a penal offence at all. Now where a wife leaves her husband, it has become all too easy for the husband to go to the police and file a complaint against her for committing *zina*, whereupon the wife is arrested and jailed. Given police corruption and the interminable length of time that it takes for such cases to be adjudicated by courts of law (often years), the woman is effectively punished without even going through the due process of law. The husband can bail the wife out of jail. But when that happens, she is totally at his mercy for he could threaten to withdraw bail which would return her to prison. Thus the woman's position is made worse than that of a slave. According to Asma Jahangir, a distinguished Pakistani woman lawyer and Secretary of the Human Rights Commission of Pakistan: 'it has now become common for husbands to file a complaint of *zina* against wives wanting separation. There are hundreds of cases every year where women are arrested for *zina* on complaints filed by husbands' (*SHE*, March 1989, p. 81). It is likewise in cases of elopement, where a father refuses permission for his daughter to marry the man of her choice. The father brings charges of 'abduction' in such cases and the law presumes *zina* unless the couple can prove lawful *nikah* or marriage according to Islam.

The *Zina* Ordinance has become a 'Catch 22' for women who are victims of rape. This arises from the fact that the ordinance brings both adultery and fornication (*zina*), on the one hand, and rape (*zina-bil-jabr*), on the other, under a single law in a manner that is unsafe. Secondly, the problem arises from the type of admissible evidence which is prescribed under the ordinance. The offence of rape is defined as sexual intercourse against the will and/or without the consent of the victim, or with consent if the consent has been obtained under fear of death or hurt. It also includes, under the category of rape, sexual intercourse with consent of the victim where the offender knows that the consent is given by the victim because she (or he) believes that she (or he) is validly married to the offender, although the offender knows that they are not.

The catch in this law, which affects women cruelly who are victims of rape, is the specification of the type of evidence that is admissible for *hadd*, or 'Islamic', punishment for *zina* and *zina-bil-jabr*, which is stoning to death (under certain conditions lesser punishments called *tazir* would apply). The evidence required is either a confession on the part of the accused (for an unmarried woman pregnancy is self-evident proof) or the testimony of 'at least four Muslim adult male witnesses about whom the Court is satisfied . . . that they are truthful persons and abstain from major sins . . . (who) give evidence as eye-witnesses of the act of penetration necessary for the offence'. This is a type of evidence that is most unlikely to be found, except perhaps in the vast open spaces of the Arabian desert.

In effect, therefore, the offence of rape is unprovable and rapists now go about without fear. Accounts of such offences have become widespread. Those affected dare not complain or notify the police (cf. *Daily Jang*, London, 9 November 1989, p. 1). The law excludes the testimony of women, so that the evidence of the rape victim counts for nothing. But if she complains of rape (which she cannot possibly prove, according to this law), she is taken to have admitted to having had sexual intercourse with a man who is not her lawful husband, and hence is guilty of *zina*. For this she invites the heavy penalty of the law. A woman not only has no remedy under this iniquitous law for the sexual violence done to her, but she herself becomes a victim of the law.

In one way or another, women have been victimised under the *Zina* Ordinance. Documenting the phenomenal increase, during the 1980s, in the number of women who are languishing in Pakistani prisons as a consequence of this law, Asma Jahangir points out that about 40 per cent of the convicted women whom she interviewed in Multan Jail had been sentenced for the offence of *zina*, and most belonged to low-income families. Out of thirty-seven women sixteen had a *family* income of only Rs 500 per month (the wage of a single labourer) and no one had a *family* income of more than Rs 3000 (the salary of an office clerk). Newspaper reports of victimisation of women under this law are legion. For want of space, we will give only a couple of examples to illustrate the different ways in which women are victimised in this way.

The most notorious case is that of Safia Bibi, an 18-year-old girl who is virtually blind, the daughter of a poor peasant, who was employed in the house of the local landlord as domestic help. She was raped by her employer's son and then by the landlord himself. As a result the girl became pregnant. Her illegitimate child is said to have died soon after birth. The girl's father filed a case with the police alleging rape. The court acquitted the landlord and his son for lack of evidence as required under the *Zina* Ordinance, the evidence of the girl not being admissible and four pious Muslim witnesses to the repeated acts of rape not being available. But by virtue of her accusation the girl herself, being unmarried, was found guilty of *zina*, her pregnancy being proof of it, and she was sentenced to three years in prison, public lashing (fifteen lashings) and Rs 1000 fine. In passing this sentence, the court said that it was being lenient in view of her age and disability! This case created an uproar and turned out to be an issue on which the Women's Action Forum began campaigning. In the light of public outrage, General Zia himself intervened and got the Federal Shariat Court to take over the case, *suo moto*. An exceptionally liberal judge quashed the outrageous conviction of the girl on the grounds that if in the case of rape the man (or men) were acquitted due to lack of the required evidence, the woman too was to be given the benefit of the doubt. But there was no question here of prosecuting the rapists and bringing them to justice. A rather different type of case illustrates the way in which the law is used by male relatives or husbands to terrorise and control women. A young woman of 25, Shahida, got a divorce from her husband, Khushi Mohammad. The divorce deed was signed by the husband and was attested by a magistrate. Under the law as it stands, however, the divorcing husband is then required to register the divorce papers with the local council. That he did not do. This was possibly a deliberate omission which was to give him a hold over his ex-wife. Shahida, after spending the prescribed period of ninety-six days of waiting (*iddat*), as prescribed for a divorcee, with her parents, meanwhile married Mohammed Sarwar. Khushi Mohammad, however, decided that he wanted her back or, in any case, that he would not allow her to marry again. So he took the matter to the law, charging her with *zina*. Although Shahida produced before the court the attested copy of the divorce document which was signed by Khushi Mohammad and attested by a magistrate, the court did not consider it to be admissible since it had not been registered with the local council. The court decided that the divorce was invalid and therefore that the second marriage was illegal. As the two accused, Shahida Parveen and Mohammed Sarwar had 'confessed' to living together as husband and wife, the court found them guilty, under the convoluted provisions of that extraordinary ordinance, of raping each other! Accordingly they were both sentenced to death. Happily, due to campaigning by the women's movement, this extreme sentence was eventually commuted. But not all victims of this incredible law have been so lucky.

In cases of eloping couples, parents deprived of the money that they would get for marrying off their daughter (bride price is not a normal custom) file a complaint with the police for abduction. Even if the girl has found refuge with the family of the boy or some supportive family, sexual intercourse is presumed in such cases and both the girl and the boy are penalised for *zina*. It is by no means unusual in such cases, especially if the young couple cannot be found, for the police to arrest the families who are believed to have given them support, as accomplices to *zina*.

The fact is that all such cases have affected not only the parties directly involved but have intimidated Pakistani women in general, for they dare not leave an oppressive and cruel husband or greedy and grasping parents wishing to sell them, for fear of the consequences for them under this terrible law.

Sadly, the eleven years of the so-called policy of 'Islamisation' under General Zia have produced in Pakistan a culture of intolerance. This has, above all, persecuted women and subjected them to all kinds of humiliation and ill treatment, not to speak of inhuman punishment under the *Hudood* Ordinances, as described above. The government embarked upon a mass publicity campaign, throughout the media, exhorting people to order their lives in accordance with Islam – as interpreted by Zia and his bigoted *mullahs*. Far more mischievous was Zia's call to the 'people' to ensure that their 'neighbours' did likewise. This was a charter for the mischief-makers and the bigots who took upon themselves the task of chastising women, total strangers, and molesting them under that excuse. For example, Mumtaz and Shaheed (1987, p. 71) quote an instance, which is by no means unique or isolated, when a woman who entered a bakery in an upper-class Lahore neighbourhood was slapped by a total stranger for not having her head covered. A much publicised and quite horrendous case is that of a congregation who, after leaving a mosque at the end of Friday prayers, found a new-born baby on a nearby rubbish dump. The *mullah* promptly concluded that it was an illegitimate child and, in accordance with the laws of Islam, as he understood them, led the congregation of the pious Muslims in stoning the child to death. Such outrageous conduct was the direct result of incitement by the propaganda of the Zia regime, which has created an atmosphere of bigotry and intolerance.

It was hoped that the democratic government of Benazir Bhutto would reverse this and, in particular, repeal the *Hudood* Ordinances (including the *Zina* Ordinance). But after a year in office the government has shown no inclination to change the laws. This is in part due to the paralysis of the government, caused by a complex set of political factors which we cannot go into here. Meanwhile, the terrible legacy of the Zia regime lives on and prospects for Pakistani women remain uncertain and threatening.

References

Ahmad, S. (1983), 'Women's Movement in Pakistan', *Pakistan Progressive*, 5 (1).
Alavi, H. (1972), 'Kinship in West Punjab Villages', *Contributions to Indian Sociology*, New Series, vol. VI.

Bhatty, Z. (1981), *The Economic Role and Status of Women in the Beedi Industry in Allahabad, India*, ILO, World Employment Programme, vol. 63.

Mumtaz, K. and F. Shaheed (1987), *Women of Pakistan* (London: Zed Press).

Pakistan Law Digest, various issues.

7 Competing Doctors, Unequal Patients: Stratified Medicine in Lahore

Wenonah Lyon

Medical treatment identified with that of Europe and North America has become one of the West's most desired exports; so much so that Dunn has proposed the designation 'cosmopolitan' to label the medical system (Dunn, 1976). As a body of knowledge, it may be universal. 'Treatment', however, the translation of theory into practice, responds to its cultural and social context. Hence, the nature of treatment varies from country to country, and within a country, between different localities. This chapter discusses medical treatment in Greentown, an urban working-class neighbourhood in Lahore.[1] While health care associated with the West has been imported into Pakistan, the organisation of roles and institutions which have provided (and developed) that health care have not been reproduced. In Pakistan, the roles and institutions through which theories about disease and its causes are translated into treatment are part of a wider social structure which results in a distinctive medical practice.

The people of Greentown overwhelmingly reject 'traditional' medical systems. They claim that they (and their families) use 'doctor medicine', '*engrezi* (English) medicine', 'MBBS medicine', 'allopathic medicine'. The treatment that they described, and that I observed, was very different from current orthodox treatment in the United States. This chapter is concerned with one set of factors shaping that treatment: the social stratification of medical practitioners in Lahore.

As in Pakistan, the organisational structure of medicine in the United States developed within a pre-existing social structure. As the system of health care developed, orthodox allopathic physicians in the United States developed a monopolistic control over treatment both as a commodity and a service. To establish such control, a group must eliminate competing groups, operate in a favourable legal

143

context, and identify their interests with those of powerful groups in the society (Berlant, 1975, p. 306). In the United Kingdom, Berlant argues that this development was closely tied to 'the development of stratified relationships between social groups so that quality of medical care has tended to be a prized scarcity and an object of class behaviour' (ibid., p. 305).

Oherson and Singham describe a similar development in the United States. They argue that the competence requirements, certification and discrete bodies of knowledge defined by professional bodies were 'institutionalized and provided a means of upward social mobility and status to the emergent middle class created by the industrial upheavals of the time' (Oherson and Singham, 1981, p. 230).

The organisation of medical practice in the United States, then, developed within a particular historical and cultural context. Currently, licensing laws and restricted entry into the profession, long educational requirements, high fees and tuition for medical schools in the United States tend to restrict entry to the middle class and wealthy.

The education system, the trade union movement, the development of private health insurance schemes all helped to determine the form in which health care is delivered. Crucially, in Western Europe as well as North America, medical research is primarily university based. The great majority of professionals who determine treatment, those involved in basic research in the biological sciences, are not involved in delivering that treatment. These factors, which shape allopathy as a medical system, are in fact independent of it.

Pakistan's health care system is formally modelled on that of Western Europe and North America. Its hospitals, medical colleges and laboratories reproduce, in form, those of (primarily) the United Kingdom or the United States. However, these are integrated into a more general system of roles and institutions which make the actual system of health care quite different from that of the original model.

In Pakistan, professional bodies of allopathic practitioners do not control who practises medicine or the distribution of drugs. Indeed, no professional group has an effective monopoly of medical treatment. Health care itself is stratified, with different care available to patients in accord with their wealth, education, occupation, religion and area of residence. This is certainly the case in the United States as well. However, in Lahore practitioners as well as patients are stratified. Doctors who treat Greentown patients have different training and use different methods of treatment from those treating Lahore's wealthy or educated élite, although they – and their patients – regard themselves as allopaths. Finally, the physician is only one of the professionals that supplies health care in the United States. This system of roles has not been fully reproduced in Lahore. The infrastructure on which American medical care relies is not available. The allopathic medical system in the US is dependent on standardised hospital, laboratory, educational and even transportation and communication facilities which are not available in Lahore. These factors influence not just the way in which treatment is conducted but the conception of allopathy as well.

I PLURALISTIC MEDICAL MODELS

Before the introduction of medicine imported from Europe and North America, South Asian medical theory and practice were dominated by two variants of humoral medicine: *Yunani Tibbia*, ('Greek medicine' which was introduced by Muslim invaders of the subcontinent) and *Ayurveda*, based on medical work developed in Sanskritic texts. Both these systems, as well as homoeopathic clinics and religious healers, continue to offer health care in Pakistan (Mushtaqut, 1980). People in Pakistan thus participate in a pluralistic medical system, and choose among health professionals representing different secular, as well as religious, medical traditions.

Minocha (1980), in a discussion of medical pluralism, argues that the same people perceive and interpret illness, and choose medical practitioners, from several different systems at different times. Physicians, as well, draw upon different traditions. A traditional practitioner might use a stethoscope, allopathic drugs and a 'germ' theory of disease to explain illness. In the same way, an allopathic practitioner might explain illness using a humoral theory of disease and suggest dietary restrictions based on these (Minocha, 1980, p. 217). Bhatia, working in India, reports that 90 per cent of the ninety-three full-time traditional healers he interviewed use allopathic medical apparatus (Bhatia, 1975, p. 17). Bhardwaj, in a study of practitioners and patient choice, found in a survey of four villages that only six of 104 people interviewed preferred traditional medicine exclusively (Bhardwaj, 1975, p. 610). The villagers also identified a *hakim* (a *Yunani Tibbia* practitioner) as an allopathic doctor because he administered allopathic medicine.

Is a *hakim* with a stethoscope an allopath? Presumably, the patients who choose him are expressing a preference for allopathy, but are they receiving allopathic care? South Asian medical treatment can be better regarded as an adaptation of allopathy rather than its adoption. In Greentown, allopathy has been adapted not only to South Asia but to the social and economic context of Greentown itself.

II MEDICAL CARE IN LAHORE

A young doctor describing his profession illustrates some of the problems of a doctor in Lahore:

> There are four kinds of doctors. The first are the consultants, who have private clinics and beds in the hospital. They make a lot of money and practise medicine the way it should be practised. Then there are the doctors who go abroad. They have rich families, and can take two months off to study for exams. They leave and don't come back. Then there are other doctors with rich families, who set them up in practice or get them good jobs. Then there are the rest of the doctors, like me, most of them, who can't practise medicine the way it should be practised, who have to do what their patients want and who have to practise just to make money, not caring at all about what we learned in medical school . . . I have a friend with his own private clinic. It cost 50 000 rupees [£2500] to set up. I went to visit him. He had a woman with an abscessed breast in his clinic, and I looked at her. She had been bitten and it was a bad infection. He asked me what I would do, and I said I'd drain the abscess and put her on a good antibiotic. He said he could never do that. If he drained it, it would be very painful and she'd never come back. He gave her a shot of a very powerful antibiotic. He had to give her a large dose. It is supposed to be given every six hours, but she wouldn't do that so he had her come back every evening for another shot and large bills.

The doctor emphasises a medical practice overwhelmingly shaped by economic factors: the differences between medical practice in the US and Lahore are due, most importantly, to the differences between a very rich and a moderately poor country. A multitiered system of health care based on wealth has been described by those investigating health care for the poor in the United States (see, for example, Lyons, 1971; Strauss, 1971; Harwood, 1981; Ingman, 1975). Like the United States, Pakistan offers a health system based on what one can afford. In the United States, the very poor see residents in large teaching hospitals. In Lahore, hospitals operate open air clinics which any one can attend. In the United States, one can obtain means-tested free medical care, belong to a private insurance scheme (usually offered through an employer) or pay for expensive private health care. These options are also available in Pakistan. Many of the employers in Lahore operate clinics, or even hospitals, for their employees and their families. Unlike the United States, Lahore offers a wide range of practitioners differing in charges and training. These differences establish a range of options theoretically available to patients.

Access to medical care is allocated on the same basis as access to other goods and services. In Lahore, relations between people are hierarchically arranged: wealth (most importantly), education, ethnic identity and religion determine access to medical care. The medical care is itself stratified with its practitioners, like its patients, grouped by wealth and education.

The wealthy receive medical care very similar to that offered in the United States and doctors offering care to these patients have often trained in the United States or Great Britain. These patients also go to the US and Great Britain to obtain care, particularly if they need to be hospitalised. Their doctors routinely use laboratory tests or X-rays to establish diagnosis. An office visit costs about Rs 100 (£1 = Rs 20.23) which does not include the cost of medicine or the tests.

The next level of medical treatment is that provided by the MBBS doctor, the terminal degree for an allopathic general practitioner in Pakistan. These doctors sometimes have laboratory facilities attached to their offices. Tests are not included in the charge of an office visit; medicine is not supplied by the practitioner. An office visit costs about 30 to 40 rupees.

Less successful MBBS doctors offer a different sort of care, at a smaller charge of 10 to 20 rupees. These doctors rely on a large patient group and tests are rarely carried out. If testing is required, patients are referred to private laboratory facilities which are neither licensed nor inspected. Medicine is generally provided by the doctor and its cost is included as a part of the office charge. These doctors usually do not have access to hospital beds and refer patients to other doctors if hospitalisation is required.

The people in Greentown most often used the next category of practitioner, the non-degreed allopath. These are local practitioners, charging around Rs 5 for an office visit. Laboratory tests are never undertaken and medicine is supplied by the doctor.

Formally trained doctors do not control who practises medicine in Lahore; however, they do control access to hospital beds in major hospitals there. If an illness requires hospitalisation, the patient will be treated by a formally trained allopathic doctor. Non-degreed allopaths in Greentown suggested that patients visit open air clinics in area hospitals or (more rarely) recommended a particular MBBS doctor to a patient when they felt this was required.

III   THE COMMUNITY

Greentown is a newly developed community located about 25 kilometres south-east of the old walled city of Lahore. Planning for the community by the Lahore Development Authority (LDA) began in 1970, as a housing development for low-level government employees. The LDA also wanted to clear *katchi abadi* (squatter) settlements from government owned land. *Katchi abadi* residents were given a free house for the head of the household and free plots for each male in the household over the age of 16. The government moved these people together and they live in the same area of Greentown.

In 1974, a few Bihari families (refugees from Bangladesh) were given housing in Greentown. In 1976, more Bihari refugees came to Lahore and were sold housing in Greentown at low rates. The Bihari residential area is spatially identifiable and is called Bihari Colony by its residents and their neighbours.

A local Christian missionary group bought lots in Greentown, and built housing for 106 low-income Christian families. This area, called Christian Colony, is separated from the rest of Greentown by a divided highway and large drainage ditch. A field near Christian Colony is used by a semi-nomadic Muslim group of scavengers and snake charmers living in tents.

As housing prices have increased, more lots have been sold to individuals. People from different parts of Lahore have moved in, and there are rural immigrants from the villages of Punjab, the North West Frontier and the Tribal Areas. There are also a large number of *muhajirs*, immigrants from India, primarily from East Punjab and Uttar Pradesh. Because of the way housing was allocated, the major ethnic groups in Greentown are spatially distinct. There is tension between the different groups.

Greentown is approximately .4 square miles in area. The dimensions of the planned community are 3500 × 3500 feet and the residential area is divided into plots 20 × 40 feet. There are two large market areas with small shops and vendors with push carts. In the centre of the area there is an elementary school and land has been reserved to build two secondary schools.

Houses supplied by the government have one room, a small storage room and a latrine at the corner of the lot next to the street. A number of people have added an extra room and almost all the Muslims have built a wall round their plots. When the area was built, the government supplied sewerage and water. Water comes from huge storage tanks in adjacent Model Town and Greentown itself. The water has a high mineral content but is free of contamination. Electricity is available.

Men work in Lahore or in communities around Greentown. Kot Lakphat is a few kilometres north-west of the area; this is an industrialised section of Lahore at the intersection of the rail line and Ferozpur Road. Some of Lahore's largest factories are here and in the early morning and early evening the roads to Greentown are clogged with men on bicycles wearing *shalwar qameez*, Pakistan's national dress of baggy trousers and loose knee-length shirt. The bicycles they ride may have been made in one of the factories nearby; black single-geared bikes that have been called the 'Pakistani Ford'. Late at night, after dark, the men who work as drivers and conductors for the Lahore Transit Authority come home to Greentown from the nearby Volvo Bus Terminal.

Information from a census and socio–economic survey[2] suggests a comfortable poor. In a survey of 457 households, 86 per cent (394) owned their own homes. Of the major earners in the household survey, 85 per cent (389) worked fifty-two weeks in 1981. In the larger census conducted at the same time as the socio–economic survey, 92 per cent of households reported that the major earner worked the week before. Eighty-six per cent of these earners have permanent jobs.

They are not rich. Of the 457 households surveyed, 286 had household incomes between 500 and 1000 rupees per month. Eighty-five per cent earned less than 1000 rupees a month. The average income in Greentown was very close to the national average income in Pakistan. Only six people in the sample had a car or truck but thirty-four had motorcycles and 192 had at least one bicycle. One hundred and thirty households (28 per cent) had a television set; 172 had radios; all but fifteen per cent had at least one fan.

They are uneducated. Almost half the population had never been in school but most desire, and work for, education for their children. Many pay for this education: 282 of 457 households reported paying monthly education costs for their children.

Several people living in Greentown described themselves (and Greentown) to me as 'middle class', using the English term. Sociologists and anthropologists who use class as an analytic device would probably not consider Greentown as a middle-class community; at least not without a qualifying adjective of some sort. But they are very far from the top or bottom of any kind of economic or social scale in Lahore.

Neighbours discussed modern versus traditional ways of living and described themselves as 'modern' and 'progressive'. Even those who praise traditional ways, and regret their loss, do not see themselves as living traditional lives. They perceive Pakistan (and Lahore) as changing just as modernists do and usually describe these differences as a rural and urban split: people do this in the village, while we act this way in Lahore. People in Greentown would be in the middle of an economic ranking; equally, they have taken a middling course in abandoning old ways or adopting new ones. Arguments about tradition and modernity seemed to be quite theoretical: a young neighbour who supported 'love matches' and coeducation and condemned the *biradari* system lived in an extended family and gave his father his salary. His primary opponent lived in a nuclear family and encouraged his older, unmarried daughters to work.

Even those people who missed traditional ways of living like their neighbourhood. People living in Greentown like living there. Both modernists and traditionalists praise the good bus services into the city and good shopping in Greentown itself. They describe themselves, and their neighbours, as 'good, respectable hard-working people.'

IV   MEDICAL CARE IN GREENTOWN

There are five private allopathic practitioners in Greentown. None of the five has an MBBS degree and none of these doctors could practise in the United States. One is a trained dispenser with a DMPS certificate, indicating completion of a training course in dispensing medicines. The others have picked up medical knowledge informally, usually by working at a low-level job in a hospital or with a doctor. In addition to these private practitioners, MBBS doctors work at a clinic funded and administered by a joint American–Pakistani research venture. The research group was primarily interested in malaria and the clinic offered primary health care to residents of the area. Two *hakims* had practices in Greentown and a medical store owner supplied health information and care as well as information, while the government ran a family planning clinic. Other medical care was available in neighbouring areas from private practitioners. Hospitals in Lahore have open air clinics, supplying medical care to out-patients. Some residents of Greentown had medical care supplied to their families by their employees. *Pirs*, saints who sometimes offered medical treatment, are occasionally used.

Greentown residents in general use allopathic practitioners. When *hakims* or *pirs* are consulted, it is generally for specific kinds of illness. Informants in Greentown were sceptical of the benefit of *pirs* as medical practitioners: 'They don't make you feel easy . . . what do they do? There is no benefit from *pirs* and *hakims*.' Another informant, asked if she or her relatives visited *pirs* or *hakims*, said, 'Not even a little. There is no benefit. My friends and relatives go to a doctor.' Two more residents remarked:

I believe there is one God and no *pirs*. We don't agree with *pirs*. There is one God, and he is the curer. Beside God, there is no *pir*. God is the one who makes you sick, and God is the curer.

We don't use house medicine, *taviz* [an amulet], *pir*, or *hakim* – only doctors. Some relatives use *taviz* and *pirs*. The *pir* takes the *taviz* and breathes on it. Sometimes there is benefit, sometimes not. The medicine from the DMPS gives benefit.

Other informants see religious practitioners as useful:

We moved here from Samanabad, and a fever came. A neighbour gave us a *taviz*. Before the *taviz*, there was no space in the fever. Afterwards, the fever came after a space of one or two months.

One woman thought that a *pir* was good in certain circumstances:

Pirs are good men. A doctor is a doctor. A *pir* is good if a person has hysteria or is afraid. I go to *pirs* and *faqirs* but for any sickness we go to the doctor. We take medicine from the clinic. I have my card.

Pirs are not considered specifically 'medical practitioners' in Greentown, but seem to be consulted for more general misfortune by some people; illness, like bankruptcy, is in this category. Others seemed to look on the *pir* as a kind of specialist, good for certain illnesses like hysteria. Another informant who had consulted a *pir* suggested another case in which a *pir* might be used: as a last resort.

While taking a census, I talked to a 20-year-old boy who told me he had 'fits', using the English word. After talking for ten minutes, his speech slowed, he began breathing heavily, fell silent and shut his eyes. He began to tremble and leaned against a doorway as he slid to the floor. His younger brother and I put him on a cot where he lay trembling for a few minutes, then relaxed, opened his eyes and lay dazed.

The young man said that he had gone to the clinic in Greentown, where he had been referred to a hospital in Lahore. He had stayed in the hospital a few days and nothing happened. He checked out of the hospital and had a seizure while waiting for a bus to Greentown. He left the hospital with neither diagnosis nor treatment.

He then consulted a *pir* in the old walled city of Lahore. The *pir* had given him treatment twice a week. He went to the *pir's* home, where the *pir* played devotional music on a tape recorder. *Djinns* and ghosts like sacred songs; the *djinn* or ghost possessing the boy was supposed to leave him and dance with pleasure while the music played. During this, the *pir* attempted to coax the possessing entity to leave the boy in peace.

The treatment was cheap; the boy gave the *pir* a packet of K-2 cigarettes, which cost a few pence, at each visit. Unfortunately, the treatment was also ineffective. The boy stopped seeing the *pir*.

The boy offered two possible causes for his seizures: he said that he had been very sick and had had a high fever for several days. After this illness, the fits began. He also said that he had had a twin brother who had died; perhaps this twin was 'seizing' him, causing the illness. The boy said he did not know which was the actual cause.

The first suggested cause of his illness was compatible with allo-pathy; a doctor might have suggested it. The second cause was compatible with cultural beliefs about possession. The *pir* might have suggested this. The boy's concern was not theoretical; he was willing to accept either possible cause, just as he was quite willing to pursue both forms of treatment. Cause was important only as it influenced ridding oneself of symptoms. As he pointed out, he could not marry, get a job or even leave the house. He knew he had fits and wanted them to go away. Culturally, the boy was offered two different theories of disease causation. Socially, the structure of medical practice in Lahore allowed him to choose between two different practitioners: allopath and *pir*. He chose to consult an allopath first, and if his symptoms had disappeared he would have gone no further. Neither practitioner provided relief and he had not yet consulted other practitioners, either *pir*, allopath, homoeopath or *hakim*, who were available.

Two *hakims* had offices in Greentown. The first was a fulltime practitioner who refused to be interviewed. The second was a parttime practitioner who was very friendly and interested in exchanging information about medicines. This *hakim* received his training from his father who operated a clinic in Lahore. He had few patients: he said he saw three or four people a week and they gave him what they wished as a fee. His patients were either his neighbours or people too poor to pay anything at all. He approved of allopathic medicine and thought it was 'very good, very strong'. He saw the differences in allopathy and *Yunani Tibbia* as differences in the medicines used.

The *hakim* gives medicines that cure all diseases. The MBBS has medicines for all diseases too. The *hakim* controls the disease very late but the MBBS controls sickness early. The *hakim* uses *juributi* medicine. [*Juributi* apparently means plants.] If he's a good *hakim*, he gives good medicine. These medicines are hand-made, he makes them himself. The MBBS doctors use the stems and leaves of plants, but the *hakim* uses all the parts of the plant. He uses stems and leaves and roots as well. He uses the bark of the tree. Quinine, for malaria, comes from the bark of the tree. There are many good medicines from plants. All plants are given by Allah, and all are good for something, but we haven't discovered some of the uses yet.

When his wife had kidney stones she went to an open air clinic in Lahore for treatment. He himself had been to the clinic in Greentown when he was ill. He said he had a fever and thought it was probably malaria. He was diagnosed as having malaria and the doctors gave him cloriquine.

The doctors there study malaria. They must know about it, and have good modern medicine to treat it. If the medicine is good, then the doctor is good. There are good medicines in every place. But you must be careful with allopathic medicines. They are sometimes too strong for children. They work very well and quickly, but they have many side effects. Sometimes a person is cured of one disease, but they become ill with something worse.

An allopathic medical student at a medical college in Lahore described the differences between *Yunani Tibbia* and allopathic medicine in much the same way. Like the *hakim*, he said that allopathic medicines were powerful but dangerous. He said that Western medicines only cured the symptoms of disease but the *hakim's* medicine cured the disease itself, 'truly cured.'

In a survey of eighty-eight households in Greentown,[3] informants were asked about the last time someone in the household was ill. The name, location, qualifications and cost of the doctor were established. Informants were asked the symptoms, causes and names of their illnesses.

People visit doctors frequently. One informant had just returned from the doctor; eleven had seen a doctor the day before. Fifty-four per cent had seen a doctor within the past week, and 90 per cent had seen a doctor within the past four months. I found this surprising, and I do not know why people visit doctors so frequently. If asked, they would say because they were ill. (Certainly a reasonable answer.) They might, indeed, be ill more often than a comparable group in the United States. (In addition, Americans could never afford to visit doctors as frequently as Greentown residents do.)

I asked initially what kind of doctor the patient saw: fifty-three informants said that he was 'just a doctor'. Twenty-three said that he was an allopath, one person saw a homoeopath, and twelve said they did not know what kind of doctor they saw. In answering a second question about formal qualifications, fifty-nine people did not know. Sixteen said that the doctors they saw had MBBS degrees; twelve said the doctor had DMPS degrees, one said 'other'.

People seem to desire allopathic practitioners, but only sixteen of the eighty-eight said that they saw an MBBS doctor. The great majority, fifty-nine, obviously did not choose a doctor because of his or her qualifications; they did not know those qualifications. Twelve saw doctors with DMPS degrees who had received training in dispensing medicine and in giving injections. One woman, who was concerned with qualifications, said:

> We always use WAPDA. [WAPDA provides its employees and their families with a free hospital.] They are good doctors, important doctors. All are MBBS doctors. My husband works at WAPDA, and I show them my papers and they have to see me. They have to take care of me, and there is never any problem with them. I have the papers, they give me the medicine.

The range of fees reported in my sample was no charge to thirty rupees. The most commonly reported fees were no charge and six rupees; both had a frequency of nineteen. Fifty-one per cent of informants paid four rupees or less for an office visit. In addition, seventy-seven (88 per cent) patients received medicine as part of the office visit.

Patients did not usually know what this medicine was. Instead, they knew only in what form the medicine was administered: tablets, powders, injections. Two received a cream. Vitamins and antibiotics were two substances informants did say that they were given: twenty-six people said that the doctor gave them vitamins, and two said they were given antibiotics. In addition, twenty-four people (27 per cent) had had drips – a glucose solution given intravenously. (My informants share what seems to be a Lahore-wide liking for drips.)

Several doctors were asked why patients were not told what medicine they were taking. They said that if the patient knew the medicine they were given, they would simply purchase it themselves without seeing a doctor the next time they were ill.

I bought medicine in Lahore. It was cheap, but not cheap enough to be supplied within this fee structure. I paid Rs 10.5 for twenty-four capsules of ampicillin. A full course of flagyl (for intestinal parasites) cost about Rs 25. It is unlikely that a doctor can profitably give very many effective medicines while charging patients three or four rupees for an office visit. (Out-of-date drugs can be bought cheaply; it is possible that some doctors use these.) It is also unlikely that the drugs available are stored properly, or that the doctor has a very wide range of medicine available in his or her office.

Few laboratory tests were ordered: blood tests were those most commonly carried out. Six patients had blood tests, and three of these were done at the clinic in Greentown for suspected malaria.

Two patients had X-rays, two were given sputum tests. One stool test and one urine test were also reported. No patient visiting a doctor in his private practice received any tests at all. The tests themselves were all reported as costing nothing. Unlike the United States, in Lahore tests are not seen as routinely necessary. Patients who reported tests received them at either the American-run clinic or local hospitals. Lack of testing reflects more than an attitude towards testing, however. Patients tended to use hospitals for more serious complaints. Patients who reported these tests had either found local practitioners unsatisfactory (they did not recover) or the practitioners had recommended they go to the local hospitals for care.

People see doctors who have offices nearby. Sixty-six went to practitioners in Greentown itself; seventy-eight of the eighty-eight questioned received care within two miles of Greentown. Proximity establishes the pool from which practitioners are chosen, but there is such a wide range of nearby doctors that other factors determine choice. Only ten people said that the doctor was chosen because he or she was near. The most common reason given for choice of a practitioner was that he or she was a good doctor. Only two people said that they had chosen practitioners because they were free.

V   THE CLINIC

The clinic operated by the research institution had closed the month before our survey was taken. Thus, it is not fairly represented in the sample. Greentown attitudes towards the clinic were complex and had little to do with allopathic medicine. The clinic, free and convenient, was rejected by a large number of the residents of Greentown. Some reasons for rejecting it were medical: patients expected certain kinds of medical treatment, injections and drips, and the American doctors in charge of the clinic thought that these were poor medical practice. The Pakistani doctors working in the clinic, in general, did not. After the clinic closed, doctors who opened private medical practices supplied their patients with injections and drips, and said that they could not have practised medicine in Lahore without doing so.

Ethnic tension in Greentown itself led to some residents ignoring the clinic as a source of medical care. It was located in Bihari Colony and some people thought it was used by Biharis only. Others said that

Biharis cursed and fought, and they did not want their wives to go to such places.

Doctors and patients both complained about each other. Doctors said that patients were dirty and ignorant. Patients said that doctors treated them in a humiliating way. For example, doctors in the clinic prescribed a ten-day course of drugs and would give medicine for only two days. Then patients were required to come back for another visit. Patients said, exasperated, that doctors thought they would sell the medicine. This was, in fact, one of the reasons given for the practice. Doctors also said that Greentown patients were too stupid and uneducated to follow directions. Use of the clinic fell drastically after several widely reported incidents in which clinic doctors treated patients with contempt. The doctors in the clinic felt, and said, that people in Greentown did not deserve MBBS doctors; people in Greentown felt, and said, that they did not deserve the kind of treatment they were given.

As a cost-cutting measure, the clinic eliminated some services and cut clinical hours. The research institute was an important employer in the area. When, as a further cost-cutting measure, almost all the Greentown employees were fired this was seen as an anti-Greentown measure. The clinic became more unpopular. In March 1982, the clinic saw several hundred people a day. In March 1983, the month the clinic closed, doctors saw sixty to seventy patients a day. Some areas of disagreement between clinic staff and residents involved medical issues, but more important sources of conflict were not medical. Social and cultural differences between doctors and patients led to misunderstanding by both. Medical disagreements could be seen as based on differences in medical practice in the United States and Pakistan. Social and cultural disagreements between doctors and patients could not.

The American administrator and doctor who had established the clinic left early in my stay. The clinic was administered and staffed almost exclusively by Pakistanis. (Only one doctor, a woman gynae-cologist from Latin America who worked part time, was not Pakis-tani.) Problems in the clinic were a reflection of roles and statuses within Pakistan, not difficulties in binational cooperation.

Relationships within the clinic, like those outside, were hierarchi-cally arranged and distance was maintained. Mutually antagonistic evaluations of doctors and patients had their roots in the broader system of relationships maintained in Lahore. Patients and doctors were integrated into a South Asian social order, one distinguished by hierarchical ranking. Doctors in the clinic and some of their patients did not agree on that ranking. A common complaint of doctors there was that patients treated them like quacks, the term used in Lahore for an untrained allopathic practitioner. Greentown people, the doctors said, did not know the difference between quacks and MBBS doctors. Doctors in the clinic said that people in Greentown were dirty, ignorant thieves. People in Greentown said that the clinic doctors were rude, greedy, self-serving and stole medicine from the clinic to sell. Doctors saw a vast social, cultural and educational difference between themselves and their patients. People in Greentown saw a much smaller one. Acting on these social intuitions resulted in unpleasant misunderstandings.

Doctors and patients agreed on how one shows respect to a superior, on the niceties of dealing with an inferior; they did not, however, agree on their relative ranking on such a scale. Behaviour was interpreted as insolent or insulting as a result of these divergent evaluations.

Social and cultural differences between doctor and patient are fewer in the case of those private practitioners whom Greentown residents generally choose to see. Thus, the potential for misunderstanding was less. Patients (and doctors) knew (and agreed) about clinical behaviour.

Paying for care was another way of avoiding a humiliation cost in medical treatment. A patient who pays has to be treated well. Payment also guarantees the patient and the patient's family more control over the treatment itself. The doctor in a private clinic treats a woman with an abscessed breast in a way that guarantees that she will come back: he does not drain the abscess because it will hurt, he does not give oral antibiotics. Instead, he gives injections adjusted to the number and timing of office visits he thinks the woman will tolerate. The doctor describing this to me thought it bad medical practice, and told his friend so. His friend agreed but pointed out that he would lose both the patient and several fees if he practised 'good medicine.' The allopathic doctor in Lahore has less control over actual treatment than his counterpart in North America.

VI CONCLUSION

In Lahore, patients and practitioners form matching pyramids; a small number of patients, the wealthy, use a small number of doctors, those at the top of their profession, who are often foreign-trained. The larger middle class has access to an equally larger number of MBBS doctors. The great mass of patients use the largest numbers of allopathic practitioners, and these are both MBBS doctors and quacks. Quacks do not normally treat the élite; highly trained consultants do not normally care for the ordinary resident of Greentown. Doctors compete for specific categories of patients. As allopathic medical care has gained in desirability and medical schools have produced more graduates, allopathic doctors cannot restrict their practice to the élite and provide care for a wider spectrum of patients. As they do so, they compete with a wider spectrum of health professionals.

This wider spectrum, in turn, complicates the mutual evaluation by patient and professional. Is a doctor a doctor, as Greentown residents thought, or are MBBS doctors quite superior to quacks, as the doctors in the clinic thought? New statuses, with a particular ranking in their place of origin, have been imported. Should a role be ranked by its country of origin or its indigenous equivalent? Quite different ranking systems have been used simultaneously in South Asia (as they have in other areas of the world). Family, education, wealth and personal piety have been (and are) used to evaluate the position of an individual within a hierarchical system.

In considering occupational hierarchy, one can say that a particular kind of person fills a particular kind of job and thus the job itself is located on a scale of relative prestige. The rank of those filling the job determines the rank of the job. Alternatively, individual ranking can be derived from work. (If working-class youths become doctors, doctoring is working-class; in the second case, if doctoring is upper class, working-class youths change class.) Both of these positions are 'traditionally South Asian'. (Consider the *Kshatriya*.) The first, however, is more significant in establishing hierarchical scales in South Asia, in Pakistan as well as India. The second is more closely identified with the process of professionalisation.

Doctors in the clinic claimed a position relative to their patients based on the fact that they were educated doctors. Patients found this criterion less important than doctors did. Patients, in general, respected doctors but not as much as doctors thought they should. People in Greentown knew little about, and paid little attention to, professional qualifications which doctors stressed. This lack of attention to formal qualifications by patients contributed to misunderstanding in patient–doctor relationships. It also influenced treatment.

Patients select physicians on the basis of cost and perceived effectiveness. Effectiveness is associated with medicine, not diagnostics. Patients in Greentown are not willing to pay for laboratory testing, and only informants who visited hospitals or the clinic received such tests. Untrained allopathic practitioners did not have knowledge of, nor did they see the need for, general laboratory testing. Neither did their patients. An MBBS doctor working in Greentown could not use such diagnostic tools in general practice and still attract patients. MBBS doctors working with the majority of people in Lahore have their treatment dictated in part by the practices of the untrained: they simply would not have patients if they attempted to practise (and charge) the same way a doctor treating wealthy patients in Lahore did.

Licensing of medical practitioners in the United States offers some protection against the grossly ignorant, if not the incompetent. There are other ways in which patients can be protected. Patient education can lead to more informed judgements concerning the quality of care given. Competition for patients discourages this as well. Patients were given very little information about their own illness or treatment.

Despite a shortage of MBBS doctors, doctors (both qualified and unqualified) competed for patients. In this situation, patients exerted great control over treatment and attracting patients took precedence over purely medical considerations. While the theoretical basis of allopathy is taught to students in medical schools, social, cultural and economic constraints make implementation of what is taught difficult.

If professional allopathic bodies in Pakistan did restrict the practice of medicine to formally trained doctors, the major part of the population would have no health care at all. There are not enough MBBS doctors to satisfy demand. In addition, MBBS doctors are not willing to work in rural areas. Professionalisation as monopoly control is not feasible. Socially and politically, homoeopathy and *Yunani Tibbia* have support. An important political party, *Jamaat-e-Islami*, operates free homoeopathic clinics throughout Lahore for the poor. Medically, legally and politically, an allopathic monopoly of treatment is not possible.

Conceptually, allopathic medicine is seen as the use of drugs and medical apparatus developed in Europe and North America. Patients interpret allopathy almost exclusively in this way, and allopathic practitioners often act as if this were the way in which they themselves interpret allopathic medicine. Medical practice, and the prescription of drugs, is not organised as a professional monopoly.

These two statements are directly related: if medicine is the tools of the trade rather than a body of knowledge, access to these tools rather than command of that knowledge establishes one as a practitioner. Conceptually, treatment *is* medicine. Patients say that it is not the doctor that cures, it is the medicine. If these tools are the hallmark of the allopath, the trained MBBS doctor has no advantage in the market place over the untrained allopath.

The full range of technology and the social organisation of medicine have not been introduced in Lahore. Those items and roles which have been introduced are integrated into a pre-existing system. Allopathic medicine has adapted to South Asia, rather than being adopted by it.

Notes

1. This chapter is based on approximately three years' familiarity with Greentown. From November 1980 until August 1981, I worked part time as Administrative Assistant to the American director of the Pakistan Medical Research Center. The Center, jointly operated by the University of Maryland, in the US, and the Government of Pakistan, focused on research into malaria. The Center operated a primary health care clinic in conjunction with a number of research projects in the area. From January 1982 until June 1982, I worked as an anthropological consultant in Greentown, where I conducted a census and socio–economic survey of the area. From September 1982 until September 1983, I conducted independent research on allopathic health care in Greentown. This was funded by a Fulbright–Hayes Dissertation Abroad Award, and findings are reported in my thesis submitted to the University of Texas at Austin. In addition, my family and I lived in Greentown from January 1983 to August 1983.
2. A census was conducted in Greentown by Michael Fischer and myself between 1 April and 31 May 1982. Approximately 90 per cent of households answered census questions. The socio–economic survey was conducted at the same time. A 20 per cent sample of the population was selected, using a map prepared by the Lahore Development Authority. Before the census, field assistants, using the LDA map, surveyed Greentown and eliminated empty lots and shops. Using the computer at the research institution, a random sample of 20 per cent of these households was drawn without replacement. Field assistants, in pairs, conducted the survey in the morning. Afternoons were spent in checking work. Discrepancies in information collected (including information from other cen-

suses and surveys) were checked in the afternoon. Random checks of field assistants' work were carried out.
3. The last illness survey was conducted from 1 March 1983 to May 1983. A 20 per cent sample of households in the economic survey was drawn, with replacement. Eighty-two of the eighty-eight households drawn responded. The survey was conducted by Wenonah Lyon and Mazhar Muhammad. Questions were written in Urdu; if the respondent did not speak Urdu, Mazhar asked the questions in Punjabi. Surveys were conducted in the morning, transcriptions and translations in the afternoon.

References

Berlant, J. (1975), *Profession and Monopoly* (Berkeley: University of California Press).
Bhardwaj, S. (1975), 'Attitudes towards Different Systems of Medicine: A Survey of Villages in Punjab India', *Social Science and Medicine*, 9 (11/12).
Bhatia, J. C. (1975), 'Traditional Healers and Modern Medicine', *Social Science and Medicine* 9 (1).
Dunn, F. (1976), 'Traditional Asian Medicine and Cosmopolitan Medicine as Adaptive Systems', in Charles Leslie (ed.), *Asian Medical Systems* (Berkeley: University of California Press).
Harwood, A. (1981), *Ethnicity and Medical Care* (Cambridge Mass.: Harvard University Press).
Ingman, S. (ed.) (1975), *Topias and Utopias in Health: Policy Studies* (The Hague: Mouton).
Lyons, R. (1971), 'A Gold Mine for Some Doctors', in P. Horton and G. Leslie (eds), *Studies in the Sociology of Social Problems* (New York: Appleton-Century-Crofts).
Minocha, A. (1980), 'Medical Pluralism and Health Service in India', *Social Science and Medicine*, 14B.
Mushtaqut, R. (1980), 'Urban and Rural Medical Systems in Pakistan', *Social Science and Medicine*, 14B.
Oherson, S. and Singham, L. (1981), 'The Machine Metaphor in Medicine', in E. Mishler (ed.), *Social Contexts of Health, Illness and Patient Care* (Cambridge, Mass.: Cambridge University Press).
Strauss, A. (1971), 'Medical Ghettos', in P. Horton and G. Leslie, (eds), *Studies in the Sociology of Social Problems* (New York: Appleton-Century Crofts).

8 Nationhood and the Nationalities in Pakistan
Hamza Alavi

More than four decades after the state of Pakistan was created it is still a country in search of an identity. This is not because the issue of our nationhood has not preoccupied our minds. To the contrary, it is one that we have been obsessed with and much blood has been spilt in the process. Political debate and conflict have revolved around the question: what is the legitimate place of subnational aspirations and demands within a larger concept of Pakistan nationhood? There is a tension and a dialectical opposition between these two levels of political identity which has never been resolved, for those in power have tended to look on subnational movements as a threat to 'the nation' and subversive of national unity.

In the eyes of the articulate leadership of subnational groups, the Pakistan 'nation' has been appropriated by Punjabis who dominate the ruling bureaucracy and the military that has effectively been in power in Pakistan since its inception: in partnership, they might say, until the mid-1970s with Muhajirs who were relatively well represented in the Punjabi dominated state apparatus. Members of the underprivileged regions have tended to see themselves as subject peoples who have not been given their rightful place in the nation. In their eyes, with a subtle inflection of meaning, the 'nation' (*qaum*) is transmuted into 'country' (*mulk*). They exist within its boundaries and are subject to its laws and institutions. But the concept of 'country' is not evocative like that of the nation. It does not draw upon a deeply embedded sense of identification; it does not have the same emotive and legitimising charge. It does not give quite the same sense of belonging and commitment as that of the nation. The Urdu language does not even possess an adequate vocabulary to articulate concepts of nationhood and nationality. The word *qaum* refers to race, nation or nationality; when asked what his *qaum* is, a Pakistani is most likely to refer to his subnational identity rather than Pakistani nationhood. The word *millat*, which in its original Persian usage refers to the secular nation, has acquired religious connotations in Pakistan and refers to the global community of Muslims. The peoples of Pakistan have not yet fused into a single community. The story of the Bengali movement, culminating in the liberation of Bangladesh, is a manifest example of this.

I 'OFFICIAL NATIONALISM'

Up to a point, it might be said that Pakistan is not alone among Third World countries in this predicament; among countries where state power lies in the hands of one dominant ethnic group, alienating the rest. In Europe, where subnational groups have also come forward in recent times with demands for autonomy and national self-determination, the historical perspective nevertheless has been rather different. There, by and large, national unification movements preceded formation of nation states so that the resulting states embraced peoples who, in the course of such movements, had developed a sense of common purpose and common identity that brought them together as nations. In post-colonial societies, such processes that weld peoples together have tended to be rather tenuous. So it was, to a degree, in the case of the Pakistan movement. Whereas in Europe, nations were constituted into states, in post-colonial societies the problem is inverted: to transform states into nations.

This problem tends to be less acute where national liberation has been achieved through a long drawn out mass struggle for independence and self-determination, which has brought peoples together to constitute nations in their march towards a common destiny. The Pakistan movement has had a trajectory that has not included such a process. In any case, the whole issue becomes more problematic where a single ethnic group finds itself in control of the state apparatus, through its disproportionate representation in the state bureaucracy and the military, as in Pakistan. Their ruling military bureaucratic oligarchies, having appropriated state power, identify the state and the nation narrowly with their own particular purposes and interests.

If, in the circumstances, it were to be claimed that Pakistan is a unified nation that would be tantamount to what Anderson (1983) speaks of as 'official nationalism', a national identity that is not spontaneously generated from below but is imposed from above by those at the heart of the power structure in the country, in reaction to powerful subnational movements that evoke a far more powerful popular response in all regions outside the Punjab. The nation, in that context, is made into a property of the privileged groups. Repression of subnational movements by the ruling bureaucracy and military, in the name of 'national unity', in the circumstances, is self-defeating for that only deepens their sense of alienation; their sense of being a subject people.

II THE SALARIAT

There is one class which has been central to this problem, both with regard to the Pakistan movement as well as regional nationalism within Pakistan after independence. This is a section of the urban middle class, those with educational qualifications and aspirations for jobs in the state apparatus, the civil bureaucracy and the military. I have called it the *salariat* (Alavi, 1987). This class has a particular salience in colonised societies with a predominantly agrarian production base where the colonial (and post-colonial) state apparatus has a dominating presence in the urban society and is the principal employer. Associated with the salariat are urban professionals, lawyers and doctors, as well as the intelligentsia, writers, poets, teachers and journalists, who share the life experiences and many of the aspirations of the 'salariat'. It is from amongst these that an articulate component of the political leadership is also drawn.

The salariat is internally differentiated, for those in its upper echelons, senior bureaucrats and military officers, hold positions of power. Their position is qualitatively different from that of lower level functionaries. But they share a common goal in the struggle for access to the limited opportunities for state employment. In that struggle the salariat has a tendency to divide and align along ethnic lines in order to draw wider support and solidarity in its struggle for a greater share of the available jobs, as well as the limited places in institutions of higher education, the source of credentials for future jobs. Students, aspiring occupants of salariat positions, are therefore aligned with the respective salariat groups and play an active role in salariat politics.

Lines of ethnic cleavage within the South Asian salariat are in large part a reflection of historical occupational specialisation in India by communities, as well as by uneven regional extension of the process of the colonial transformation of Indian society. Some communities have traditionally been associated with state employment. Under the several hundred years of Muslim rule, many Hindu communities nevertheless occupied a key role in the state apparatus, such as the Kayasthas and Kashmiri Brahmins in northern India or Amils in Sindh. It was much later that members of other communal, occupational groups began to be drawn towards salariat careers, and it is not surprising therefore that they found themselves greatly underrepresented in state employment.

An important factor in the regional equation in Pakistan was the patronage bestowed by a grateful colonial regime on Punjabis for their help to the colonial regime in putting down the so-called 'Indian mutiny', the first Indian war of independence. Punjabis, whether Muslims, Sikhs or Hindus, were rewarded in many different ways, including land grants in the newly created canal colonies of the Punjab. But that included special attention to education. This was availed of by urban Punjabis who by virtue of being drawn into the salariat followed the political leadership of the Muslim League rather than the Unionist Party that was in power in the Punjab, the party of landowners of the Punjab, a multiethnic party that defended landlord interests. Urban Punjabis, predominantly Urdu speakers, were both patronised and looked down upon by the ruling Unionists of the Punjab and their leaders like Sir Fazli Hussain, founder of the Unionist Party. By contrast Bengali Muslims were much underrepresented in salariat jobs, despite their relatively higher educational levels (Basu, 1974).

In Sindh, the urban population before Partition was overwhelmingly Hindu, as indeed was the Sindhi salariat, the Amils. But Hindus were driven out of the country, following well-organised rioting in Karachi, in January 1948, leaving a social vacuum which was filled by incoming Urdu-speaking Muhajir refugees from India. Sindhi Muslims were overwhelmingly rural and the Sindhi Muslim salariat element was very small at the time. Likewise, the Baluch and Pathans were under-represented, although the latter were well established in the military. The relatively well-educated Urdu-speaking Muslims of northern India were traditionally well established in salariat positions, and after Partition these Muhajirs shared control over state power as junior partners of the dominant Punjabis. Given the source of patronage and support, Muhajirs were with the Punjabis in supporting the notion of an indivisible Pakistan nation. But their position was shattered by the weakening of bureaucratic power by Bhutto's administrative reforms, and decisively so by the Zia regime that followed. Against that background Muhajirs abandoned their earlier position and declared themselves to be another disadvantaged ethnic group – giving rise to a new movement, the Muhajir Qaumi Mahaz (MQM), the Muhajir National Front. Ethnic politics in Sindh have followed an uneven course because at one level the small and weak Sindhi-speaking salariat in that province has found itself in direct competition at the local level with the Urdu-speaking Muhajirs, while at the national level they both find common ground by virtue of Punjabi domination from the centre.

While the salariat has been at the centre of ethnic politics in Pakistan, it does not stand alone in this. This applies in particular to sons of landowners or rich peasants, for example, who can afford to put their sons through higher education so that they may move into salariat positions, positions which they did not traditionally occupy. In such cases, we can say that there is an *organic link* that ties the salariat with the classes from which they originate. Beyond direct organic bonds, by virtue of kinship, there are also other kinds of linkages that mobilise broader sections of society behind the salariat politics which dominates our political life. This is particularly an effect of the pervasive role of government in our society and its personalised character. Linkages that create possibilities of personal access to the bureaucracy are much valued, sought after and cultivated. Persons who come within wider social networks that potentially provide such contacts and connections with actual and prospective members of the salariat, such as fellow villagers or even those who can invoke their shared ethnic identity, will tend to identify themselves as such and give their backing to the ethnic politics of the salariat. They have a stake in their installation in public office and their promotion to higher positions within the bureaucracy, for they can then hope to invoke their mediation and help that would provide for them a point of fruitful access to the bureaucratic machine.

In the case of subnational movements for regional autonomy, ambitious politicians are also drawn into the game of ethnic politics. Where they have little hope of gaining power at the centre, an alternative is to profit from possibilities of acquiring influential public office at a local or provincial level. They have a stake in the goal of greater provincial autonomy which would put greater power and more resources at their disposal. They resort to chauvinistic rhetoric as a powerful means of mobilising support when they have little else to offer the common people. On the other hand, one can see the logic of the politics of members of privileged and dominant ethnic groups who hold key positions in the bureaucracy and the military, and thereby are in control of state power, who feel threatened by the politics of ethnicity and denounce such political appeals as parochial and particularistic. They invoke instead appeals to loyalty to larger entities such as the 'Pakistan nation' or the 'brotherhood of Islam' in the name of which they try to delegitimise regional ethnic demands. They invoke an 'official nationalism'.

Finally, in considering the reasons for Pakistan politics being overshadowed by the politics of ethnicity, we must consider our long history of authoritarian government by a bureaucratic and military oligarchy, seen to be predominantly Punjabi. There have been few opportunities, therefore, for the common people to participate in democratic processes. They feel alienated from the political system with no sense of participation in it.

III SALARIAT-BASED NATIONAL MOVEMENT

The salariat was at the heart of early Indian nationalism whose main slogan was not yet independence but rather 'Indianisation' of government service and 'self-government' within the empire. Under conditions of colonial rule the salariats from different parts of India were, initially, united in that common goal. Yet even at this early stage ethnic competition within the Indian salariat was beginning to make its appearance. The movement of the Muslim salariat that ultimately culminated in the formation of Pakistan was only one of several such movements. By itself the salariat provided a very narrow political base. This limitation is reflected in the history of the Muslim League too. It did very badly in the elections of 1937 and, ironically, it was at its weakest in the Muslim majority provinces of India. It was by virtue of certain special circumstances which surfaced when independence was in sight, circumstances which brought about a swing in political alignments of powerful landlord groups in the Muslim majority provinces, that enabled the Muslim League to muster the forces lying behind the creation of Pakistan.

The heart of Muslim nationalism in India was in the United Provinces and Bihar, both Muslim minority provinces. Muslims there had held a lion's share of government jobs. But with the switch to an Anglo-vernacular system of education and changes in the colonial administrative and legal systems, as well as the very rapid expansion in the size of the salariat in the latter half of the nineteenth century, parallel with the construction of a new colonial economy in India (cf.

Alavi, 1989), there was a relatively greater increase in the non-Muslim component of the salariat. Muslims saw themselves losing their pre-eminence. Their share in the highest ranks of government service declined from 64 per cent in 1857 to about 35 per cent in 1913. This was a remarkable *decline in privilege*, for Muslims were only about 13 to 15 per cent of the total population of the UP in that period. Under the leadership of Sir Syed Ahmad Khan they demanded a parity in quotas for government jobs, arguing that Muslims made up in quality what they lacked in overall numbers! Aligarh and Lucknow were the main political bases of the Muslim salariat who hijacked the Muslim League as soon as it was founded (cf. Alavi, 1987). Jinnah, a leader of the Indian National Congress, was invited to join them in 1913. It is a component of the Muslim salariat that was later to come to Pakistan as *muhajirs*.

In the Punjab the Muslim salariat was also quite sizeable, for about 32 per cent of those educated in English in the Punjab were Muslims, rather less than their share of the total population which was over 52 per cent (Census 1931). The Punjabi Muslim salariat joined that of the UP and Bihar in the Muslim national movement, declaring that they were under-represented by way of their proper share of government jobs. These relatively more advanced components of the Muslim salariat in India were the main base for the Pakistan movement. It was a very limited base.

The salariat-based Indian national movement was able to extend its base both by virtue of getting the backing of the Indian national bourgeoisie, anxious to get the colonial regime off its back, and by virtue of the politics of mass mobilisation inaugurated by Mahatma Gandhi which triggered off the active support of the subordinate masses behind the movement for independence. That was not the style of politics of the Muslim League leadership. Mass mobilisation being absent in this case, the requisite political weight was secured only when a deal was made by Jinnah with the landlord leadership of the Muslim majority provinces, especially in the Punjab and Sindh. That secured, nominally at least, the adoption of the Muslim League label by right-wing, landlord-dominated governments that were in power in those provinces and gave the Muslim League some kind of mandate on the basis of which it was able to secure the final result. But the Muslim League's dependence on landlords of Sindh and Punjab for securing its goals and its inability to mobilise the Muslim masses were to have far-reaching consequences for the state of Pakistan.

Politics of ethnicity, based on the problems and aspirations of different salariat groups, have developed differently in India and Pakistan in two respects. First, ethnic movements in Pakistan have taken the form primarily of subnationalism, although a secondary theme of localised ethnic conflicts and competition has not been absent. In India, by contrast, politics of ethnicity have, by and large, been displaced on to local arenas, taking the form of communalism and inter-communal conflict over quotas for jobs and places in institutions of higher education that lead to salariat and professional careers.

Secondly, we find that in the case of Pakistan there has been a succession of ethnic definitions and redefinitions, according to changing contexts of ethnic politics. To begin with, the salariat groups behind the Pakistan movement were defined and unified by a religious *ethnic* criterion, namely, 'Muslim'. Pakistan was not created, as is ideologically represented by some interests in Pakistan today, to create an 'Islamic' state (cf. Alavi, 1987). The Pakistan Muslim League was held to be the champion of *Muslim* nationalism. But the social roots of Muslim nationalism were quite shallow. It is quite remarkable that the Pakistan movement was at its weakest in Muslim majority provinces. As has been pointed out, political power in the Punjab lay in the hands not of the Punjabi salariat but, rather, in the hands of powerful landowners who were organised behind the right-wing landlord party, the Unionist party, the party of Hindu and Sikh as well as Muslim landowners who despised the urban salariat groups even when they patronised them.

In Sindh, the pattern was virtually identical, except for the fact that an ethnic Sindhi-speaking Muslim salariat was virtually non-existent. Muslims in Sindh were either landlords or peasants, the *waderas* and *haris*. Sindhi urban society was overwhelmingly Hindu, except for a certain number of non-Sindhi Muslims who had migrated to the cities of Sindh in the wake of colonial development. It is only in relatively recent times that Sindhi-speaking Muslims, who were predominantly rural, have begun to come forward to claim their share of salariat positions. Muslims of Baluchistan were likewise backward as also those of Sarhad, although some subregional variations existed. In these regions, the Muslim League was to be at the mercy of landlords and tribal leaders. The claim of Muslim nationalism in India was that Indians were divided into two nations, the Hindu nation and the Muslim nation. The moment that Pakistan was established Muslim nationalism had fulfilled its objective and had outlived its original purpose. There were two interesting responses to this new situation. First, Jinnah himself buried the two nation theory in his inaugural speech given on 14 August 1947 to the newly established constituent assembly of Pakistan. In that historic speech he declared in the clearest possible terms his commitment to the idea of secular citizenship in Pakistan. From the principal forum of the new state he declared:

> You may belong to any religion or creed. That has nothing to do with the business of the state . . . We are starting with this fundamental principle, that we are all citizens of one state . . . I think we should keep that in front of us as our idea and you will find that in course of time Hindus will cease to be Hindus and Muslims will cease to be Muslims, not in the religious sense because that is the personal faith of each individual but in the political sense, as citizens of the state. (Choudhury, 1967, pp. 21–2)

Jinnah's speech was a clear declaration of secular citizenship in the new state, a speech that ideological vested interests in Pakistan have a hard time explaining away.

IV ASSERTION OF REGIONAL IDENTITIES

A rather different response to the creation of Pakistan was the affirmation of their own regional identities, as against the common identity of 'Muslim', by underprivileged regional salariat groups in Pakistan *vis-à-vis* the dominant Punjabis. There was a fresh reckoning of the distribution of privilege and deprivation. Virtually overnight there were ethnic redefinitions. The salariat groups of East Bengal, Sindh, Sarhad, and Baluchistan promptly redefined their identities as Bengalis, Sindhis, Pathans and Baluch and demanded fairer shares for themselves in jobs in the state apparatus. The respective regional, subnationalist, movements exploded into view the day after Pakistan came into being. The state of Pakistan was now represented by them as an instrument of Punjabi domination, with their control of the bureaucracy first under Secretary-General Choudhury Muhammad Ali and later under Governor Ghulam Mohammed. The fact that neither General Iskandar Mirza nor General Ayub Khan, who held the reins of power after them, were Punjabis made little difference to that perception, for given the

Punjabi positions within the bureaucracy and the military, power was seen to be securely in Punjabi hands.

The articulation of Bengali and Pathan identities, respectively, on the basis of both region and language, was relatively unproblematic. The first expression of the demands of the East Bengal salariat came when Shaikh Mujibur Rahman, as a young student leader, put the aspirations of the people of East Pakistan before Jinnah when he visited Dacca. The powerful Bengali language movement, symbolically so, for language is above all the instrument of the pen-pushing salariat, was triggered off by the announcement in 1952 that Urdu would be the national language of Pakistan. The Bengali movement demonstrated its power in the East Pakistan elections of 1954 when the 'ruling' Muslim Party secured no more than ten seats out of a total of 309. Here the Bengali salariat was far more effective in the political arena than the Muslim League had been in the 1937 elections. In 1937, the social base of the victorious Krishak Proja Party in Bengal was made up of rich peasants and *jotedars*, who demanded abolition of *zamindari*, to get rid of the overlords who dominated their lives. That objective was achieved by *zamindari* abolition in East Bengal in 1951. In the elections in East Bengal in 1954 and subsequently, the leading issues were salariat demands. The rich peasants and *jotedars*, whose sons made up the East Bengal salariat, were solidly with them. Hence their landslide victories. These were solid votes against 'Punjabi' domination.

The problem of ethnic identity is rather more complicated in Sindh and Baluchistan. In Sindh, especially, it is an explosive issue that has torn that province apart in violent conflict. In Baluchistan, if cultural criteria were to be interpreted too rigidly, as differentiating criteria of ethnic groups, a number of separate groups can be demarcated, namely, Baluch proper, Brahuis (or Brohis), Lassis, Makranis and in the north-eastern districts Pushtuns who are Pathans rather than Baluch. The literature of Baluch nationalism repudiates angrily attempts to fragment them on the basis of such criteria. Instead they have produced historical accounts of convergent origins of these different sections of a single people, the Baluch. It is the dominant Punjabi ruling groups, they argue, who emphasise and try to exploit such differences to disrupt Baluch unity. The Baluch, on the other hand, resist such attempts to divide them and stridently proclaim their unity. The only exception that some of them are prepared to make is in the case of Pushtuns, and they accept the idea of Pushtun areas of Baluchistan being amalgamated with the neighbouring Sarhad province. Affirmations of Baluch unity are directed against

Punjabis and other outsiders who monopolise jobs and the most profitable occupations in Baluchistan, to the exclusion of the Baluch.

V THE CASE OF SINDH

It is in Sindh that the worst contradictions of the politics of ethnicity in Pakistan are concentrated and they take violent forms. Sindh is truly a multiethnic province. In a sense it has always been so, for historically it has been inhabited by a substantial number of Baluchi-speaking people who, although they may speak Baluchi at home, are nevertheless regarded as Sindhi; some of them are Sindhi nationalist leaders. Likewise, there are migrants from Cutch in India (business communities) who have lived in Sindh for many generations and have played leadership roles in Sindhi politics. For example, Mahmood Haroon, who is from such a background, was among prominent delegates at a conference organised at Sann, the home of G. M. Syed, when the Sindh National Alliance was founded in 1988. Feroz Ahmad, a militant Sindhi extremist, who is an Ismaili, also belongs to this category. Hence we can see that Sindhi identity is a mixture of many different elements, a product of historical evolution.

But a distinction *is* made in the case of those who have come to Sindh after Partition. They are not categorised as Sindhis although they have lived in Sindh for decades. These include Muhajirs, Urdu-speaking refugees from India who came in at Partition and also Punjabis and Pathans who have migrated to Pakistan since then. Forty years ago when a flood of refugees uprooted from India poured into Pakistan (similar numbers of Hindu and Sikh refugees were uprooted from Pakistan and driven across the border to India), the Punjabi dominated ruling oligarchy ensured that refugees from East Punjab, and in the main only those, were settled in West Punjab so that ethnically and linguistically Punjab remained homogeneous; only a handful of refugees from other parts of India found their way into that province. All refugees other than those from East Punjab, that is, mainly the Urdu-speaking refugees from northern and central India, were settled in Sindh, although Punjab, being a much larger province, had a greater capacity to absorb these refugees and offer them a livelihood. With Sindhi Hindus, the predominant element of Sindhi urban population having been driven out and the influx of Muhajirs into Sindh, the ethnic composition of Sindh was radically altered.

Some of the Urdu-speaking refugees from India who were

funnelled into Sindh settled on the land. But the bulk of them took the place of urban Sindhi Hindus, either as traders or professionals in the big cities and small towns of Sindh. The Urdu-speaking Muhajirs also initially provided the bulk of the urban working-class in Sindh. The Sindhi-speaking urban population in Sindh thus became quite minute. Whereas before Partition Sindh's cities were predominantly non-Muslim, now they are predominantly Urdu speakers. As Sindhis started coming up in the salariat, they found that they had not only to deal with Punjabi domination of the state apparatus but also to compete with the relatively more advanced Muhajirs. Although initially (after Partition) the population of Sindh's cities was over-whelmingly Muhajir in composition, their ethnic composition changed substantially with the influx of Pathan and Punjabi workers who provided additions to the workforce for the growing industries.

As a result, according to the 1981 Census only 52 per cent of the population of Sindh consisted of those whose first language was Sindhi. Urdu speakers were more than 22 per cent of the total. But they predominated in the urban areas of Sindh where they were reckoned to number over 50 per cent of the population. The Muhajir urban majority is less pronounced as one moves to smaller towns which, after all, are mere extensions of the rural society. But along with Punjabis and Pathans they are an overwhelming majority in the three major industrial cities, namely Karachi, Hyderabad and Sukkur.

In Karachi, the capital of Sindh, a metropolis of over 8 million people, 54.3 per cent of the population (in 1981) were Urdu speakers, namely Muhajirs. A total of 13.6 per cent were Punjabi speakers and 8.7 per cent Pushto-speaking Pathans from the Sarhad. In that capital of Sindh, those whose first language was Sindhi numbered a mere 6.3 per cent. That is the grievance of Sindhi nationalists. They have become strangers in their own land. However, it might be said that the census figures probably underestimate, as some experts believe, the numbers of Pathans and Punjabis in Karachi, many of whom live in *katchi abadis* or shanty towns where there has been an under-enumeration. An estimated 40 per cent of the city's population live in these slums. By contrast, Sindhis who live in Karachi belong to the lower middle class and above, many of them being absentee land-lords and their retinues. Likewise in the other major cities of Sindh, Hyderabad and Sukkur, native Sindhi speakers are in a very small minority.

A rather different kind of complication in the ethnic composition of Sindh arises from the influx of privileged groups from outside. These are mostly Punjabis. Large tracts of land in Sindh, brought under irrigation since independence, were allotted by the ruling bureaucratic military oligarchy to senior officers of the bureaucracy or the military or their relatives, rather than to Sindhis. These new landlords in Sindh tend mostly to be absentee landlords and they brought with them Punjabi tenants or labourers, whom they could better control and rely upon than local Sindhis. So this is a double deprivation, of lands as well as jobs. In urban areas, too, valuable land and property have been allotted to persons in these categories. Punjabis are taking over industries and large businesses also from the (mainly) Cutchi businessmen of Sindh. Because of proliferation of state controls of various kinds, over the operation especially of industrial enterprises, the established businessmen have found it increasingly more difficult to cope with them, the more so during the eleven years of Zia's military dictatorship when rule of law gave way to arbitrary decisions taken by military officers. As a result, many of the traditional businessmen have retreated into trade and many have transferred their operations abroad. In their place a new class of Punjabi capitalists has taken shape. These are not just any Punjabis, but rather they are close kinsmen of senior bureaucrats and military officers. Their kinship links play an important part in their ability to negotiate bureaucratic hurdles which the old established bourgeoisie found it difficult to negotiate. *Both* Sindhis and Muhajirs have found themselves pushed into the background and resent these developments.

VI MUHAJIR POLITICS

The ethnic orientation of both Sindhis and Muhajirs has undergone significant changes in recent years, dramatically so in the case of Muhajirs. As the time of Partition Muhajirs were well established in the bureaucracy, though not in the armed services which is estimated to be around 85 per cent Punjabis, most of the rest being Pathans (these are not confirmed or verifiable figures). It must be said, however, that there does exist a number, though a diminishing one, of very senior Muhajir officers and generals; General Mirza Aslam Baig, Zia's successor, is, for example, a Muhajir. However, as the significant alignments in the military are those amongst Punjabi officers and generals, Muhajir officers do not represent a power base on their own. They are rather often the 'least evil' choice of powerful rival groups of Punjabi officers. Muhajir presence in the bureaucracy was an important source of patronage for them. In the circumstances they identified politically with concepts of Pakistan nationhood and some even with Islamic ideology, and opposed demands of regional ethnic groups. This ideology was in continuity with their political orientation in the past for, along with urban Punjabis, Muhajirs were the bulwark of Muslim nationalism in India and provided many of the principal leaders of the Pakistan movement. In Pakistan they were largely non-political, for their linkages with the bureaucracy were personal and particularistic. In so far as they were drawn into the political arena, they tended to back Islamic ideological parties such as the Jamaat-e-Islami or the Jamiat-e-Ulema-e-Pakistan.

The bureaucracy, with its important Muhajir component, used to be presided over by the tightly organised CSP, the Civil Service of Pakistan, successor to the colonial ICS, the so-called 'steel frame' of colonial rule. For two and a half decades after independence, it was the senior partner in the bureaucratic military oligarchy that ruled Pakistan (cf. Alavi, 1983). It was powerful enough to keep the military at bay even during the martial law regime of General Yahya Khan. The situation changed radically after Bhutto's administrative reforms broke its back, and the bureaucracy ceased to be the powerful entity that it used to be. Ironically, this opened the way for unrestrained military rule under General Zia for the one great barrier in the way of military hegemony was removed. With the collapse of bureaucratic power, it was also the case that the Muhajirs lost their patrons in the structure of state power which now passed into unchallenged Punjabi hands.

It took a little time for these changes to manifest their effects in Muhajir politics – although it must not be forgotten that Muhajirs played a big role in movements against Ayub Khan which led him to transfer the capital away from Karachi, the principal Muhajir centre. Soon Muhajirs were to abandon their preoccupation with affirmations of Pakistani nationhood and they abandoned, in the process, their support for Islamic fundamentalist parties. They lined up behind the politics of ethnicity.

Hitherto, Muhajirs had agitated against the quota system for jobs and admissions into institutions of higher education, which are at the core of ethnic politics. As late as December 1986 a Jamaat-e-Islami Urdu weekly, read mostly by Muhajirs, carried an article entitled:

'Quota System: Denial of Justice and the Sword of Oppression' (*Kota Sistam: Adal ki Nafi Aur Zulm ki Talwar* in *Takbeer*, 24 December 1986). But the Muhajirs were to change this stand. The quota system in Pakistan dates back to the 1950s when it was introduced in deference to East Bengali ethnic demands. Unlike the system in India where quotas are based on local communal criteria and are left to local authorities to work out and implement, in Pakistan they are regional, 10 per cent of the places being awarded 'on merit', 50 per cent for the Punjab, and 19 per cent for Sindh, of which 11.4 per cent was for 'rural Sindh' and thus for predominantly Sindhi speakers, and 7.6 per cent for urban Sindh, mainly Muhajir. A quota of 11.5 per cent was fixed for Sarhad and 3.5 per cent for Baluchistan and the rest for Azad Kashmir and the Federally Administered Territories. However, there were problems with implementation of the quota system. Given Punjabi control over the administrative machinery, it has not been too difficult for a Punjabi to poach places from the other groups by obtaining false 'Certificates of Domicile' in say Quetta in Baluchistan or Hyderabad in Sindh, thus depriving the locals.

With the total collapse of bureaucratic power and with consolidation of the power of the Punjabi dominated army, Muhajirs began to feel that they were losing ground heavily and their bureaucratic patrons were no longer able to help them quite as much as before. They had little to gain, they felt, from agitating for abolition of the quota system. In March 1984, a new movement called the Muhajir Qaumi Mahaz (MQM), that is, the Muhajir National Front, was set up, its main impetus deriving from a Muhajir students' organisation. They now demanded that Muhajirs be recognised as the fifth nationality of Pakistan and that they should be allotted a 20 per cent quota at the centre and between 50 per cent and 60 per cent in Sindh. They also demanded some assurance that quotas in Sindh reserved for Sindhi speakers and Muhajirs, respectively, would not be poached by Punjabis. The MQM took the urban centres of Sindh by storm.

VII EMERGENCE OF MUHAJIR QAUMI MAHAZ

The MQM has emerged through the 1988 elections as the third largest party in the country – one might even say that in effect it is the second largest, for the Islamic Democratic Alliance, reckoned second, is itself no more than a precarious patchwork of nine parties, cobbled together under pressure from above, to present a viable opposition to the Pakistan People's Party (PPP). Since its foundation by some Muhajir students' groups in 1984, the MQM's rise as a major force on the national scene has been quite dramatic. This dramatic rise was precipitated by certain events in September 1986 when a planned Muhajir protest march from Karachi to Hyderabad was stopped by the police at Sohrab Kot, the 'gateway' to Karachi, and the participants beaten up. This was the catalytic moment in its subsequent meteoric progress.

The emergence of the MQM as a major political force was not merely a matter of Muhajirs getting organised as such. It marked a sea change in their political attitudes. So far Muhajirs had championed the cause of Pakistan nationhood and were a major source of support for extreme right-wing Islamic fundamentalist parties such as the Jamaat-e-Islami. But now the national identity was dropped. Only a few months earlier it would have been thought unbelievable for Muhajirs to rally behind a slogan which proclaimed: 'We have not signed a contract to uphold Pakistan and Islam!' (*Ham nain Pakistan aur Islam ka theka nahin liya hai*). Having for decades declared quite militantly that their identity was Pakistani and Muslim and that they opposed all ethnic movements as communal, they now decided to pursue communal politics. Overnight there was an ethnic redefinition for they now declared themselves to be Muhajirs rather than Pakistanis. Instead of moving towards an end to communalism and to ethnic conflict, the rise of the MQM, in the face of strident Sindhi nationalism, further consolidated the hold of communalism in Pakistan politics.

Sindh politics, however, have been in a state of flux. In 1983, the Movement for the Restoration of Democracy in Pakistan was to launch a nationwide protest against Zia. In the event, it was in Sindh that an exclusively Sindhi movement arose, with great fury and power. Based on Sindhi speakers, it turned out to be narrowly a rural movement for it failed to rally the urban population, mainly Muhajirs, because of its sectarian Sindhi slogans. Nevertheless, it was a most powerful movement that stretched the repressive state apparatus to the limit in trying to contain it and put it down. Attempts were made by the Zia regime to turn that movement into communal rioting and there was plenty of evidence of *agents provocateurs* at work. The leadership of the Sindhi movement succeeded in securing the help of local level Muhajir leaders and prominent members of their community to stand with the Sindhis on their platforms in order to prevent their struggle against the central government from degenerating into an intercommunal conflict. That experience had some impact on the thinking of some sections of the Sindhi leadership, especially its more radical sections. They began to realise that their movement had failed because of their inability to rally the urban population without which no movement in Sindh could succeed; and that if they had managed to involve the Muhajirs, their movement would have been irresistible. They began to see that Muhajirs were a part of the peoples of Sindh, indeed a part of the Sindhi people.

An important and influential section of the Sindhi leadership began to redefine Sindhi identity. Historically, Sindhi identity had always been rather problematic in that multiethnic province. Many people from other regions have settled in Sindh, such as the Baluch who still speak Baluchi at home but are recognised as Sindhis – many Baluchis are in fact in positions of leadership in Sindh. There are also Cutchis in Sindh, as already mentioned. Cutch is a bridge between Sindh and Gujarat (in India) and the Cutchi language is cognate with Sindhi. There are other groups of early migrants in Sindh. These include those who are (putatively) of Arab origin, the Syeds, who came with the Arab conqueror of Sindh in the eighth century AD, Mohammad bin Qasim. Amongst these would be counted G. M. Syed, the father of Sindhi nationalism.

VIII EXTENDING SINDHI IDENTITY

In 1986, one found Sindhi leaders and intellectuals engaged in discussing criteria on the basis of which Sindhi identity might be redefined so as to include also Muhajirs who are now an integral part of the population of Sindh, and whom they would like to carry with them in their struggle for provincial autonomy. One can recognise that achievement of greater provincial autonomy would benefit the rural Sindhi speakers more directly because of the rural bias in the political system and the franchise. If unity with Muhajirs brought them nearer to that goal, it is the Sindhi speakers who would stand to gain most, even if the benefits were to be shared with Muhajirs. Together they would get the dominant Punjabis off their backs. At that time, many Sindhi leaders were keen to extend the concept of Sindhi identity, accordingly, although there were a chauvinistic few who campaigned vigorously against it. In the case of at least one of these in the latter category, suspicions were voiced that he was an employee of the ubiquitous inter-services intelligence, the notorious

ISI (which was reported by the London based *Financial Times* to have 100 000 persons working for it). Such a possibility is not at all unlikely and cannot be ruled out. It would have suited the interests of the Zia regime to generate conflict between Sindhis and Muhajirs and even now that would serve the purposes of those who would like to see a weak government in power, even if it is a democratically elected one.

Sindhi leaders, who favoured extending the concept of Sindhi identity, argued that being a Sindhi was not a matter of place of origin or one of language that one spoke. If that were so, how could the Baluch in Sindh be accepted by them for so long as fellow Sindhis and so many of them acknowledged and honoured as Sindhi leaders. They argued that the Baluch in Sindh were Sindhis because they had *roots* in Sindh. They would extend that principle to Muhajirs. Muhajirs, they argued, were uprooted 'by fate and the forces of history' from their own soil in India and deposited in Sindh. They had struck fresh roots in Sindh as the Baluch and the Cutchis had done before them. These Sindhi leaders and intellectuals repudiated quite forcefully the paternalistic designation of Muhajirs as 'new Sindhis', a term that was widely used in the past but which, implicitly, denies Muhajirs full status as Sindhis. They insisted that they are full Sindhis, without any qualification. Descent, they said, was no criterion of ethnicity nor was it religion or language. It was a question of *roots*.

Applying that criterion of rootedness to other groups in Sindh, they took the view that Punjabis in Sindh would not qualify for inclusion within the expanded notion of being Sindhi. Punjabis in Sindh are mostly bureaucrats and members of the armed forces or their close relatives who have secured large grants of land from the government, and who have brought with them their retinue of Punjabi sharecroppers and labourers. These Punjabis, the Sindhi leaders and intellectuals argued, have come to Sindh as conquerors and usurpers, on the strength of state power. They remain Punjabis for they have their roots in Punjab which is exploiting the resources of Sindh. They should therefore be expelled from Sindh and the land restored to Sindhi hands, the sons of the soil.

Such Sindhi ethnic redefinitions, impelled by recognition of the need for political realignments, are most interesting to see. Muhajirs were similarly impelled to respond to political circumstances; both to realignments of the Sindhi position and, especially, to changes on the national scene. This included the change in the ethnic self-definition of Muhajirs and the dramatic rise of the MQM in the mid-1980s. The Muhajirs now abandoned their opposition to the very conception of subnationalities. Earlier Muhajirs had repudiated the idea of ethnic identity or nationality in favour of Pakistan nationhood and Islamic brotherhood for which such divisions were repugnant. The MQM demanded instead the recognition of Muhajirs as the fifth nationality of Pakistan and virtually overnight Muhajirs rallied around it over-whelmingly. The process of ethnic redefinition continued further. In the face of Sindhi moderation, and realising that their own future is tied up with the future of Sindh as a whole, a future which cannot be resolved except in company with Sindhi speakers, Muhajirs changed tack once again. More confident after their resounding success in the local elections in the spring of 1987, they reoriented their approach to prepare the ground for closer political cooperation with Sindhi speakers. Now they declared that Muhajirs were not a nationality by themselves. They were only a subnationality within the larger Sindhi nationality, Sindhi speakers being the other subnational group. *Together* they constituted Sindhi nationality. Given Sindhi reorien-tations too, for a time it looked not at all unlikely that the two would move closer in the political arena towards some kind of a United Front in order to win concessions from the centre. However, the political situation was to change once again after the death of Zia and the elections of 1988. The self-definition of Muhajirs as a sub-nationality was therefore short-lived. With the new realignments, they reverted to their claim to be the fifth nationality of Pakistan.

IX   STRANDS IN SINDHI LEADERSHIP

Sindhi realignments were taking shape also. A conference was held in Sann, the home of G. M. Syed, the grand old man of Sindhi nationalism, where the Sindh National Alliance was founded. It was a very broad-based conference where delegates comprised the whole political spectrum among Sindhi speakers. A central issue in the debate turned out to be the name of the alliance, whether it should be *Sindh* National Alliance or *Sindhi* National Alliance. The former would leave the door open for Muhajirs to be invited in, and several speakers suggested that they should be. The latter alternative was designed to close the doors on Muhajirs being brought into the alliance at all. It is significant therefore that it was the former option which was adopted.

There are elements within the Sindhi leadership who have resorted to extreme chauvinistic rhetoric *vis-à-vis* Muhajirs. Some of them speak of 'Muhajir separatism' which is both an absurd and also a mischievous notion. It is intended to arouse Sindhi fears that Sindh will be dismembered. This is nonsense because the cities in which Muhajirs predominate cannot be lifted out of their rural environment in order to constitute a Muhajiristan. Moreover, a very large proportion of Muhajirs do not live in the three large cities but are dispersed throughout Sindh in small provincial towns where their livelihoods depend on their relationships with Sindhi speakers who predominate there. Indeed these Muhajirs, now in their third and even fourth generation in Sindh, have learnt Sindhi at school and have been undergoing a process of Sindhification. In the 1983 movement, despite attempts to promote Sindhi–Muhajir riots, to split and disrupt the powerful Sindhi movement, Muhajirs and Sindhis stood united, a fact which does much credit to both the Sindhi and Muhajir local level leadership. But it is sad, in the circumstances, to find scholars such as Feroz Ahmad fanning the fires of Sindhi chauvinism and progressive journals publishing such material.

On the other hand, there are Sindhi leaders whose eyes are focused on the problem of getting the authoritarian hand of the central government off their backs and winning a greater degree of regional autonomy for Sindh. These more pragmatic leaders of Sindhi speakers cannot be unaware of the fact that, given the rural bias in our political system, it is they rather than the Muhajirs who would predominate in the government of Sindh, as is the case at present. They have nothing to lose by an alliance with Muhajirs and indeed much to gain *vis-à-vis* the centre.

The motives of the leaders of Sindhi speakers who resort to an extreme chauvinistic rhetoric and violent anti-Muhajir slogans must remain much more suspect. In the case of many of them, leaders whose political fortunes have waned, this strategy of outbidding more 'moderate' leadership by extreme slogans would, hopefully for them, revive discredited political fortunes and foster personal political ambitions. There is at least one Sindhi chauvinistic leader who is preaching what is tantamount to fascism. He is demanding that all those who are not native Sindhi speakers should be expelled from Sindh. In the case of non-Sindhi industrial workers he declares: 'Let them take their industries with them. We do not want them here.' Likewise, he demands that Muhajirs should be expelled from Sindh. When asked where they might go – for by now we have third and fourth generation Muhajirs who know no other home than where they are – this leader replies that this should be no concern of his or the Sindhi people: 'Hand them over to the United Nations High Commissioner for Refugees. He should find some place for them somewhere in this world. That is his job.' This mischievous and vicious campaign offers nothing concrete to the Sindhis. Those who know the political leaders who are conducting such a campaign saw the hand of the Zia government in this and are able to point out concrete examples of patronage and positions of very considerable profit that have been bestowed on such individuals and their close relatives by a grateful government. Such campaigns directly benefit central power by causing disruption, divisions and conflict amongst the people of Sindh and undermine possibilities of united action on their part in the interest of the region as a whole.

X THE NAÏVETY OF THE LEFT

Paradoxically, objectively at any rate, the authoritarian centre is helped ideologically in this by groups on the Left, mainly in the Punjab, who tend to take utterly naïve and quite misinformed positions *vis-à-vis* the Sindhi movements. They feel ideologically committed to the right of oppressed nationalities to national self-determination and regional autonomy. But when they look at Sindh, they see only the movement of Sindhi speakers as a legitimate movement. They have not yet overcome their suspicion of Muhajirs to recognise that they too are an oppressed nationality, standing side by side with Sindhis. Their suspicions of Muhajir politics are grounded in the fact that until the mid-1980s, Muhajir politics were hostile to the idea of national self-determination. In the name of Pakistani nationhood and Islamic unity Muhajirs had supported central authoritarian rule and Islamic fundamentalism. When the MQM appeared on the scene they were taken unprepared for it and have not yet figured out how to evaluate it. They have yet to come to terms with the sea change in Muhajir politics, their abandonment of Islamic fundamentalism and their emergence as a subnational group whose claims, hardly less valid than those of Sindhi nationalism, need to be located justly and fairly within the overall picture.

At this point, one might add that the ethnic problem in Sindh does not involve only the contending claims of the rival salariat groups, although that class has been at the core of ethnic politics. It concerns also a complex mixture of ethnic groups that make up the industrial working class in Sindh, concentrated mainly in Karachi, Hyderabad and Sukkur. Ethnic divisions have been exploited to break up the unity of the industrial working class, whereas in periods of militant working-class action, as in the early 1970s, ethnic conflicts tended to recede into the background and to disappear from sight.

Industrial workers from Sindh are, almost entirely, non-Sindhis. Before independence, the working class in Karachi, engaged mainly in transport (railways, the docks and various forms of urban transport) were overwhelmingly Baluch (Makrani) migrant workers. Immediately after Partition, Muhajirs made up the bulk of the working class in Sindh's industrial cities of Karachi, Hyderabad and Sukkur. As industrialisation progressed in the 1950s and 1960s, more workers were pulled in from densely populated agricultural regions of Sarhad and the Punjab (i.e. its extreme north-western districts in the Potowar area) where farms were small and fragmented, incapable of providing a livelihood, so that traditionally there has been a 'push effect' forcing members of farm families to look for employment outside. In Sindh, by contrast, there was no such push effect so that members of farm families did not seek outside work and the working class in Sindh was therefore not recruited from the immediate hinterland. It is only in very recent years that farm mechanisation by Sindhi landlords is causing eviction of Sindhi sharecroppers, the *haris*, who are being forced to look for urban employment in a period of relative industrial stagnation.

Powerful vested interests are at work in Karachi which have generated ethnic conflict between working-class ethnic groups, notably Pathans, against Muhajirs. Rioting has become endemic in Karachi and the people are terrorised by gangs equipped with automatic weapons, transported around in trucks. Some brilliant investigative journalists, especially those who have contributed to the monthly *Herald*, have exposed the hand of well-organised drugs mafia and those engaged in trade in illegal arms and, not least, racketeers in urban land, who were behind these so-called ethnic riots. Karachi has large areas of vacant land around it, into which the rapidly expanding city has been pushing. Vacant land is seized by the racketeers, developed as housing projects and the houses sold at great profit to themselves. The city administration has been able to do nothing, for it is itself under the control of the mafia. Given extraordinary levels of official corruption, the mafias also control the agencies of 'law and order', both the police and also the military at the local level. In the circumstances, they have a relatively free hand. They do not tolerate any official projects that might interfere with their own very profitable operations. The organised violence of these mafias has sometimes been explained away as ethnic conflict, which masks its real purposes on behalf of powerful interests. But once violence begins, inevitably, in the wake of such conflicts ethnic antagonisms escalate.

XI THE 1988 ELECTIONS

More recently, in the context of the 1988 elections, some remarkable changes in alignments have taken place. Despite the powerful thrust of Sindhi nationalism, it was the Pakistan People's Party (PPP) that got solid support from the Sindhi-speaking part of Sindh's electorate. Those Sindhi nationalist candidates who insisted on standing in the elections were routed.

The PPP and notably its Sindhi leadership had consistently distanced itself from Sindhi nationalism. When approached by some chauvinistic Sindhi nationalist leaders in 1987, who invited the PPP to join them in sponsoring the Sindh National Alliance, the PPP Sindhi leaders spurned them saying that they were a 'national' party and could not therefore espouse regional causes. The PPP refused to align itself with particularistic Sindhi demands. The PPP also kept out of the Sindh National Alliance. There is an understandable logic in the PPP's anti-communal position. If it was to come to power at the centre, it had to carry the electorate of the Punjab, and the Punjab was hostile to regionalist movements that challenged Punjabi domination.

Despite that consistent position of the PPP leadership, already in 1986 there were clear indications that if general elections were to be held, Sindhi votes would go to the PPP. In my discussions with Sindhi intellectuals and Sindhi nationalist leaders in 1986 in Hyderabad, they all put it in somewhat emotive language legitimising their decision to abandon, temporarily at least, their Sindhi nationalist cause. They said that 'We have a debt of blood to discharge. Therefore this time it will be the turn of the daughter of Zulfiqar Ali Bhutto. Our turn will come the next time.' Bhutto had given his life for them, they said. That debt must be repaid by voting for his daughter.

Behind that ideological justification for their electoral tactics, practical reasons for taking such a course were quite evident. Sindhi nationalists could have no hope of forming a government at the centre and without that nothing would be delivered. Voting for Sindhi nationalist candidates would therefore be an empty gesture. On the other hand, Sindhi leaders occupied powerful positions in the PPP, not least Benazir Bhutto herself. Even if in deference to her 'national' position she would not go quite so far as they might wish, it would not be unreasonable, they thought, to expect that she would go some little way at least to redress Sindhi grievances.

Ethnic strategies were reassessed in the context of the 1988 elections. Despite the more florid rhetoric of some Sindhi nationalists, in the face of the consistent position of the PPP in distancing itself from them, Sindhis, nevertheless, voted solidly for the PPP. Those few Sindhi nationalist leaders who insisted on standing on a nationalist platform, faced ignominious defeat. Half a loaf was still something, as far as the Sindhi electorate was concerned. Just protest would achieve nothing. There are so far few signs that Sindhi nationalists will get even the few concessions that they hoped for and their disaffection is already making itself felt.

Defeated and discredited Sindhi nationalist leaders are using this to try to stage a comeback. Their rhetoric has taken on a more chauvinistic tone. A wave of rioting has been sweeping through the cities of Sindh, following attacks by motorised armed gangs equipped with automatic weapons who have driven, with impunity, through the wards of the cities of Sindh, killing indiscriminately. As the history of communalism on the subcontinent has shown, once such violence is unleashed, it becomes self-generating and communal riots escalate with mutual reprisals.

Against such a background of intercommunal tension and indeed bloody violence, a demonstration was organised in Karachi in the name of the Sindh National Alliance, 'the first big demonstration of its kind', as it was reported (*Jang Daily*, 3 April 1989). This would not be quite true, for in 1987 an even bigger demonstration, in the form of a Peace March, was organised in Karachi after some extremely vicious communal rioting. That demonstration and procession was led by leaders of all communities, Sindhi, Muhajir, Pathan and Punjabi, and to good effect.

Be that as it may, the recent Sindh National Alliance demonstration was led by defeated and discredited right-wing leaders such as Hamida Khuro and Hafeezuddin Pirzada in company with ultra-chauvinists such as Rasool Bux Palejo. But it was addressed also by saner voices such as that of Abdul Wahid Aresar, chairman of the largest of the Sindhi nationalist parties, the Jiye Sindh Mahaz. The demonstration was organised against continued immigration and settlement of outsiders in Sindh but for the chauvinists it was clearly an anti-Muhajir event. On the other hand, Aftab Meerani, a senior minister in the PPP-led Sindh government, declared that the demonstration was a conspiracy against the democratic government of the PPP. The speech of Abdul Wahid Aresar, chairman of the Jiye Sindh Mahaz, was in marked contrast to that of some of the others mentioned above. He said that just as the people of Sindh, while voting for the PPP on pragmatic grounds, nevertheless, could not be identified with the PPP, so also the fact that the Urdu-speaking Muhajirs had voted solidly for the MQM did not mean that they did not have their differences with the MQM or that they should therefore be identified with that party. The fact that there had been an electoral polarisation did not mean that these two peoples of Sindh were therefore aligned against each other in rival camps. He continued that political conditions do not remain constant and fresh alignments would emerge. He appealed to both Sindhis and Muhajirs to stand shoulder to shoulder in their struggle to solve the collective problems of Sindh and he was confident that they would do so. The solution of Sindh's problems did not lie in rioting and conflict between Sindhi and Urdu-speaking people of Sindh. It was a courageous speech in the context of attempts to arouse Sindhi chauvinistic feelings. What is significant is that this speech from the leader of the most important of the Sindhi nationalist parties (and groups) was received with enthusiasm. However, no Muhajir leader has emerged taking such a courageous line for peace and unity. The province of Sindh has been experiencing communal violence on an unprecedented scale.

References

Alavi, H. (1983), 'Class and State in Pakistan', in H. Gardezi and J. Rashid (eds), *Pakistan: The Roots of Dictatorship* (London: Zed Press), pp. 40–93.

Alavi, H. (1987), 'Pakistan and Islam: Ethnicity and Ideology', in F. Halliday and H. Alavi (eds), *State and Ideology in the Middle East and Pakistan* (London: Macmillan), pp. 64–111.

Alavi, H. (1989), 'Formation of the Social Structure of South Asia under the Impact of Colonialism', in H. Alavi and J. Harriss (eds), *Sociology of Developing Societies: South Asia* (London: Macmillan), pp. 5–19.

Anderson, B. (1983), *Imagined Communities* (London: Verso).

Basu, A. (1974), *Growth of Education and Political Development in India, 1898–1920* (Delhi: Oxford University Press).

Choudhury, G. W. (ed.) (1967), *Documents and Speeches on the Constitution of Pakistan* (Dacca).

9 Factionalism and Violence in British Pakistani Communal Politics*

Pnina Werbner

In a serious affray in the Central Mosque in Manchester, in 1985, a man died of a heart attack (*Arabia*, 1985). In 1988, during a fight between two opposed British Pakistani neighbourhood-based associations another man died of a coronary, after being punched in the chest (*Manchester Evening News*, 1988). At certain phases in the history of the local British Pakistani community, political violence in the public arena has seemed close to the surface. Pakistani public meetings are often confrontational and charged with passion. The intensity of political action is a potent and tangible current running through these events.

Throughout Britain similar confrontational politics within British overseas Pakistani communities have increased. In this chapter I ask the question: why are overseas Pakistani local-level politics, often concerned with apparently minor or even trivial issues, so volatile and potentially violent?

In a sense it may be argued, as indeed local people have argued in response to my question, that this is the way politics are conducted in Pakistan as well. In other words, the *political culture* is a volatile and potentially violent culture. It can also be argued that the marked encapsulation of overseas Pakistanis in Britain, and in Manchester, their remoteness from positions of status and honour within the wider British society, make positions *within* the community prizes of immense significance and worth competing for. A man's status derives from his internal position, the offices he holds in key local Pakistani associations.

I   BLOCS AND FACTIONS

Two major debates focus on the processes and organisation of South Asian politics. The first surrounds Barth's model of political bloc formation among the Swat Pathan, the second, factional coalitions in Indian politics. On the whole, the two literatures have remained surprisingly discrete, although in reality they relate to a single phenomenon constituted by the same basic cultural principles. Since my study focuses on overseas Punjabi Muslims, I shall take as my starting point the various studies of their western neighbours, the Pakhtun, especially as they are analysed in the works of Barth, Lindholm, Ahmed and Asad, and of their eastern neighbours, the Punjabi Sikhs, studied by Pettigrew. More generally, I shall refer to some studies of factions among overseas Asians and to Jones's analysis of Indian urban politics, in order to highlight the potential complexity of the overall political arena in South Asian politics in general, and overseas Pakistanis' communal politics in particular.

Barth's model is remarkable both for its economy and lucidity (Barth, 1981a). The unilineal descent group, rather than defining 'a hierarchy of homologous groups' and their fusion within a merging series, 'defines rivals and allies in a system of two opposed political blocs'. The principle by which the system operates is as follows:

Closely related descent units are consistent rivals; each establishes a net of political alliances with the rivals of allies of their own rivals. In this fashion a pervasive factional split into two grand alliances of descent segments emerges, with close collateral segments consistently in opposite moieties. (ibid., pp. 55–6)

As Lindholm (1982) and others (e.g. Ahmed, 1976) have shown, these principles are culturally articulated through two notions. The first is of the relationship of enmity between consanguineous patrilineal relatives (brothers, patrilateral parallel cousins) which is known as *tarburwali*. The second is of a dual set of alliances or 'blocs' known as *dala*. Lindholm notes that these dual parties are spoken of as 'concrete entities' (ibid., p. 79) and 'each individual sees the tribal world as divided into those who are in his party and those who are against his party' (ibid). Each village *dala* 'ramifies in a net of alliances throughout the region'.

Barth's model is thus as much a *cultural* model as a sociological one. Comparatively, as Lindholm rightly recognises, Swat Pathan is a vengeance rather than a feud society (cf. Black-Michaud, 1975). In such societies, vengeance killing is the prerogative of individuals and not of larger corporate groups, and the composite groups within an alliance can consequently be quite shallow genealogically. Feuding normally occurs between much larger corporations, and it is between these that alliances are formed (Peters, 1959, 1967).

Although this has not, to my knowledge, been documented in the anthropological literature, Muslim Punjabis have an analogous set of concepts relating to cousin enmity and alliance. Enmity between cousins is known as *sherika bazi*. 'Sherika' means family, and 'sherik' is a patrilineal brother or cousin of the same blood. Such enmity arises, as among the Pakhtun, from disputes between close agnates over inheritance, property or leadership. 'Bazi' which literally means 'fun' refers here to conflict. Political bloc alliances in rural Punjab are known as *pattiwal*. Like Pakhtun *dala* they are made up of coalitions of rival groups determined at the lowest level of segmentation.

Barth contended that Pakhtun bloc alliances showed considerable stability over time. This, despite the possible defection of strong leaders to the weaker bloc in order to swing the balance (Barth, 1981a, p. 166). However, he argues, such defections may be risky or dangerous, particularly so for small leaders, and are in any case unlikely as long as one's close collateral rival is in the other bloc (ibid., p. 169). One major strength of Barth's model is that it relates political alliance to *violence* or potential violence, a feature analysed extensively in segmentary societies. This focus on violence is often lacking in discussions of Indian factionalism.

Nevertheless, the persistence of factional alliances is a feature also noted in most studies of factions in Indian politics. Pettigrew argues strongly that 'some factions, and the strife between them, endure for many decades' (1975, p. 65); even, she argues, beyond the life of their leaders. She documents the history of one such factional division in the Punjab which persisted for ten years.

The major difference between factions in Indian politics and among the Pakhtun relates not to the underlying principle generating the groups ('my enemy's enemy is my friend') which is common to both, but to the multiplicity of political arenas in which factional divisions are manifested in the broader context of state politics (see Jones, 1974). In Swat society, kinship defines both territoriality and individual property rights. Factional opposition is thus articulated by an inclusive idiom (that of unilineal descent) which encompasses the political, economic and personal relationships of group members within a single uniform framework (but see Ahmed, 1976, pp. 103–22 for a contrary view). Not so in Indian politics. Factions in the Punjab, for example, manifest themselves in a variety of contexts or arenas: the Punjab state, the Sikh community, the Congress party, the state administration (Pettigrew, 1975, p. 68). Each of these arenas determines a framework of rules, values and ideals within which factions operate (ibid., p. 64), whether this be the unity of the Punjab, the Khalsa, or the party or the need for administrative impartiality (ibid, p. 68).

Pettigrew identifies certain key features of factions: they operate within the framework of rules, values and ideals of the larger whole. They are in competition for control over resources and are based, to use Jones's term, on 'distributive policies' (i.e. patronage. See Jones, 1974, p. 365. According to Jones, class politics, by contrast, are based on 'redistributive' policies). They are relatively persistent. They consist of persons tied horizontally and linked vertically to one another on a *variety* of bases (this is the feature most commonly stressed by other students of factions). They are kept alive through a series of mobilisation events in *different* political arenas. This is particularly important for an analysis of urban contexts. They are not simply leader-focused but leaders embody the power of the faction and the resources under its control. The faction, as a coalition, operates through both *vertical* links and *horizontal* ties. Factions are thus internally divided into *different* '*levels*': upward links are crucial to local leaders if they are to maintain their downward links (ibid., pp. 64–74). Finally, factions are integrative, in the sense of creating alliances which cut across villages (or classes and neighbourhoods) and link together both villages and cities.

These features taken together give a clue to the organisation of factional alliances in a modern state. Yet in a sense they ignore Barth's insight that bloc alliances are composed of opposing groups at the lowest level of segmentation. Close rival collaterals compete rather than align even in broader contexts. The same principle may be applied to a more complex political field in which each arena is characterised by a series of segmentary oppositions determined by ideological or primordial affinities and divisions. In the following discussion, I return to the communal politics of overseas Pakistanis in Manchester in order to clarify this proposition.

II THE THREE ARENAS

There were, in 1987–8, three major contexts or political arenas (Bailey, 1969; Swartz, 1968; Jones, 1974) in which Pakistani community politics were publicly conducted in Manchester. Each arena not only had different selection rules, values and objectives, but each related to a different definition of 'community'. There were, of course, many other more specific – or lower level – contested arenas, but these three arenas were all marked by their city-wide territorial catchment area and publicly supervised election procedures.

In terms of value, the most important arena was the religious one, or mosque politics, with the focus being on the Central Mosque, the *Jamiat el Muslemin* and control of its Management Committee. Since the Central Mosque supposedly serves all Muslims in Manchester, irrespective of school or denomination, it is also the scene of contested Islamic religious approaches. The history of the mosque in Manchester is a fraught one, and particularly so from the mid-1970s onwards (cf. *Arabia*, 1985 for a description of one serious conflict in the mosque). The emergent divisions within the mosque and the community represent a recent historical development. The local Muslim community started as a unity with a single mosque. The elaborate national and most recently sectarian divisions have emerged gradually.

During the 1980s the mosque has been the scene of violent confrontations, extended and expensive litigation, and external intervention by the police, the Mayor of Manchester, and the Pakistan Ambassador (who reputedly intervened at the instructions of the higher echelons of the Pakistan government). The mosque was built entirely with funds raised within the community (see Werbner, 1985, 1990) and was considered by most local Pakistanis to be one of the most beautiful and important mosques in Britain. Officially, the mosque of the whole Muslim community, it was effectively controlled by Pakistanis. In recent years, several other important mosques have been built representing various Islamic approaches or orders. None, however, has usurped the symbolic primacy or hegemony of the Central Mosque.

Elections to the mosque have been sporadic and fraught with conflict. Although elections were supposed to be held annually, no elections were held for a lengthy period during the 1970s while the mosque was being built. Two or three elections were then held in succession, the last being the scene of a major confrontation and outside intervention. At this point the constitution was changed and elections are now held every three years. The last elections were in 1985 and the next elections were due in August 1988 (they were, in fact, delayed a whole year).

The second political arena, the Pakistani Community Centre, has emerged more recently. The centre was built with funding from the state (known as Urban Aid) and the grant – ultimately received by a local literary society – was hotly contested by a united front of the more established old-timer associations (see Werbner, 1991). The building of the Community Centre has only recently been completed and it has held, in 1987, only one prior seriously contested public election. This was, however, apparently the scene of a *halagula* (a noisy public dispute) to be followed by another such *halagula* during elections for a Longsight Community Representative for a municipal body. The centre has a formal constitution which lays down strict election procedures, and this has been used in the past by the established Executive Committee to disqualify both voters and candidates. It has also ensured that procedures are respected and closely supervised. Membership to the centre is open to all members of the Pakistani community in the city (and even to interested non-Pakistanis), the boundary of the city being defined in very broad terms.[1] In accordance with its charitable status, elections to the centre are held annually as part of the Annual General Meeting in which an annual report and audited accounts are presented. The executive meeting is held monthly and is, officially, open to all members of the centre.

The third potential political arena, the Race Subcommittee, formed by the local City Council, has also only recently been established. It was set up by the radical left Labour party group controlling the council and functions as an advisory body composed of elected ethnic community representatives and chaired by a councillor. Each ethnic community in the city – West Indian, African, Chinese, Indian, Pakistani, etc. – is allocated a number of seats and 'Community Reps', as they are known, are elected annually in elections supervised by the council through its recently established Race Unit. The Race Unit with several full-time workers also services the subcommittee, prepares lengthy agendas, minutes, etc. advises Community Reps on matters of procedure and substance and attempts to carry out policy decisions. The meetings of the subcommittee, held monthly, are extremely formal and require quite detailed knowledge of the rhetoric of public administration and the functioning of the council. The Longsight elections were the first publicly proclaimed and supervised.

The Pakistani community is currently allocated four seats on the subcommittee, based on four territorial divisions: 'Central', 'North Manchester', 'Longsight' and 'Whalley Range'. The three latter divisions centre around the three major Pakistani residential clusters in the city, the fourth being something of a catch-all and including the business community in the city centre. Although the boundaries of these divisions were initially left vague, pressures have increased, as we shall see below, to define them unambiguously as elections have come to be seriously contested.

Elections to the subcommittee are thus based on local territorial subdivisions within the wider community. Pakistanis referred to elected representatives as 'councillors' and appeared to make little distinction between them and official councillors, elected during local authority elections. There was in any case only one Pakistani councillor in the whole of Manchester in 1987, elected the previous year.[2]

Each political arena is defined in relation to different 'communities': the religious arena is defined in relation to the Muslim community; the community centre arena defines the Pakistani community as a whole; the Race Subcommittee defines neighbourhood Pakistani communities. Each political arena also focuses around different ideological and ascriptive affinities and divisions. The mosque is the scene of religious dispute and secessions by different groups with different religious approaches or organisational affiliations. The Community Centre reveals something of the tension between the secular and religious, the cultural and religious or the 'rich' and 'poor' (i.e. workers and businessmen) among Pakistanis, but has remained somewhat obscure ideologically. The third arena, that of elections to the Race Subcommittee, focuses on issues of race and ethnicity. At the local level, however, competing associations and their leaders were defined by ascriptive affinities such as area of origin in Pakistan and caste. This is thus the scene of local 'village politics' which find their expression in the elections for Community Reps. Following these, the community centre elections constitute a testing ground, a rehearsal for the mosque elections. During the mosque elections, territorial divisions, ascriptive links and ideological orientations all converge in a single unifying major arena.

These ideological and ascriptive divisions can be conceived of as a set of segmentary oppositions (see Figure 9.1). Turning to the divisions within the Muslim community, it is divided first by nationality, then by major denominational affiliations (such as Sunni or Shi'a), then by religious approach and locality (scholastic/reform versus mystical), and finally by subdivisions within these major approaches corresponding to specific mosques (Deoband, UK Islamic Mission, Tabliqui and Ahl-i-Hadith versus Barelvi sufi orders).

Although during the 1970s the major ideological dispute was between Barelvi and Deoband, the actual factional division in the mosque was between the 'moderates' group, advocating the preservation of the openness and universal nature of the mosque as a central mosque, equally accessible to all Muslim groups in the city, and those committed to specific, first Deoband then Barelvi, traditions.

The result of the disputes has been, however, the establishment of separate mosques in south Manchester dominated by different approaches: Deoband, UK Islamic Mission and Tabliqui Islam. The Central Mosque *maulvi* himself belongs to the Sufi Qadriya order centred on the (British) head of the order in Walthamstow, London. The most recent mosque to be established is located quite close to the Central Mosque, right in the heart of Longsight, the earliest and most populated Pakistani residential enclave. This mosque was founded and is controlled by a member of the Naqshbandiya order centred on the (British-based) head of the order in Birmingham. Although ideologically the closest to the Central Mosque, it is its major rival for support, members, and religious hegemony. This is partly because a large majority of local Pakistanis follow Barelvi traditions, but it also stems from the advantageous location of the new Longsight Mosque and its success in establishing a harmonious, non-politicised, atmosphere.[3] The mosque in Longsight has been particularly successful in building up its afternoon Islamic instruction classes and currently has some 300 local children attending classes daily, and a group of older students studying for Urdu O and A levels. It is a relatively well attended mosque, with an attendance during Eid of just under 1500 persons (the Central Mosque probably has around 4–5000 during Eid).

Here, in other words, is an instance in which close collaterals with ideological affinity are major rivals, whereas ideologically opposed groups are allies (in this case, this was particularly true of the link between the Shi'a community and the Central Mosque, and between it and at least one of the branches of the UK Islamic Mission). The rivalry between the two mosques was not normally conducted within a single arena but it fed into the factional divisions within the community and was discussed quite openly by those in the know. Like the Muslim community, the Pakistani community as a territorial entity can also be represented in segmentary terms. The divisions here are cross-cut by ascriptive divisions based on area of origin and caste. Broadly speaking, the two coincide. There are three large caste groups in Manchester: the first is the Arain caste, originating from East Punjab and settled in Pakistan in the cities and the canal colonies (Faisalabad, Sahiwal, Multan, Bahawalpur). Many of the Arain businessmen have moved out of inner city areas and live scattered in the city suburbs. The other two major groups are Gujar and Rajput, originating primarily from the Jhelum District and surrounding districts (Gujrat, Gujar Khan, Chakwal). These migrant settlers, who of course were never refugees, still have deep roots and extensive links in their villages of origin and are intensely involved in Pakistani political rivalries at home. They are also the group who most universally dream of returning home one day.

All three caste groups call themselves 'Chaudhri' (i.e. headmen) and are regarded as *zamindar* (landowners). While the Arain caste's status in West Punjab was, before Partition, much lower, their achievements both in Manchester and Pakistan have placed them high within the landowning group. The Arain in Manchester tended to move into business quite early after arrival (cf. Werbner, 1990) and most of the wealthy businessmen, particularly in the clothing and garment trade, are Arain. Jhelmis worked longer in factories and many are today smaller businessmen: market traders, taxi drivers, small manufacturers, grocery store owners. Although Manchester, as a large city, has migrants originating from all over Pakistan and from a large number of caste groups, it is these three main caste-cum-district groups which seem to count – as groups – in the political arena. Professionals, who hold office in associations (particularly as secretary or treasurer), tend to originate from cities and from the higher castes (Pathan, Sayyid, Qureshi, Siddiqui, Moghul, etc.) but they are few in number and seldom have large *biradaris* locally.

This, then, is the context in which the communal politics take place and factional alliances emerge.

III   THE EMERGENCE OF NEW FACTIONAL ALLIANCES

A faction is a network of networks in which the constituent groups at its base are relatively small. The shifting composition of opposed blocs stems not so much from the shifting of whole groups and their leaders from one bloc to the other, as Barth and others suggest, but from internal disputes within the base groups which lead to secessions and splits (see Pocock, 1957), with the losing subgroup inevitably shifting to the opposed faction. Quite often these splits occur as a natural response to the growth of constituent groups. The shift of part-groups in response to internal splits is evident in the Manchester case.

It is normal in discussions of factionalism to focus on specific leaders and their strategies. Mancunian British Pakistani communal politics suggest, however, that no single leader really controls a faction. Most often several leaders cooperate to form a kind of oligarchy with an internal division of labour. The point was made quite explicitly by a leader of one of the factions (an influential large wholesaler) who explained that 'X deals with the town hall, he is our foreign minister; I am more in the community'. The third leader, a *maulvi*, dealt with religious matters, and with religious followers. Different leaders are deemed more suited to represent the group in different arenas. Often the 'kingmakers', as they are known colloquially, stay behind the scenes. Despite this, certain personalities do emerge as foci of interest and gossip. They may have stronger or more enigmatic and intriguing personalities; these are discussed, analysed and gossiped about more than others. The point is, however, that they, as individuals, emerge through structural cleavages in specific arenas. They cannot be regarded as the reason for the emergence of groups or their persistence for lengthy periods.

The emergence of two new political arenas – the Community Centre and the Race Subcommittee – has been associated with the emergence of a new factional constellation. Although the opposing factions have certain continuities with the past, and the past is indeed constantly *referred* to, the introduction of new political prizes and institutional contexts has introduced a radical break with the past.

During its formative years, from 1950 to 1980, the community was controlled by a group of oldtimers. Of these the most powerful and influential member was a large pioneer wholesaler and his associate partner. The wholesaler not only had an enormous turnover (and thus many suppliers and customers dependent upon him), but he and his partner also benefited from their status as founder-members of the community who had helped many later immigrants to settle or start businesses. Both partners were East Punjabi Arain and had a large number of relatives and *biradari* members in Manchester and other parts of the North West (particularly Rochdale). The wholesaler was energetic, sophisticated and powerful while his partner was highly respected for his wisdom and dedication to community causes. In the early 1970s, the partnership split up somewhat acrimoniously and the wholesaler's brother became a full partner. Before the split the wholesaler had had a dispute with a fellow villager, also an East Punjabi Arain, then a market trader, who had taken him to court and won his case against him. He was never forgiven for his temerity. This market trader later became a highly successful wholesaler and the dispute was to have repercussions in the 1980s.

Clearly then, even at this early stage, cracks and potential lines of secession were discernible in the solidarity of the controlling Arain group. The economic power of the pioneer wholesaler, his clear pre-eminence and philanthropic generosity in the community, and his avoidance of office, kept potential dissenters under control. The 1970s was a period of construction and relative harmony. The sum of £250 000 was raised from within the community (a relatively small one, then only about 10 000 strong), a beautiful mosque was built, and Manchester's reputation as one of the most successful Pakistani communities in the country was unassailed. There were, of course, disputes since this was a period of religious ferment throughout Britain, in which the division between Deoband and Barelvi surfaced and caused rifts in many of its major cities. In Manchester, the dispute focused on the *maulvi* of the Central Mosque, a committed and open Deobandi who refused to allow Barelvi practices in the mosque. He was a man with an international reputation as an Islamic scholar, and indeed he was subsequently appointed head of the *Shari'a* Court set up to prepare Pakistan's legal transition to an Islamic state. Allegations against him led to a court case which he eventually won. He did, however, leave his post as *maulvi* and he subsequently founded a separate mosque and Islamic Academy which engaged in scholarly research and teaching.

Other points of dissension during this period focused on the refusal of the Management Committee to hold public elections. They preferred, rather, to coopt new groups and associations on to the committee. The excuse for the delayed elections was that these would disrupt the building process. The ruling Arain faction was itself divided on the religious issue, most members being Barelvi. Some of the other office holders, and particularly the chairman felt that the mosque should be open and non-denominational, and refused to support the attack on the *maulvi*. In any case, the underlying ferment never coalesced into a clear opposition faction and the disputes and divisions were contained and did not erupt into real violence. This was due, in my view, primarily to the great economic power and influence wielded by the head of the ruling faction and by its evident contribution to the corporate wealth of the community. Subsequent developments appear to confirm this.

It is noteworthy that during the whole of this period resources, power and patronage were *internally* generated. The influence of the British state was minimal and it was not regarded as an important source of economic prizes. All this changed during the 1980s. First was the success of the Literary Society in obtaining a large state-sponsored Urban Aid grant for a community centre (see Werbner, 1991). It later became evident that smaller welfare grants and jobs, including state subsidised jobs for registered unemployed (provided by the Manpower Services Commission set up by the British government) would be made available with support from the Local Authority. In the meanwhile, the wholesaler's economic empire collapsed suddenly and unexpectedly and no other Pakistani emerged to replace him. Some of the largest wholesalers in Manchester today are Hindus, while one of the most wealthy Pakistani wholesalers in the city is a non-Punjabi, a recent newcomer to the city, and an openly non-observant Muslim to boot. All this has meant that there is no clear centre of exclusive patronage power *within* the community, and no one with sufficient resources to disburse or give away in competition with state largesse.

The implications of the collapse of the pioneer wholesaler's empire were not immediately evident. After the building project was completed the whole committee resigned *en bloc* and did not stand for re-election. The wholesaler's brother replaced him on the committee, however, and became its chairman. Key members of the old committee, including the pioneer wholesaler, remained trustees of the Central Mosque building, responsible also for the financial handling of its affairs. It was during this period that the divisions within the Arain establishment manifested themselves publicly. The wholesaler's brother was reselected in the next election, but then the joint business folded up. The brother abandoned his old allies (and, it would seem, his brother, the original kingmaker) and aligned himself with other oldtimers who had until recently been excluded from mosque politics. Among these was the market trader, now a large wholesaler himself, who had sued the pioneer wholesaler's firm some years before. The brother explained to me that his motives, in abandoning his erstwhile allies, were to save the community and reunite it. In the event, he failed to achieve this unity. The following Central Mosque elections and disputes surrounding the trusteeship to the mosque resulted in a violent confrontation, a tragic death, a major investigation called by the Lord Mayor, and intervention by the state of Pakistan.

I must stress here that although the details of this prolonged dispute are well known to many members of the community, it is difficult to piece the whole picture together. This is because most Pakistanis are ashamed of the current disharmony in the public domain and do not want it publicised, whatever faction they support. The pride they felt in their achievements as a community has been undermined by the unpleasant events of the past few years, and although they are naturally committed to their particular point of view, they do not wish the divisiveness of the community to be known beyond it.

When I first started fieldwork at the end of 1986, I found that the ruling faction was attempting to spread its control to all major institutions in the community. Wherever I went, organisational leaders told me of pressure that had been exerted upon them by the Central Mosque. The key targets for control were the Community Centre on the one hand, and the neighbouring Barelvi mosque, the Dar-Ul-Aloom, on the other. This predatory attitude was evident throughout the fieldwork, although the confidence of the ruling faction came to be progressively undermined by internal divisions and by the creation – at first somewhat tentative – of a new viable opposition.

The new factional alignments can be presented diagrammatically (see Figure 9.1).

The new alliance was born out of disputes and secessions within the Central Mosque itself. These disputes were made public during elections in 1987 for a Longsight Community Rep which took place at the Community Centre. There were three candidates standing for elections: a representative of group (A) which had seceded from the Central Mosque and whose candidate was a supporter of the rival Dar-Ul-Aloom; a representative of (B) who was initially set up by the mosque to oppose (A); and a representative of (C) who supported the *maulvi*'s subfaction within the ruling faction, and was set up in opposition to (B) as well as (A).

This chain of secessions explains why there were three candidates for the Longsight Community Rep position, and why the leader of

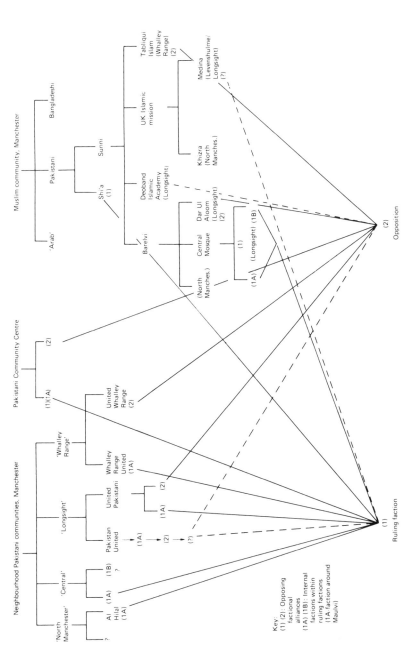

Figure 9.1 Factional alliances, 1987–8

(B) chose to ally with a more distant collateral against a closer, more recent, rival. (A) of course could have chosen to ally himself with either (B) or (C) who were equidistant collaterals. He was, indeed, under some pressure from his group to go along with (C). All were Jhelmis, and they all knew each other well. He chose (B) because (C), a Rajput, had insulted him on the low caste origins of his wife, and because, as a member of the Dar-Ul-Aloom, he represented a close collateral rival to the Central Mosque represented by (C).

It was at this point that (B) emerged as a major leader and unifier of the opposition faction, determined to defeat the *maulvi*'s group controlling the Central Mosque. In order to broaden his alliance he contacted a group in an adjacent neighbourhood in the city, Whalley Range. This group was itself a seceding group, bitterly opposed to the mosque vice-chairman and by extension also to his allies, the *maulvi* and a local race activist. The split in Whalley Range had its origins in a dispute which had occurred in Pakistan and had centred around a division within a single village in Jhelum. The two Whalley Range rival groups in Manchester were thus part of an 'international' village factional dispute which refracted the unity of the group both in their village in Pakistan and in Manchester. The vice-chairman of the Central Mosque in Manchester had for several years been the acknowledged leader of local migrant-villagers living primarily in the Whalley Range residential cluster in Manchester. A recent leadership dispute and factional split in their village had, however, split the group in *Manchester* into two opposed factions. (B) helped the seceding faction to form an association rivalling that of the vice-chairman and his allies in the mosque, thus undermining his hitherto complete political monopoly in Whalley Range.   .

In the meantime, a close cousin and ally of the vice-president from the same village was selected as Community Rep virtually unopposed in Central District, thus strengthening the power of the *maulvi*'s ruling faction. Three out of the four Community Reps on the Race Subcommittee were currently from this faction with only one in opposition, the Longsight Rep (B). He too, as we saw, was initially selected by the ruling faction, and had only quarrelled with them in the course of preparations for the elections.

This new factional constellation brought Jhelmi men, previously content to provide votes rather than assume office, very much into the centre of the political arena. Most came from dominant castes in their home villages, which were providing (in Pakistan) more and more elected councillors and Members of Parliament or of Provincial

Assemblies. They began to realise that in Manchester too they could challenge the Arain business community's hegemony with their superior numbers and organisational talents. Many of them had also become businessmen themselves. There was, in any case, no real need for fund-raising since the Central Mosque had been built, the building opposite it lost, and funding regarded now as a matter of state largesse and successful political manoeuvrings in City Hall (this, following the astonishing success of the little known Literary Society in receiving its enormous grant for the construction of the Community Centre).

Among those forming the opposition alliance were some with strong ideological commitments, including the local Pakistani Councillor and his supporters and some religious leaders. The first main objective of the group was to win the control of the Community Centre. Although the centre had been built by a group strongly opposed to the (old) ruling business faction of the Central Mosque, now that they were the 'establishment' themselves, they had formed an alliance with the new ruling mosque faction and particularly its *maulvi*. This was mainly because members of the Community Centre Executive, initially really only a *tonga* association (i.e. a restricted group), had a very small constituency and could not mobilise the votes needed to win a major election. They were willing to let the mosque into the centre in order to retain their control. This, despite the fact that the Community Centre was explicitly requested from the council as an alternative meeting place to the mosque.

During the period running up to the Community Centre elections, membership of the centre rose from a few hundred to almost one thousand. Both factions – the mosque and the opposition – frantically enlisted supporters for what promised to be a closely contested poll. The opposition led by (B) even managed to enlist the rival association (A) in Longsight (as it proved, temporarily).

In the upshot, the elections proved to be a fiasco for the opposition, as mutual disqualifications based on constitutional technicalities decimated their list. The meetings held a few days before the elections erupted into loud shouting matches. Clearly, contested elections were bound to turn into a confrontation between supporters of the two groups. To avoid this, the councillor and his faction decided to withdraw with good grace. Supporters were told that there would be no contest and the majority stayed away. The atmosphere in the election hall was tangibly bitter but very restrained. Many fence-sitters were glad that a major confrontation (which could have involved 1000 registered members) had been avoided. A year later the same councillor was elected as chairman of the centre. During 1988 it was unclear whether the opposition alliance would be able to survive the earlier blow. It is made up of several groups only loosely linked together. Although the Jhelmi leader (B) has created an umbrella organisation uniting them (of which he is chairman), they had not really secured the support of any major leaders outside the smaller local associations. The hope that the two Arain businessmen of the ruling faction would abandon the *maulvi's* faction did not initially materialise. By July 1989, however, the opposition faction had created a viable and powerful bloc, including (B), these two Arain businessmen and key members of the old ousted faction. The test of the opposition was imminent with elections to the Central Mosque about to take place as this chapter goes to press.[4]

These are the bare outlines of factional formation in Manchester. Both the complexity and the intensity of political activity cannot be conveyed in such an account. What is evident, however, is that personal ambition or enmity *and* ideology are both important features of the formation and persistence of factions. Disputes with the ruling faction reflected attitudes by association (A) in particular towards the business élite in the community, and towards the handling of Central Mosque finances. The division in the Community Centre surrounded the right of the mosque to intervene in the centre's affairs directly. The division between the *maulvi* and group (B) surrounded the right of religious officials to intervene in communal politics. These are important issues, widely debated and crucially affecting the community's development. In my discussions with the various adversaries it was clear that they felt extremely strongly about these matters, and were willing, at least officially, to make strategic compromises only within the clear limits set by their respective principles.

Pettigrew rightly argues that studies of factions have tended to stress the centrality of leaders and the different bases on which they recruit followers. The emphasis is on the utilitarian bases for these groups which seem to cut across ideological commitments and render them irrelevant. But even in Pettigrew's account, factions are regarded as formed in relation to patronage and distributive policies. It seems to me that this continuing focus on the Machiavellian talents or rivalries of individual leaders and on the instrumental aspects of factionalism has meant that the relation between factional politics and ideology has not been adequately addressed. Asad (1972) made an initial attempt to do so, and in the following two sections I attempt to probe further into this relationship.

IV PATRONAGE AND LEADERSHIP

There is little doubt that notions of patronage underlie factional structures. A leader must be seen to provide his followers with tangible advantages. To do so he must be seen to have access, if he is a local leader, to higher-level sources of patronage. At an even higher level, he may be in the position to disburse such resources himself. Overseas Pakistanis operate their factions, rightly or wrongly, as though such patronage channels are equally significant in the British political context. They *perceive* this to be the case, even though the vertical channels of patronage are by no means as clear. Thus, they spend a great deal of time hosting and entertaining both high-level visiting Pakistani and high-level British officials – ministers, councillors, ambassadors and the like. Their hosting of the Pakistani dignitaries will, they believe (apparently with some justification), provide them with patronage in Pakistan (in the form of business licences, state allocated building plots, etc.).

The relationship between visiting Pakistani dignitaries and local community leaders is in reality, however, rather ambiguous. Overseas Pakistanis are not part of these dignitaries' electoral constituencies and the factional power of local leaders is thus of little interest to them. A top Pakistani official may be just as interested in a convivial host or in being entertained in the grand home of a wealthy British Pakistani businessman. Such officials clearly enjoy their trips to Britain and the fuss made of them, and thus the symbiotic relationship between local leaders and visiting dignitaries persists, the prizes being as much symbolic as practical.

Vertical links to Pakistani dignitaries are complemented by vertical links to British dignitaries. These too are fraught with ambiguity. The British system of grants and allocations is hedged with bureaucratic procedures and direct patronage is rare. This is particularly so for community leaders (as against black political representatives). Once again, much of the gain in knowing MPs, Lord Mayors and ministers is symbolic. Nevertheless, acquaintance with councillors and MPs does make some difference, as grants must be taken through the different representative bodies and gain council subcommittee approval. MPs can help with particularly difficult immigration matters.

Hence followers regard good vertical links both with visiting Pakistani dignitaries and with local politicians as essential for a leader. They also believe that these connections will, ultimately, bring patronage rewards. Most leaders attempt to establish upward vertical links and the *level* of these links is a test of the status of the leader. Many aspiring leaders engage in voluntary immigration advice since this ultimately becomes a source of immediate patronage and an excuse for forging links with MPs and other concerned politicians. The more successful they are in this advisory work, the more likely they are to establish such vertical links.

There is, of course, also the direct patronage provided by large clothing wholesalers which may, and sometimes does, create a loyal clientele. A more recent source of patronage is associated with British state grants through the Manpower Services Commission to workers in the community, recruited from the ranks of the unemployed. In the one instance I know of, in which several MSC jobs were in the control of a local Pakistani office holder, he managed to get *two* family members appointed to key positions (albeit low paid and temporary). He did so despite the apparent objectivity of an interviewing selection panel! Such MSC jobs are becoming more common in community associations and may certainly provide a fertile source of patronage.

It should also be remembered, however, that running a faction is an *expensive* enterprise. Leaders host both dignitaries and supporters to large-scale dinners. They usually pay the membership fees of followers to the Central Mosque or Community Centre (registering 500 members can be a very costly affair!). They pay for the printing of embossed invitations to such dinners and ceremonial celebrations. Being a leader is thus an expensive business and a faction can only be viable in the long run if at least some of its key members have enough reserve capital to pay for such expenses. In Britain, these expenses necessarily come out of leaders' own pockets. They are a matter of *noblesse oblige* (see Werbner, 1990).

While factions direct their energies towards winning elections in key arenas, the intervening periods between elections are interspersed with activities, internal elections and public events and celebrations held by the various associations making up a factional alliance. Now and then one of these events erupts, there is a *halagula*, a public commotion or noisy argument, which is discussed and gossiped about, analysed and recounted. Indeed, I have been told cynically by some local people that 'it is impossible to hold a public event in

Manchester without some trouble erupting'. My own impression is that most events pass relatively harmoniously as long as they are dominated by a single faction or group. There is no doubt, however, that the potential for violence seems close to the surface in the more open events.

Apart from incidental or open events there are also parallel events that are held by the different associations to mark specific Pakistani public holidays such as Pakistan Day or *Quaid-e-Azam* Day. Among all these events during my fieldwork, three were seriously disrupted. The first was the Longsight Community Rep elections referred to above; the second was a *halagula* occurring not long before it during a public Eid celebration held in one of the municipal libraries. The most violent event was a confrontation between two factions in Whalley Range (who had previously been united) in which a great deal of property damage was caused, and an elderly man died of a coronary.

This event was significant for another reason, for it highlighted the way factional disputes within the city and even in a single neighbourhood are 'penetrated', to use Jones's expression, by wider networks and divisions elsewhere. The leaders of the opposed groups in Whalley Range were, as mentioned, from a single village in Jhelum District and had previously been part of a single faction there, supporting the same candidate for council and provincial elections. The division in Manchester appears to have been precipitated by a division in Pakistan, following the death of a local notable and kingmaker. His sons led the secession and mobilised support among those disgruntled with the current leadership. Following the fight in Whalley Range in which the man died, a petition was organised blaming the leaders of the opposed faction (currently the controlling faction in the Central Mosque). The petition was signed by persons throughout the North West of England who were linked to the group in Manchester. In the following council elections *in Pakistan* the ruling faction was routed, 'finished', and this triumph much strengthened the political hand of the local opposition faction in Manchester, as they gained local British Pakistani defectors keen to join the now successful extension of the group in Pakistan.

Links beyond Manchester to its outlying regions are evident in many public confrontations, and a recurrent complaint is that those attending local election meetings are from 'Blackburn', 'Bolton' or 'Rochdale'. A local leader bragged to me that he could mobilise support throughout the North West and listed a series of small towns where he had supporters. The link between the politics of Pakistan and Manchester are evident in a poster printed by the Whalley Range United Association which sponsored a large well race fair in their village (in which buffalo are raced around an artesian well), held in the name of the leader's father. The event, which cost the British Pakistani promoters several thousand pounds (in addition to fares), was attended by members of *both* the Whalley Range factions. Each videoed the event separately, and the two competing video versions were circulating among supporters and adversaries throughout Manchester and the North West. Among men in these groups were several who hoped to return to Pakistan in order to hold political office, and indeed one local migrant appears to have succeeded in winning a place in the present council elections. The complexities of elections in Pakistan, such as those held in 1988 following Zia's death, are discussed endlessly in Manchester. The current leader of the seceding faction had his telephone cut off after, as he explained, he had accumulated an enormous bill during the recent Pakistani (and Manchester) confrontations.

Apart from such major fights which have long-term implications, there were also more minor fights during committee meetings or at the Central Mosque, and these too were publicised through word of mouth. The various communal public events during my fieldwork are listed in Table 9.1.

Table 9.1   Mobilisation events during 1987–8

Public disputes and elections		*Ceremonial events and meetings*
May 87	Eid Party public argument	Eid parties (1, 4)
		Dar Ul Aloom anniversary (2) [1]
June 87	Race Subcommittee elections	Pakistan cricket team parties (1, 4, 5)
July 87	Race S.c. 2nd Elec. Longsight	Election Victory celebration (2) Pakistan Day ceremonial dinners (1, 2)
September 87	Whalley Range meeting and violent fight	Outgoing councillor party (3) Petition Town Hall (2) [2]
October 87		Eid Milad-ul-Nabi ceremonials and public processions (1, 2) [3]

December 87	Pakistani provincial and local elections	Quaid-e-Azam ceremonials (1, 2, 3) [4]
January 88	Public dispute over the disqualification of candidates to community centre	Muslim development centre Town Hall conference on Asian Business (1) [5]
January 88	Community Centre elections (no contest)	Longsight Association Dinner (2) [6]
March 88		Confederation elections (2) Pakistani Minister's visit (1) [7] Pakistani Minister's visit (2) [8]

Key
1 Controlling faction
2 Opposition faction
3 Old controlling faction
4 Elite Pakistanis not involved in community politics
5 Youth organisations or initiatives

Notes
[1] (2)'s event attended by local MP for Longsight and other dignitaries.
[2] Involved appeals to the MP and council chair and confrontation in Town Hall.
[3] (1)'s event held at the Town Hall and attended by local MP and new Pakistani subconsul.
[4] (1)'s event held at the Town Hall and attended by the Pakistani ambassador. (2)'s events held at the Pakistani community centre and in Whalley Range, the latter attended by the Pakistani subconsul and several Pakistani barristers. (3)'s event held at a hotel and attended by the Pakistani ambassador.
[5] (1)'s event held the following day at the Town Hall, attended by the Mayor, several councillors and the Pakistani ambassador.
[6] Attended by a visiting dignitary from the Pakistan Embassy, London.
[7] This took place at the Town Hall.
[8] This took place at the community centre.

The events keep the associations and factional alliances alive and provide public clues to shifts in allegiances. Some groups do indeed shift, and most people regard acts of betrayal and disloyalty as inevitable. Most commonly, as mentioned, the shift is not by a whole group but by a disaffected section of it. Given these underlying utilitarian features of factions, and the anticipation of betrayal, what is striking is the stress put on principles, values and loyalty. Again and again faction leaders stressed to me their constancy, the fact that they stuck to their side through thick and thin. One leader said of a man who had shifted twice – 'he is not a man of the world. In politics you need to have some principles and to stick to them.' This sentiment was echoed many times by different group leaders.

V   IDEOLOGY AND LEADERSHIP

Factions are usually described as pragmatic, utilitarian groups, based on self-interest and thus non-ideological. Just as factions cut across class, so too they cut across or combine various ideological commitments. Groups and individuals may shift from one party to another, and the dominant party is itself riven by factionalism. Asad has argued, though, that such manoeuvrings disguise the real opposition and growing polarisation between landowners and tenants in Swat society. In other words, the major division is in reality a *horizontal* division, on the basis of ownership of the means of production. Barth, he argues, ignored these historical processes of polarisation and exploitation underlying the surface manifestation of factionalism.

Asad's critique has, however, itself drawn criticism from both Lindholm and Barth himself, in a recent critical reappraisal of his own work (Barth, 1981b). Indeed, according to Lindholm the Pakhtuns' integration into modern Pakistani politics and the undermining of the Badshah's power, rather than leading to horizontal polarisation, has resulted in an 'equalisation' of holdings among leading Khans. He goes on to say that

> rather than becoming more centralised, Swat appears to be going backward to the era of local parties without central leadership. Although it is possible that class polarisation will increase in Swat, it is just as likely (if not more likely) that either class differences will be coopted into a struggle between power hungry junior Pukhtun and the already powerful élite or that the situation will regress entirely and the old segmentary system will be reaffirmed in the face of external pressures from the state. (Lindholm, 1982, p. 92)

Factional alliances normally cut across class interests (but see Jones, 1974 on a powerful labour faction in Indore). They are vertical rather than horizontal political alliances, and as such they undermine the solidarity of propertied dominant groups in the society. Rather than paternalism, patronage reigns supreme. Both the evidence from the literature and events in Manchester suggest that as ideologically weak vertical structures, factions allow *primordial* ideologies stressing divisions along ethnic, religious or language lines to flourish. Because of their essentially *vertical* structure, factions often tend to become fertile ground for quasi-nationalist movements, rather than intensifying class conflict. In Indore, for example, Brahmins were divided between two opposing factions but were united on an ethnic/linguistic basis. In the Punjab, Sikhs shifted between the Akali Dal and Congress but it is unlikely that many Hindus were members of the Akali Dal. In Manchester, while local leaders have engaged in power struggles, the various religious leaders who have figured at one time or another in these factional disputes have built up a formidable array of Islamic institutions. Each *maulvi* who has resigned or abandoned the Central Mosque has set up a new, viable alternative to it. While erstwhile factional leaders have long been forgotten and past disputes mainly buried, these religious institutions have grown and flourished. We have seen, moreover, that kinship or regional loyalties and caste (i.e. quasi-tribal) divisions figure in such factional disputes as much as class does.

Lindholm points out that the division between close collaterals as members of opposing blocs breaks down in cases of homicide, and violence against persons. A close collateral will not remain an ally of a group which murdered a person within a certain kinship range. The system thus retains some segmentary features. Similarly, an external threat to the whole ethnic group appears to rally the group behind a unified leadership (Ahmed, 1976). This may be a key to the way factions ultimately come to be linked to 'vertical' ideologies (based on ethnic, linguistic or religious loyalties), often progressively extreme. Violence in factional disputes sets limits to the shifting of groups back and forth, as primordial bonds are evoked linking followers to the victim by ties of substance. Progressively serious revenge violence between factions comes over time to define a 'structure of fear'. When this happens, the pragmatics of alliance are replaced by the politics of fear and the emotional rallying of support. This follows any incidents in which members of the ethnic/religious or language group are physically molested or murdered.

The polarisation that emerges is not along class lines but along communal ascriptive lines. Factions may not seem ideological but they enable subgroups to foster ascriptive ideologies and to build up,

almost surreptitiously, powerful organisations which are *not* frac-
tionised but are, instead, highly unified and ideologically committed.
The rise of the Pathan *Badshah* (ruler) as described by Ahmed
illustrates an instance of this process: he succeeded to power on the
basis of external threats to the integrity of the state. Moreover,
whereas propertied classes have a stake in maintaining stability,
factional political rhetoric is more prone to appeal to people's
passions, fears and primordial attachments if these are perceived to
be an effective way of mobilising support, and to be exploited by
unscrupulous politicians out to gain power at the expense of communal consensus. It is not that faction leaders are not committed
ideologically or that class divisions are not important. It is more that
moderate pragmatists often lose out to 'extremists' in the long run in
their ability to rally supporters.[5]

People in Manchester, as elsewhere, think of the political history
of their community retrospectively as a series of *personalised* leadership struggles, victories and downfalls. The details and personalities
in these disputes all appear terribly important to them and rather
trivial and confusing to bystanders. But the real historical process
would seem to be one of increasing *religious* domination. The enormous efflorescence of mosques and their growing influence in communal affairs is not a peculiarly Mancunian affair: it is evident
throughout Britain, always apparently generated by local personal
disputes. The ideological divisions within South Asia have been
reproduced in Britain, and the true leaders of this ideological movement are the religious officials. If there is a counter-movement, it is
towards greater involvement in the British political arena. In this
Manchester lags behind Bradford, Birmingham or London. But the
trend is there and is likely to gather momentum, irrespective of the
individuals, groups or factions fuelling its progression. At present in
Manchester local politics are inseparable from religious politics.
Local members of the community can easily ignore factional disputes
and, indeed, many choose to do so. But whenever they set foot in a
Pakistani controlled mosque they are making a *political* choice,
whether they like it or not. As observant Muslims, and they are
increasingly so, they cannot entirely escape from factional politics.

VI   POSTSCRIPT: THE AFTERMATH OF VIOLENCE

In 1987 when this paper was first written, it seemed that the violent divide within the Manchester Pakistani community which had emerged in the course of the previous year would create a spiral of further violence. Following events proved that this assumption was too simplistic. The death in Whalley Range, following the earlier death at the Central Mosque, and the election *halagula* at the Community Centre, appeared to drive home the cost of violence for the community and its reputation. Leaders embarked on a cautious reappraisal of strategy and a greater consciousness of the consequences of spontaneous physical aggression. They began to preach self-control. Events during the following year were marked by careful and considered preparation. Elections were universally felt to be best held through the ballot box rather than by a show of hands. An attempt was made to settle election results by compromise before the actual event.

Three potentially violent events during the course of the following year were held peacefully. The first – the elections to the Community Centre, started rather badly with abuse and shouting matches between factional leaders during the pre-election meetings. In the upshot, however, the losing faction decided to accept in good grace what amounted to a technical constitutional defeat. This despite the fact that they had spent a good deal of time and money in mobilising support. In the following event – the second elections of a Longsight Community Representative for the Race Subcommittee, the two main candidates reached a compromise agreement minutes before the elections were due to be held.

The third event, the election of a Whalley Range Community Representative, was bitterly contested. It ended quite remarkably in a dead heat with both candidates receiving exactly the same number of votes, and a handful of ambiguous spoilt ballots. One of the factions did, however, win the *Deputy* Community Representative seat, by one vote. Here was a potentially explosive situation. Among the people who had gathered outside to hear the election results were men from both Whalley Range and Longsight, as well as from other parts of the city. A great deal of time and effort had been invested in the election campaign. The result was highly ambiguous, the animosities deeply felt. Yet here too the men restrained themselves. There was no violence and no shouting. I was told later that elections to the Central Mosque were being delayed in order to avoid violence, and to prepare for a peaceful and orderly campaign.

Yet beneath the surface, the hidden spark of spontaneous communal violence, with young men at its forefront, is undoubtedly a feature of British Pakistani political culture. The initial response to challenge is again and again in the idiom of honour and revenge. It is only later that more consensual and less emotional considerations may prevail. At the time of writing, the Salman Rushdie affair bears tragic witness to this process on a global scale: spontaneous protests, almost uncontrolled, and calls to violence have marked the initial response to the book's perceived attack on sacred Islamic values. This has been followed by a more cautious reappraisal by some community and Islamic leaders in Britain, and growing attempts by them to channel passion into legal protest. The lesson that political violence entails heavy costs must, it appears, be learnt again and again.

Notes

* Earlier versions of this chapter were presented at the Pakistan Workshop at Satterthwaite in May 1988, and to the Punjab Research group in July 1988. I am grateful to participants in these workshops and to Hastings Donnan, the coeditor of this book, for their penetrating comments. I would also like to thank Mr Munir Choudhri for his immense help during the research and the insight he gave me into the political culture of local British Pakistanis.

1. The boundaries of the community centre membership were discussed in an Executive Committee meeting in which it was decided to leave them deliberately vague.

2. In 1988, another was elected. Both are university educated youngish men originating from Africa, one from Kenya, the other from Mauritius. The Kenyan councillor has, however, lived in Pakistan for part of his life, and speaks fluent Urdu and Punjabi. The third Asian councillor, a woman, is an Indian Muslim Gujerati. All represent the Labour Party.

3. This harmony was irrevocably shattered by a dispute surrounding the Central Mosque's *maulvi*. This split occurred towards the end of my fieldwork and its implications go beyond the scope of this chapter.

4. Elections to the Central Mosque are due to be held on 18 August 1989. At present it appears that the opposition faction, including some key seceding members of the ruling faction, are likely to win them.

5. I define moderation as a tolerance of divergent points of view and an attempt to work within a broad consensual framework. Extremism is defined as a commitment to a specific ideology as the only legitimate truth which others must conform to or be excluded altogether.

References

Arabia (1985), 'Old Differences Make a New Start in Eid Violence', October.

Ahmed, Akbar S. (1976), *Millennium and Charisma among Pathans* (London: Routledge & Kegan Paul).

Asad, Talal (1972), 'Market Model, Class Structure and Consent: A Reconsideration of Swat Political Organisation', *Man* (NS), 7 (1), pp. 74–94.

Bailey, F. G. (1969), *Strategems and Spoils: A Social Anthropology of Politics* (Oxford: Basil Blackwell).

Barth, Fredrik (1981a), 'Segmentary Opposition and the Theory of games' (1959). Reprinted in *Features of Person and Society in Swat: Collected Essays on Pathans* (London: Routledge & Kegan Paul), pp. 55–82.

Barth, Fredrik (1981b), 'Swat Pathan Reconsidered', in *Features of Person and Society in Swat: Collected Essays on Pathans* (London: Routledge & Kegan Paul).

Black-Michaud, Jacob (1975), *Cohesive Force: Feud in the Mediterranean and the Middle East* (Oxford: Basil Blackwell).

Jones, Rodney W. (1974), *Urban Politics in India: Area, Power and Policy in a Penetrated System* (Berkeley: University of California Press).

Lindholm, Charles (1982), *Generosity and Jealousy: The Swat Pukhtun of Northern Pakistan* (New York: Columbia University Press).

Manchester Evening News (1988), 'Man Dies from a Punch in the Chest', October.

Peters, Emrys L. (1959), 'The Proliferation of Segments in the Lineages of the Bedouin of Cyrenaica', Curl Bequest Essay, *Journal of the Royal Anthropological Institute*, 90, 1, pp. 29–53.

Peters, Emrys L. (1967), 'Some Structural Aspects of the Feud among the Camel-herding Bedouin of Cyrenica', *Africa*, XXXVII, 3, pp. 261–82.

Pettigrew, Joyce (1975), *Robber Noblemen: a Study of the Political System of the Sikh Jats* (London: Routledge & Kegan Paul).

Pocock, David (1957), 'The Bases of Faction in Gujerat', *British Journal of Sociology*, 8, pp. 295–306.

Swartz, M. J. (ed.) (1968), *Local Level Politics* (London: Aldine).

Werbner, Pnina (1985), 'The Organisation of Giving and Ethnic Elites', *Ethnic and Racial Studies*, 8 (3), pp. 368–88.

Werbner, Pnina (1990), *The Migration Process: Capital, Gifts and Offerings among British Pakistanis*, Explorations in Anthropology Series (Oxford: Berg).

Werbner, Pnina (1991), 'The Fiction of Unity in Ethnic Politics: Aspects of Representation and the State among British Pakistanis', in Pnina Werbner and Muhammad Anwar (eds), *Black and Ethnic Leaderships in Britain: The Cultural Dimensions of Political Action* (London: Routledge).

10 *Ulema* and *Pir* in the Politics of Pakistan*
Saifur Rahman Sherani

Since 1947 Pakistan's political history has been largely a continuous struggle between religious orthodoxy and secularism. Sometimes overshadowed in this debate is the curious paradox that the most traditional section of the religious leadership supports secularism against the fundamental Islamic leadership. This has been obscured in recent studies of Pakistan's religious leadership by a tendency to group together as *ulema* all religious leaders regardless of differences of opinion among them. By identifying the different types of leader, and by focusing particularly on one of them, the *pirs* or 'saints', this chapter seeks to clarify the role of religious leaders in Pakistani politics and social structure.

The chapter also seeks to clarify the nature of the relationship between *pirs* and successive governments in Pakistan. Ewing has argued that the governments of Ayub Khan, Zulfiqar Ali Bhutto, and Zia-ul-Haq each adopted a similar policy towards *pirs*, using them, as well as the government department responsible for administering their shrines (the Department of Auqaf), as a vehicle for modernisation (Ewing, 1983, p. 252). However, I will suggest here that the policy towards shrines was actually designed to strengthen government rule by rallying support in the countryside, and that far from modernising the country, this retarded modernisation and democratic growth.

I MYSTICISM IN THE SUBCONTINENT

It is well known that early Muslim mystics, popularly known as sufis due to their style of dress (Chishti, 1976, p. 329), were responsible for converting large parts of the Indian subcontinent to Islam (Mujeeb, 1967, p. 21ff; see also Titus, 1959, p. 36). These sufis, or saints as I will also refer to them, professed different mystic doctrines known as *tariqah*, the basis of the mystic orders. The two earliest mystic orders to flourish in the subcontinent were the Chishtiyya and Suhrawardiyya, but sufis from a wide variety of orders and sects established centres in their respective areas.

Gradually, the original reform-minded sufis were replaced by their descendants and a new class of hereditary religious divine, the *pirs*, began to emerge. Some saw this as a deterioration, remarking how sufi institutions had 'degenerated into speculation, semi-religious ceremonies, a kind of brotherhood, a source of inactive and easy life, a means of begging, a cause of revolution, a way of deceiving gullible, illiterate and simple minded people' (Shushtery, 1966, p. 380). The religious scholars (the *ulema*) considered these institutions alien to Islam (Kagaya, 1966, p. 72–4) and a conflict developed between *ulema* and *pir* over the status of sufis. Despite this conflict the sufis, almost all of whom were *Sayyids* (descendants of the Prophet), were greatly revered by all classes of orthodox *ulema*. There is no quarrel over the accomplishments of these saints but there is strong disagreement on the strategies they followed and on how they should be venerated. This is the basis of the most wide-spread and ubiquitous religious conflict in present day Pakistan.

There is some confusion concerning the definition of 'sufi' among Western scholars. Sufis are considered to be 'generally less learned . . . popular religious leaders possessing divine grace' (Keddie, 1972, p. 1). Similarly, Ewing holds that 'The saint, by performing specific disciplines prescribed by the Sufi Order of which he is a member, has had *baraka* (God's blessing) bestowed upon him' (Ewing, 1984, p. 107). These definitions separate sufis from the *ulema* and present Sufism as something alien to Islam. Social anthropologists have identified two main divisions in Muslim society; one represented by the *ulema* stressing the importance of the revealed text and an urge to translate it into practice, the other represented by the sufis, giving primacy to mystical experience, intercession with God, performance of miracles and syncretic tendencies by which pre-Islamic beliefs and rituals have been interlaced with Islam. These divisions in Muslim society have been conceptualised as official and popular Islam (Waardenburg, 1978), as urban and tribal Islam (Gellner, 1982), and as scripturalist and syncretic Islam (Geertz, 1968), with the former represented by the *ulema* and the latter by the sufis, respectively. But this distinction is confusing and misleading. By dividing Muslim society into these polar positions some Western scholars have tried to demonstrate that

Islam until recently and in certain regions still today has been an agglomeration of very different kinds and sorts of religion. A certain unification and levelling of them is taking place now, due among other things to the communications media and especially the political change since World War II, connected to the political Independence of the Muslim countries. (Waardenburg, 1978, p. 332)

This means that what for centuries was an agglomeration of different religions is now emerging as Islam, thanks to the modernisation taking place in Muslim countries as a result of contact with the West and Western technology.

However, the categories of *ulema* and sufi are not as mutually exclusive as usually presented. Both have their roots in Islamic law or Shari'a. Without knowledge of Shari'a it is impossible to become a sufi (Nasr, 1966, p. 121). Similarly, many of those considered *ulema*, those expert in divine law, such as the founders of Islam's major schools of jurisprudence, were also sufis. In fact, many of Islam's early missionaries were simultaneously *ulema* and sufis. According to some Muslim scholars, sufism is thus not an alien intrusion into Islam but an integral part of it (ibid., p. 125; see also Muhammad, 1970; Shahab, 1987, pp. 1112–28).

It is true that some sufis developed their own idiosyncratic versions of sufism based on their interpretations of other religions and philosophies, but such heterodox sufis were condemned by Muslim sufis and *ulema* alike (see Ahmad, 1964, p. 186, 193). Indeed, some Muslim scholars argue that the prime objective of sufism, their role in conversion notwithstanding, was purification of the Muslim masses from pre-Islamic influence (Haq, 1972; Nadwi, 1969).

Throughout history there are many examples of those combining the roles of *alim* (singular of *ulema*) and sufi reformer: Shah Waliullah in eighteenth-century Delhi; Shah Waliullah's followers who founded the Muslim seminary at Deoband in 1867; and the founder of Tabliqui Jamaat, the largest reform movement among Muslims today (Haq, 1972). Beyond the subcontinent the *ulema* have also shown an interest in mysticism (see Gilsenan, 1973, p. 12).

This suggests that it would be wrong to characterise sufism simply as 'popular' or 'syncretic' Islam. According to some *ulema*, the sufis have actually employed their energies to suppress popular tradition against the 'true Islam'. In *Tareekh-i-Dawat-wa-Azeemat* Abul Hassan Ali Nadwi describes the role of the great sufi masters in purifying

Muslim society from popular or superstitious beliefs and rituals through-out the history of Islam. All the above mentioned sufis have criticised the *pirs* and their rituals in the most caustic terms, even equating some practices with polytheism and declaring them beyond the pale. Many sufis were thus first of all great scholars, whose basic objective was to establish 'true Islam' among Muslims in the subcontinent.

II SAINTS, SUFIS, *PIRS* AND *ULEMA*

It is necessary to distinguish between *pir* and sufi or saint, since these are sharply contrasted categories according to the *ulema*. The *ulema* argue that all the Muslim saints were great preachers of the pure and pristine belief and were thus exemplary Muslims, who never deviated from the Prophet's path. Such saints were neither absolute ascetics who abstained from all of life's pleasures nor mere mystics who claimed esoteric knowledge, but were true fundamentalist scholars and great reformers. Their mission was to establish the true faith by living among people and training a few selected students of outstand-ing abilities to carry on the Prophet's work. According to this view, found in the work of many *ulema*, sufis and Muslim scholars (see Muhammad, 1970; Nadwi, 1969; Nasr, 1966; Shahab, 1987), none of the saints performed miracles simply to impress the masses, or claimed special access to God.

This is in contrast to popular religious belief in Pakistan which can be described with reference to *pirs* and shrines. *Pir* is a Persian word meaning 'an old man, a founder or chief of any religious body or sect' (Steingass, 1947, p. 264), but in Pakistan refers to a person believed to possess occult powers inherited from a great sufi ancestor. Here the term *pir* applies to a mystic who separates *tariqat* from Shari'a, and who claims revelation of esoteric knowledge, the ability to perform miracles and to communicate with God, and the power of intercession on behalf of fellow human beings. While his claims may be valid, the fact that a *pir* neglects the Shari'a would exclude him from the rank of sufis. Descendants of sufis and custodians of their shrines, who claim to have inherited the spiritual power of their ancestors but do not conform to Shari'a, are also considered *pirs* and they constitute the vast majority of *pirs* in Pakistan. Their main source of legitimacy is the hagiographies of their ancestors rather than their knowledge and practice of Shari'a. They have large follow-ings among those who believe in their powers of divine intercession.

It is possible, therefore, to draw a clear distinction between *ulema* and sufis on the one hand and *pirs* on the other. The *ulema* and the sufis represent the formal, legal tradition preserved in the Qur'an and the Sunna (the traditions of the Prophet). They emphasise preservation of the ideal beliefs and conformity to the ideal practices transmitted through scriptural authority. The *pirs* on the other hand, legitimise the popular, prevalent beliefs and practices in society at large and in so far as these are opposed to Islamic beliefs and practices, they could be called 'superstitious'. In some studies of Islam the concept of 'official religion' as opposed to 'popular religion' has been used to make a similar distinction (Waardenburg, 1978), as has Redfield's typology into Little and Great Traditions (Ahmad, 1971; Gellner, 1982).

Pirs and their rituals thus tend to cultivate and perpetuate beliefs and practices which could be called 'superstitious'. European visitors to Muslim countries, as recently as the Second World War, described 'customs and practices, beliefs and loyalties which one would call *now* "popular Islam"' (Waardenburg, 1978, p. 318, emphasis added) as the most degrading 'superstition'. Thus one author wrote that Muslims in west Punjab

> are singularly lax and unobservant of the ordinances of their faith . . . most are still very much linked with the Hinduism they once professed, but all alike are sunk in the most degrading superstition, and are in the most abject submission to their spiritual pastors or pirs. (O'Brien, 1911, p. 509)

Now some scholars insist that these 'degrading superstitions' represent another kind of Islam – syncretic or popular – in contradiction to orthodox Islam. I have argued that this division of Islam is not justified because the 'scripture', the 'legal–formal', the 'official' and the 'Great Tradition' Islam stresses the ideals which *ought to* guide behaviour. Any Muslim, however superstitious and non-conformist, who accepts this ideal as a valid model *is* a Muslim and no authority can brand him otherwise.

III   THE POWER OF *PIRS*

In any society beliefs and practices which do not conform to what is considered 'rational' are termed 'superstitious'. This polarisation exists everywhere no matter how unfounded from a scientific point of view. In Pakistani society, many people believe in the mystical and spiritual power of *pirs* and shrines. Some also believe that metaphysical forces can work only if one has a strong belief in them. As one visitor to a shrine told Darling (1929, p. 231), 'If . . . faith is strong, God will fulfil our purpose.' Strong and firm belief is the first requirement by which a *pir* is assigned the highest place nearest to God. A Pushtu proverb reflects the same thing: 'Though the *pir* himself does not fly, his disciples would have him fly.' These beliefs are inculcated by the existence of lavishly decorated tombs and shrines, folklore, hagiographies and the living examples of people who claim that they owe everything to the blessing of a *pir*. Any hagiographical account will describe the miracles of the saint, and all saints seem to have performed the same or very similar miracles. All these miracles are repeatedly described by the *mullah*[1] and thus become seen as factual events of the recent past. According to widely known and popular accounts, saints have raised from the dead the only son of an old woman, protected visitors bringing tribute to shrines, given sons to infertile women, or travelled very long distances in a few seconds. There are saints who have crossed the River Indus on their prayer carpet or in a stone boat, or who have crossed the deep waters with their followers as if walking on sand. There are stories of saints who rode on a wall or on wild animals like tigers and who used snakes as whips.

Many festivals are held on the sites of famous shrines, the largest being the *urs* or death anniversary of the saint. At the *urs* all types of *pirs* and *mullahs* give eye-witness accounts of the miracles performed by dead and living *pirs*. There are several *urs* in one year at any big shrine, and all types of ritual traders earn their livelihood on these occasions by selling amulets and charms, portraits of saints, hagiographical pamphlets and many other articles of ritual significance which help to perpetuate the beliefs or superstitions associated with *pirs* and their occult powers. In this context, the *pir* – the symbol of all these powers – becomes the central figure whose protection and help is sought in coping with the uncertainties of life.

The *pirs* are not magicians with secular powers. Their thaumaturgical powers are legated to them by the sufis and the Prophet and are acts of God. This power is called *barkat* which is distributed among all the progeny of the saint and harnessed by the few who fulfil religious obligations and meditate on the tomb of the saint in order to perform miracles. In theory this *barkat* descends from God, through the Prophet and through the saint to his progeny. According to Barelvi beliefs (see below), the Prophet can be made present anywhere through the performance of certain rituals and the *pir's* direct communication with him allows the *pir* to dispense divine favours. Indoctrination into this belief is provided in month long celebrations of the birthday of the Prophet (*milad sharif*). Every night during this month a *milad sharif* is held in the mosque at shrines and in all other Barelvi controlled mosques. During the *milad sharif*, near the pulpit of the *mullah*, a highly decorated and comfortable raised seat is arranged for the Prophet, who comes to occupy it when the *mullah* describes the events of his birth. At this point, the congregation stands as a mark of respect and professional singers intone *salam* – a poetic prayer for the Prophet. The *mullah* then prays for the organisers of the event and everyone responds with 'amen'. This indicates that the *pir* has direct contact with the Prophet and can forward supplications of the faithful to God with a fee slightly higher than a long-distance international telephone call.

In an underdeveloped and overwhelmingly rural society with marked inequality, social services are few and mainly cater for the needs of urban middle classes (Gardezi, 1973). The rural and urban poor cannot afford modern medical treatment because the medical services are extremely limited and inadequate. In Pakistan, in 1972, there was one doctor for 4132 persons and one hospital bed per 1846 persons and there were only 503 dentists for a population of 65.3 million (Government of Pakistan, 1984, p. 112; see also Government of Pakistan, 1972, pp. 4, 215–16 and 1987, p. 185). For many complicated ailments requiring specialist diagnosis and treatment – which more than 90 per cent of the population cannot afford[2] – the remedy is the *pir*, his shrine, and his charms. Some shrines are famous for ritual cures of infertility, the bites of mad dogs, rheumatic pains, skin diseases, epilepsy and all sorts of mental ailments, while in most villages one can find *pirs* who cure toothache, migraine, snake bites and certain other types of common diseases.

Throughout much of Pakistan mental illness is regarded as the effect of *djinns*. According to the Qur'an, *djinns* are beings created from fire who possess all human capabilities and will be called to account on the day of judgement (Al-Qur'an 15 (26) 72(11–15); see for detail Tabatabai, 1975, pp. 235–7). There is no evidence in the Qur'an to suggest that *djinns* can possess human beings and make them sick. The *pir's* spiritual superiority rests on communication with the *djinns* who are subservient to his commands. Belief in *Jumma*

Jinn (a *djinn* named Jumma associated with shrines) is widespread throughout Punjab, though with local variations (Darling, 1929, pp. 242–3). In a country with very little knowledge of the nature of mental illness, and with only a handful of mental hospitals and a few psychiatrists, mental illness is presumed to be the work of a *djinn* and remedy is sought from the *pir*. In rural society where 85 per cent of people are illiterate (see Table 10.2), men and women are married mostly without their prior consent and often shortly after puberty. Establishing mutual understanding and adjusting to new roles and relationships in the midst of excessive family and social pressures are difficult, and as a result psychological problems are common. If a woman is not pregnant a couple of months after marriage, about which elderly female in-laws constantly enquire, then the woman is thought to be infertile. In these circumstances a *pir* may be approached for a cure. Similarly, relief for all sorts of matrimonial and emotional problems or family quarrels can be brought about with the help of a *pir* and his charms.

In commerce, business, professions, examinations, and the search for a job, the *pir* is the ultimate source whose blessings can guarantee success. Not only in this life, but in the hereafter, the *pir* will work as an advocate and pleader in the Court of the Almighty to save his followers from the sojourn in hell. Many rich men leave money to *pirs* or shrines in their wills in order to secure their services on the day of judgement. While a *pir* may have some basic religious knowledge, his real potency lies in his claim to competence in esoteric doctrines and to metaphysical powers (Ali, 1975). A *pir* equipped with these powers is viewed by his followers as superhuman, equal to the Prophets of God and a little less than the Almighty God, although for some 'he has taken the place of Allah' (Darling, 1929, p. 276). For his followers a *pir* is all-powerful to do whatever he pleases. All the follower's fortune is due to his favours. He can protect followers from all afflictions, cure any disease both in men and animals, and can give a boost to a bankrupt business. He can bestow offspring to barren women, and a son to a woman who has had many daughters. His followers will venerate him irrespective of his actions and will even praise his more ignominious behaviour, viewing it in the most favourable light. This is a status which no other secular leader nor the most prominent and erudite of the *ulema* can achieve. It is acquired due to the *pir's* sacred genealogy and his special relationship to God and the Prophet through his ancestor's soul.

Succession to the office of *sajjada nashin*, the person who owns and controls a shrine, is often troublesome since Islamic law does not favour primogeniture. Brothers struggle to succeed and if they are minors their uncles and cousins may try to usurp the position. In this case claims are referred to courts and the legal wrangling continues until the final appellate court decides the rightful heir. Litigation can be prolonged and during this period the management of the shrine is sometimes taken over by the district administration. This conflict may be productive for the contending parties if it results in a division of followers (*mureed*) between them. When the final appellate court decides in favour of one heir, the unsuccessful heir establishes his own shrine and becomes a rival *sajjada nashin*. The establishment of a *pir* is known as the *khanqah* and consists of the tomb of the saint, a mosque, several rooms which are reminders of the saint's miracles, a free public kitchen (*langar*) and free accommodation for the visitors. The *pir's* residence is near the shrine and is surrounded by the living quarters of his staff which includes servants and retainers, secretaries and maintenance staff, as well as by his vehicles and other equipment. The *pir* has no sectarian preference and is never involved in political controversy unless it is absolutely necessary to protect his power and privilege.

IV TYPES OF *PIR*

There are many kinds of *pirs*: 'some are quiet hermits, others active preachers; some take a useful part in the secular affairs of neighbourhood, some are mischievous stirrers of trouble, and some are charlatans pure and simple' (O'Brien, 1911, p. 509). Various terms are used to describe different types of *pirs*. Mayer and Wilber both differentiate between *pir* and *murshid*. Wilber distinguishes between the *pir* as the centre of the cult of saint worship and the *murshid* as the spiritual preceptor and member of the sufi order (Wilber, 1964, pp. 100–6). Analysing the statements of Punjabi villagers, Mayer concludes 'that all those with spiritual powers are *pirs*: but each of them is a *murshid* to his disciples and only a *pir* to other followers' (Mayer, 1967, p. 163). Several other terms are also used like *shaykh*, *faqir*, *mian* and *makhdum* but most of these are local variants for the term *pir* and are used interchangeably. Since they are all traders in spiritual blessings and performers of miracles, any analytical distinction between them must refer to the level and degree of their influence. On this basis we can distinguish between the following categories of *pirs*, although we should remember that there is some overlap between each category.

The *sajjada nashin pirs* are the most popular and powerful *pirs* and they exercise considerable influence on Pakistani politics. They are the descendants of famous Muslim saints who either converted people to Islam or began reform movements. Unlike their saintly ancestors who lived as ascetics, these *pirs* benefited from royal patronage, often receiving landed estates or money to build beautiful mausolea and shrines in memory of the saints. The ruling classes forged an alliance with these *pirs* who commanded a vast body of hereditary followers all of whom gave unswerving allegiance to them. *Sajjada nashin pirs* inherited neither the knowledge nor the piety of their ancestors, only their tombs, shrines and devotees. Since they include very rich landlords who married into leading landlord families, they do not visit their followers to collect their tributes. Instead their followers visit them every year on the *urs* of the saint and offer them tribute. These *sajjada nashin pirs* are politically active and are leaders of religio–political parties like the Jamiat-e-Ulema-e-Pakistan, the Jamiat-e-Mashaikh, the Pakistan People's Party and the Pakistan Muslim League. Some of them have formed their own parties from their followers (Gilmartin, 1979; Talbot, 1982, 1983). Despite party affiliation, they have tended to support the government in office, as have other large landlords and tribal leaders of different political parties. These *pirs* have large numbers of minor *pirs* and *mullahs* among their followers. They command the allegiance of many local, provincial and national level political leaders and government officials. Since they are not religious scholars, they employ *mullahs* to preach the hagiolatry and hagiology, particularly of their ancestors.

A second type of *pir* consists mostly of relatives of the *sajjada nashins*, but they command a relatively small number of followers and are not very rich. They have smaller shrines, although this does not mean that they are viewed as spiritually inferior to the *sajjada nashin pirs*, and they are famous for their amulets and charms. These *pirs* annually visit their followers to bless them and to collect their tribute. They exercise political influence at the local level and in local government institutions.

A third type of *pir* is without any sacred genealogy. These *pirs* trade their blessings and make high-sounding claims. They have a small following which they try to increase by claiming spiritual powers and sacred descent. These *pirs* claim to cure certain diseases and exorcise victims of the *djinn* (see Ewing, 1984 on these *pirs*).

A fourth type of *pir* emerges from the most unusual channels and gains instant reputation as problem solvers, largely because of the frequent eye-witness accounts of their spiritual powers in the press. Such *pirs* gain popularity overnight and thousands of people throughout the country seek their blessings. These *pirs* are usually from humble origins and without any claims to Shari'a or *tariqat*. Their reputation for spiritual power declines rapidly after a few reports of disappointment. They are often accused of being charlatans and may disappear from public memory as rapidly as they emerged. The most recent examples of this type in Pakistan are the *dabba pir* and *pir sipahi* described below.

A fifth kind of *pir* is without much influence, but has a little popularity and a following mainly in his own rural locality. They are poor and lowly mendicants who practise exorcism to earn their livelihood. Despite their claims, they convince few of their spiritual powers (see Ahmad, S., 1971, pp. 73–104).

V   TYPES OF *ULEMA*

The *ulema* are scholars, learned in Islamic sciences and able to interpret the sacred text and its historical context. Their influence 'primarily rests on the quality of their scholarship and their piety, for they are religious men and are expected to act upon their preaching . . . Their training is that of lawyers and jurists' (Qureshi, 1974, p. 9). There are four major types of influential *ulema* in Pakistan.

The 'fundamentalist reformers' are the *ulema* who use every means of propaganda, the press, cassettes, and radio and television, to preach their interpretation of Islam. They regularly address meetings in different mosques. Although they oppose many other classes of *ulema* and *pirs*, their main concern is propagation of their doctrines which they say would lead to a 'true Islamic State' in Pakistan. These *ulema* are founders and editors of journals and own publishing agencies. Their interpretation of Islam is most relevant to current discussion of religion in Pakistan and they have large followings among the urban literati and intellectuals. Some of them have bases in several cities where they regularly travel to preach. They are leaders of highly disciplined religious or religio–political parties.

The second type of *ulema*, the 'orthodox teacher', are founders of the Islamic schools called *madrassah*. They are followers of the revivalist orthodox tradition. The fundamentalist reformers consider this type old fashioned and conservative (see Maududi, 1960, p. 51). Despite the opposition of the fundamentalists, these *ulema* have a large following, and politically they have scored more electoral victories than their rivals. Their support comes from the vast network of *madrassah* and their followers are mostly conservative rural and urban masses.

The 'sectarian orthodox' *ulema* belong to the second category above but have a propensity to highlight sectarian dissent. They become popular with one sect and are frequently invited to deliver speeches in other places. They are leaders of the sectarian religious parties and are also associated with the political parties of the *madrassah*.

Finally, the 'preacher orthodox' *ulema* are also similar to the second category, except that they remain completely aloof from politics and sectarianism. Their main activity is advocating regular ritual observance without expressing any sectarian or political bias. Probably for this reason they have the largest following in every region and among all classes in rural and urban Pakistan.

The contrasts between *ulema* and *pir* are summarised in Table 10.1.

Table 10.1 Distinguishing features of *Ulema* and *Pirs*

Variable	Pir	Alim
Status base	ascription	achievement
Establishment	*khanqah*	mosque, *madrassah*
Religious orientation	traditional non-sectarian	sectarian orthodox
Power base, influence	problem solving intercession with metaphysical forces	reformer, publisher, public oratory
Economic position	from mendicant to rentier	modest means
Religious following	hereditary followers	convinced by preaching
Religious outlook	syncretic	revivalist
Political organisation	unity of establishment	competitive party politics
Oratory	apolitical	strongly political

VI BARELVI AND DEOBANDI

Pakistan was demanded in the name of Islam to which 96.7 per cent of its population adheres (Government of Pakistan, 1985, p. 13). The majority of these are Sunnis and only about 15 per cent are Shi'a (Richter, 1981, p. 153). There are several sectarian divisions among the Shi'a but except for the Shi'a Asna Ashri these are quite small. There are several big sectarian divisions among the Sunni of which the Deobandi, the Barelvi and the Ahl-i-Hadith are important. Historically, there is a division between the Shi'a and the Sunni but the majority of Sunnis would hardly identify their sect membership, unless they were religious minded or in some way involved in the sectarian controversy. The main division is between Deobandi and Barelvi. Deoband and Bareilly are the names of two towns in the United Provinces of India where two different schools of Islamic learning flourished. Deobandi refers to the orthodox revivalist movement which dates back to the fundamentalist reformer Shah Waliullah of Delhi (1704–64). His followers opened an Islamic seminary at Deoband in 1864 and founded a movement aimed at purifying Muslims from what they saw as un-Islamic practices. Their main targets have been shrines and saint worship. Ahmad Raza Khan of Bareilly (1856–1921) began a crusade against the revivalist attack on the institution of *pirs* and shrines, and 'gave coherence to a distinct group both intellectual and social' (Metcalf, 1982, p. 297). As a consequence, *pirs* and their followers became known as Barelvi. Although the Barelvi prefer to call themselves the Sunni and their opponents the Wahabi, this term is not widely used.

Over 70 per cent of Pakistan's population live in villages, the majority of whom depend on agriculture for their livelihood. The literacy rate is relatively higher in towns than in rural areas and among males than among females (see Table 10.2). Religious sects fall into two categories: followers of *pirs* afterwards called Barelvi, and followers of revivalist orthodox afterwards called Deobandi. All the Shi'a and the Sunni Barelvi fall within the first group and the rest into the second group. If we map these divisions on to the rural–urban composition, we find an overwhelmingly large rural population included in the first group. Probably the *pir* has dominated the whole countryside since the advent of Islam. However, it would be a mistake to identify towns as exclusively Deobandi, since many of their inhabitants are recent rural migrants. The percentage of the population in cities increased from 17.6 per cent in 1951 to 28.3 per cent in 1981 mainly because of rural–urban migration (see Table 10.3). Nevertheless, the Deobandi tradition is relatively strong in towns mainly because of the large Islamic schools of the revivalist orthodox orientation that are actively engaged in increasing their

Table 10.2   Literacy ratio by sex and rural and urban areas of Pakistan, 1981

Sex	Pakistan	Urban	Rural
Both sexes	23.3	43.4	14.8
Male	31.8	51.5	23.1
Female	13.7	33.7	5.5

Source: Government of Pakistan, 1987, p. 178.

Table 10.3   Urban composition of the population of Pakistan, 1951–81

Year	Population	Rural	Percentage	Urban	Percentage
1951	33.74	27.78	82.4	5.99	17.6
1961	42.88	33.22	77.5	9.65	22.5
1972	65.30	48.72	74.6	16.6	25.6
1981	84.3	60.09	71.7	23.7	28.3

Source: Government of Pakistan, 1985, p. 3.

constituency. A reasonable estimate would suggest that in contemporary Pakistan, with due regard to regional variations, more than three-quarters of the population in the countryside are Barelvi, while the corresponding proportion in towns would be 50 per cent. With certain reservations as we will see below, this even distribution in towns may be attributed to the higher rate of literacy, and to the vigorous campaigning of several competing revivalist orthodox and fundamentalist religio–political interests.

VII   ULEMA AND PIRS IN THE POLITICS OF PAKISTAN

The ulema have played an important political role throughout the history of Islam, being members of the state establishment and the custodians of orthodox Islam. In contrast, the pirs rarely played a political role at national level until the advent of colonialism and the formation of the Pakistan movement. Like landlords, pirs supported the colonial power, while most of the ulema were diehard opponents of 'Christian rule'. Some pirs were appointed as provincial and viceregal dubaris and honorary magistrates according to their position and influence. Some of the ulema admonished Muslims against recruitment in the British Indian Army and strongly opposed the use of Muslim troops against Muslims in the two World Wars, while some *pirs* gave life-saving amulets and charms to these same troops to protect them against enemy attack. *Pirs* with landed estates served their own class interest by supporting the colonial power, which recognised these *pirs* as members of the 'landed gentry', protecting their lands under the Punjab Alienation of Land Act 1901. The majority of *pirs* were thus loyal servants of the British Empire and did not participate in the nationalist movement until the end of the *raj* was imminent.

Some *pirs* were 'closely connected by marriage to the leading landlord families' (Talbot, 1983, p. 245), and in Punjab they supported the National Unionist Party, the coalition of Muslim, Sikh and Hindu landlords. In the Punjab elections of 1937, fourteen leading *pirs* issued an election appeal on behalf of the Unionist Party. In this election the Muslim League, who appealed in the name of Islam, won only two of the eighty-six Muslim seats and quickly realised that electoral success would be impossible without the help of the *sajjada nashins*. Consequently, after 1940 when the Muslim League adopted Pakistan as its objective, it courted the support of the *pirs*, and met with greater success in the Punjab elections of 1946 under the leadership of the westernised landlords and professionals (see Gilmartin, 1979; Talbot, 1983). In the course of the struggle for Pakistan, the Muslim League issued emotionally charged appeals in the name of Islam and in the Punjab elections of 1946 appointed a *Mashaikh (pirs)* Committee to enlist the support of the rural masses, many of whom were ardent supporters of saints. The *Mashaikh* Committee included some genuine *pirs* like the Pir Sahib of Manki Sharif, Pir Jamaaet Ali Shah, Khawaja Nizamuddin of Taunsa Sharif and Makhdum Raza Shah of Multan, but because of the potential electoral power of saintly association, the leading westernised landlord members of the committee were also assigned mystical titles (see Government of the Punjab, 1954, p. 255). The backing of the *pirs* was clearly important to the league whose success in the referendum to determine the future of Sarhad in 1947 was largely due to the support of Pir Sahib of Manki Sharif (Weekes, 1964, p. 29).

Electoral appeals in the name of Islam also allowed the league to refer to their opponents as 'the enemy of Islam' (Sayeed, 1967, p. 52), although the *ulema* regarded leaguers as 'ignorant of even a rudimentary knowledge of Islam and its laws' (Sayeed, 1957, p. 62). In the final phase of the struggle for Pakistan, the identification of the league with Islam and the support of some *ulema* and *pirs* generated the mass mobilisation of Muslims necessary for the creation of the country. In these circumstances it is hardly surprising that shortly after Pakistan's creation Jinnah was greeted by a large peasant crowd with the slogan of 'Maulana Muhammad Ali Jinnah Zindabad' ('Long live the distinguished religious scholar Muhammad Ali Jinnah') (Bolitho, 1954, p. 213). The Islamic propaganda of the league was so powerful that in the view of the illiterate masses, the head of the new Muslim state must have been a distinguised scholar of Islam. For years the *ulema* had preached that God would give them power if they became good Muslims; thus in some circles the emergent Muslim government was described as the 'Government of God' (Sayeed, 1968, p. 180). There were frequent attempts by the *pirs* and their followers to eulogise the Quaid-i-Azam as a religious leader. Pir Jamaaet Ali Shah, member of the *Mashaikh* Committee of the Muslim League, went a step further and presented Jinnah as one of the great saints when he declared that 'think of Jinnah Sahib whatever you like, but I say that Jinnah Sahib is "Wali Allah"' (the greatest of all sufi titles) (Gilmartin, 1979, p. 510). Such were the cultural imperatives that even the westernised secular political leaders were referred to as *pir* or *alim*.

There was a sharp contrast between the roles of *pir* and *alim* in the new state. The *pirs* were powerful leaders in their respective areas, and had considerable influence with the local authorities and the government (O'Brien, 1911, p. 514), while the *ulema* were acquiring influence with the ruling circles for the first time. The Punjab government created and funded a Department of Islamiat and employed revivalist orthodox *ulema* to deliver lectures on theology in schools, colleges and jails. When the Constituent Assembly met to frame the constitution for the new state, the *ulema* demanded a greater political role; in fact, they demanded that under the Islamic Constitution all effective power should be in their own hands. Fundamentalists engaged in a lengthy debate with the secular leaders but it soon became evident that the issue could not easily be resolved. The westernised leaders made an alliance with the *pirs* but treated the *ulema* with contempt and tried to define and restrict their role in state and society.

The *ulema*'s frustration over the constitutional issues found its way into the bloody anti-Ahmadi agitation that resulted in the promulgation of martial law in Lahore in 1953. This agitation was unique in so far as it united all shades of religious opinion including the *pirs* against the Ahmadis. The movement was crushed with the brutal use of force. Many people were killed and the martial law tribunals passed death sentences on two leading *ulema* and awarded lengthy prison sentences to many others. Those *ulema* who had entered the political arena in the new state were condemned and forced to retreat while the influence of *pirs* remained unchanged (see Binder, 1963).

In 1955, the provinces of West Pakistan were merged into one unit and the new West Pakistan Assembly formed. The *pirs* were back in the political arena with the landlords and tribal leaders. The new house of 310 members was composed of 200 landlords, 30 tribal leaders, 30 refugee leaders (Maniruzzaman, 1966, p. 86), and 16 *pirs* (Mayer, 1967, p. 166). Once the *ulema* were removed from politics, the *pirs* cooperated fully with the ruling bureaucratic oligarchy who wanted to govern the country in colonial style, patronising influential men without ever allowing them to become powerful enough to challenge the government. The result was that governments formed by the landlords and *pirs* remained adjuncts of the military and the bureaucrats.

The promulgation of martial law in 1958 by General Ayub Khan did nothing to change this situation. Ayub's image was one of a great secular modernising leader (see Huntington, 1968, p. 251) and he tried, albeit unsuccessfully, to remove the prefix 'Islamic' from the Republic of Pakistan. He also introduced reforms in other walks of life, including those for the administration of saints' shrines. For this purpose a West Pakistan Auqaf Department was created and entrusted with managing the *waqf* (endowed) properties. By taking over the management of shrines, it was claimed, the department would loosen the hold of *pirs* and *sajjada nashins* over 'the unwary masses' (Government of West Pakistan, 1960, p. 162).

The department started functioning in 1960 and after one year had received 4000 declarations of endowed property, although it accepted responsibility for only 800 of these. In fact, these reforms were a further step in strengthening the hold of shrines and *pirs*. Ayub made an alliance with the most conservative and powerful section of the religious establishment to reinforce his somewhat secular and arbitrary rule.

The *sajjada nashin* are large landlords, and their personal land holdings are immense when compared to the endowments of the shrines. At the turn of the century, the descendants of the great sufi Baba Fareed of Pakpattan owned 43 000 acres of land, those of Shah Jiwana Bukhari owned 10 000 acres, those of Jahanian Shah 7000 acres (Talbot, 1982, p. 13), and those of Taunsa Shareef 12 500 acres. The *pirs* of Sindh were among the largest landlords of the country. The Auqaf accepted responsibility for administering a limited number of the largest shrines, carrying out 'highly visible repairs and improvements' at them (Ewing, 1983, p. 262). Contrary to the government's expectations, this enhanced the *pirs*' prestige, because the followers were convinced that the government had at last recognised their importance. The economic and political power of the *pirs* were unaffected by the activities of the department. The *mureeds* are tied to the *pir* and pay their tributes directly to him and not to the shrine. At the shrines, the department appointed staff to organise the 'traditional' rituals and practices like the *nazar, niaz* (ritual offerings) and special ceremonies performed on the eleventh night of every lunar month, practices which were condemned by the *ulema* and considered 'exploitative' by the government.

The department's activities at the shrines popularised these practices instead of educating the masses against the 'exploitation' which they were thought to represent. The Auqaf department took control of mosques and trained and appointed *imams* (prayer leaders) and other staff. The government thought that by becoming a state employee the *mullah* would be less militant towards them. But this policy had no impact, since Auqaf controlled less than half of 1 per cent of the mosques in the country. The department also published a small number of books on Islam and biographies of saints, but most of these were too scholarly and beyond the comprehension of ordinary people (see, for example, Chishti, 1976).

Ayub Khan soon came into conflict with the *ulema*, first over the Muslim Family Laws Ordinance in 1961 and then over his attempts to secularise the constitution in 1962. Other fundamentalists like the Jamaat-e-Islami rallied to the opposition and Ayub, forced to seek popular support, turned to the *pirs* for help. In this he was successful, and he managed to forge alliances with some of Pakistan's greatest *pirs* whose followers numbered many thousands (Sayeed, 1966, p. 411).

Interesting evidence of the political power of *pirs* is provided in the presidential elections of 1964. President Ayub Khan was opposed by Miss Fatimah Jinnah as a candidate of the Combined Opposition Parties (COP). Ayub relied heavily on *pirs* for support in the election, particularly on the Pir of Dewal Sharif who became head of the *Jamiat-e-Mashaikh*, the party of the *sajjada nashin pirs*. *Pirs* in Pakistan have two political parties. One is the Jamiat-e-Ulema-e-Pakistan, established by the refugee *pirs* from India. It claims allegiance mainly from Urdu-speaking refugees from United Provinces. This party was small, insignificant and soon became moribund as most of the Punjabi, Sindhi, and Pathan *pirs* did not accept its membership. The other is the Jamiat-e-Mashaikh, led by Ayub's close ally, the Pir of Dewal Sharif, and which most of the *pirs* joined because of the President's need for support. The Jamiat-e-Mashaikh claimed 20 000 of the total 80 000 members of the electoral college as its members in 1964. This meant that Ayub Khan already had a solid 25 per cent of the votes. The Pir of Dewal Sharif further claimed that 'in the course of meditation, the Almighty had favoured him with a communication which indicated divine displeasure with the Combined Opposition Parties' (Feldman, 1972, p. 73). This *pir* used all his spiritual powers to intimidate voters who still supported candidates of the COP, and only one prominent *sajjada nashin pir*, Khawaja Nizamuddin of Taunsa, dared to support Miss Jinnah (Mayer, 1967, p. 166). Another *pir* even suggested that to perpetuate his power Ayub should declare himself a monarch (see Meer, 1985). *Pirs* thus played a major part in Ayub Khan's re-election as President in 1964, despite his claims to be a modernising and secular leader.

Capitalist development in industry, and since the late 1950s in agriculture, has increased the class contradictions in Pakistani society. In particular, the advocacy of 'functional inequality' (Maddison, 1971) as the basis of economic growth created support for revolutionary ideology and a desire for fundamental structural change. It is important to note here that the Pakistan People's Party (PPP), which emerged as a revolutionary party, was a conglomerate of conservative elements and left-wing groups headed by a staunch feudal-type landlord, Zulfiqar Ali Bhutto. Its leadership consisted of large landlords, *pirs*, *mullahs*, as well as many liberalist secularists and revolutionary socialists. This particular combination was a clear indication that landlords and *pirs* would effectively inhibit any real revolutionary change in the country, despite the party's rhetoric. The party adopted what it called 'Islamic Socialism' as its slogan to mobilise mass support. This notion was widely denounced by the *ulema*, who declared that anyone believing in socialism was an infidel (Mortimer, 1982, p. 213).

Despite this opposition, PPP won the elections and came to power after the traumatic events of 1971. Bhutto faced great opposition from the fundamentalist Jamaat-e-Islami and later from the Jamiat-ul-Ulema-e-Islam. Like Ayub, he sought an alliance with the *pirs*, vigorously exploiting the popular beliefs in saints and showing great reverence for them. His favourite slogan was *Dama Dam Must Qalandar* (Qalandar will take care, do not despair). The National Institute of Folk Heritage was created by the government to popularise mystical poetry in different local languages. Recordings of mystical poetry in all the regional languages flooded the market. This was welcomed by everyone, by regional and parochial intellectuals, as well as by the ordinary followers of *pirs*. While talking about radical reform, Bhutto's government officially patronised the most traditional rituals and practices of saint worship: ministers inaugurated important *urs* ceremonies and presided over the washing of the tomb and the placing of decorative covers on it. Bhutto ordered two golden gates from Iran for the shrines of Data Ganj Bakhsh in Lahore and Shahbaz Qalandar of Sehwan in Sindh (Syed, 1984, p. 148). During this time publications of the Auqaf highlighted the egalitarian aspect of sufi teachings and described sufi concern with the uplift of the down trodden masses. It is no wonder that after his execution Bhutto became a saint. A mausoleum was built for him which party activists thought would be used for political mobilisation. In rural Sindh, Bhutto is now known as the *Shaheed Baba* (martyred saint) or 'Chairman Badshah Shaheed' (Martyred Chairman/king) (Richter, 1981, p. 152) and is thought to be a great saint like Shah Lateef and Shahbaz Qalandar. Sindhi villagers venerate his tomb and make vows in his name.

The 1977 movement which toppled the Bhutto regime and replaced it with martial law was initiated in the name of *Nizam-i-Mustafa* (the 'rule of Muhammad'). This became the slogan for the party of *pirs*, the Jamiat-e-Ulema-e-Pakistan, who opposed the fundamentalist demand for an Islamic state. It is the contemporary tradition of *pirs* to portray the Prophet as the highest figure, in many respects equal to God. The Prophet is the patron of saints and has an intimate relationship with God. The Prophet is the perfect example and so is his system, though none of the *pirs* has ever tried to explain how this system can be fitted to modern times. According to the President of the Jamiat-e-Ulema-e-Pakistan in the 1950s, because the Prophet is the perfect example and the Qur'an the complete book of law, there is no need for the legislature in the Islamic state (Government of the Punjab, 1954, p. 102). Since the *pir* is semi-literate and his followers illiterate, they are unable to comprehend the jurist's interpretation of Islamic political theory; as a result, they invented a convenient and popular slogan.

The military government of Zia-ul-Haq, after abandoning its promise to hold elections in 1977, made strong appeals in the name of Islam. In 1978, it appointed civilian ministers from the Pakistan National Alliance parties, two of which, the Jamaat-e-Islami and the Jamiat-ul-Ulema-e-Islam, clearly represented the Deobandi point of view. This

> became a cause of resentment for the Barelvi religion, which is the faith of the overwhelming majority. One of the minor government functionaries in Karachi issued instructions to officially-administered mosques for them to make sure that Barelvi practices were excluded from the prayers. (Asia 1979 Yearbook, 1979, p. 269)

After a strong protest from the Barelvi group these orders were promptly withdrawn and the government introduced some non-sectarian Islamic reforms. The radio was ordered to broadcast the Muslim call to prayer five times a day. All government offices were ordered to open official correspondence with the *Bismillah* (Islamic prayer for beginning anything). Female television announcers were required to cover their heads. Restrictions were imposed on hotels and cinemas which now had to remain closed during fasting in the month of Ramazan and punishments were prescribed for eating, drinking and smoking publicly during fasting hours. Some of the Islamic penalties and the introduction of Islamic taxes created hostility among different sects. In search of popular symbols and support to calm this opposition, the government patronised Barelvi practices in a different manner. Instead of encouraging popular saint worship, it patronised processions of *Milad-ul-Nabi* – a Barelvi practice in all towns and cities to celebrate the Prophet's birthday. Even the fundamentalist Jamaat-e-Islami appealed to its followers to join these processions and Zia-ul-Haq chose this day to make all important policy statements and decisions concerning Islamisation. In the absence of popular support, the military government vigorously exploited its Islamisation programme to win the support of the '*mullah* and *pir*-ridden' masses.

In 1980, a traffic police sergeant of Multan claimed that he had acquired spiritual power to cure the sick. In the midst of Zia-ul-Haq's Islamisation programme, the vernacular press gave wide publicity to his claims and he became famous as *Pir Sipahi* (policeman *pir*) almost overnight. A large number of followers and patients flocked to him in every city, bringing with them bottles of water. As *Pir Sipahi* blew into the microphone, the water was transformed into a remedy for almost all types of ailments. In every big city his arrival caused huge traffic jams on the roads adjacent to the site of his performance. The government took no action to restrict these activities until *Pir Sipahi* announced that someone else had usurped his mystical powers. After several months, the public also lost enthusiasm and the police authorities ordered *Pir Sipahi* to return to duty.

The government of Zia-ul-Haq instituted many pieces of Islamic legislation, such as the creation of Shari'a (Islamic law) courts and appointments of Shari'a benches in the high courts. Pir Karam Shah of Bhaira, a popular *pir* of Punjab, was appointed judge of the Shari'a court. In face of opposition from the Movement for Restoration of Democracy (MRD), Zia-ul-Haq made an alliance with the Muslim League of Pir Pagaro.[3] Pir Pagaro is probably the most influential *pir* in Pakistan. In the non-party elections of 1985, which the MRD boycotted, the religious elements secured the largest number of seats in the national and provincial assemblies and in the senate. The election boycott of MRD failed, as there were 4917 candidates for the 700 seats of the national and provincial assemblies (Rizvi, 1986, p. 248). Since the leftists had no candidates of their own party, they supported the *pirs* and the Muslim League candidates against their arch rival Jamaat-e-Islami. For example, in one national assembly constituency, NA 124, Jamaat-e-Islami's candidate was elected against the *pir* in the 1970 elections. In the same constituency in 1985, however, the *pir* secured victory over the Jamaat-e-Islami candidate with a majority of 35 536 votes.[4] Because the opponents of Jamaat-e-Islami had boycotted the elections, their supporters vigorously campaigned in favour of a semi-literate *pir* against the lawyer candidate of the Jamaat-e-Islami. Probably the same thing happened in many other constituencies. As Rizvi notes, the absence of political parties from the elections and the restrictions on political mobilisation 'enabled the feudal and tribal élite to emerge triumphant in the polls' (ibid., p. 249). In 1985, the new civilian government was formed by the Muslim League of Pir Pagaro with Muhammad Khan Junejo, a follower of the *pir*, as Prime Minister. Support for Zia-ul-Haq also came from the same class, as the 'Pakistan Muslim League tends to be a party of "*Pirs*, *Makhdums*, and landlords"' (Richter, 1981, p. 152).

In her analysis of the politics of sufism, Ewing largely refers to newspaper articles, reports about the *urs* ceremonies, and publications of the Auqaf department to claim that successive Pakistani governments have tried to redefine the saints and shrines in accordance with their ideology and goals. The policy towards saints initiated by Ayub Khan and followed by his successors to the present day 'used the shrines directly as a vehicle for modernisation' (Ewing, 1983, p. 252). However, it is difficult to understand the concept of modernisation as employed by Ewing, since she reports neither changes in the rituals at the shrines nor in the practice of *pirs* and their followers. Yet she claims that this 'modernisation' indicates that there was a 'direct assault on the traditional meaning of *pir*' (ibid., p. 260). This strange conclusion is supported only by English language publications on shrines and *urs*, publications which have a doubtful impact on the '*piri-mureedi* industry' (Darling, 1929). The English language press in Pakistan has a very limited circulation when compared to the vernacular press with its wide circulation in all regions of the country.

Increased literacy rates and the development of education are considered major ingredients of modernisation (Dube, 1971) and it could be argued that these would reduce the influence of *pirs*. Even a keen observer of the rural scene like Darling has recorded some minor changes in this respect as early as 1929, although his diary is replete with instances of government officials involved in *piri-mureedi* practices (Darling, 1929). He also mentions university graduate *pirs* and university graduate *mureeds* who needed charms for their success. Similarly, O'Brien mentions government officials who insisted on the occult powers of *pirs* and their charms (O'Brien, 1911).

Waardenburg (1978, p. 318) argues that belief in *pirs*, shrines and the performance of rituals associated with them have declined 'with more schooling and greater literacy, with a more rationalised way of life, and with more penetration of western ideas'. But this assertion is not supported by evidence. My argument here remains that education and increased literacy have further strengthened the belief in *pirs*, and in the practices of saint worship. We would contend that the contrary observations mentioned have been too hasty, and that neither education nor the institution of Auqaf have brought about any significant change in this respect. In fact, there is convincing evidence to suggest that education and the Auqaf have perpetuated existing beliefs and practices. An examination of the three major national Urdu daily newspapers with the largest circulation in 1983, the daily Jang, Mashriq, and the Nawa-i-Waqt, enables us to assess the impact of the press on people's attitudes. Content analysis of the three dailies reveals four regular weekly features: first, hagiographical stories of the saints, life histories and accomplishments of the more recent *pirs*; second, a 'problem page' in which *pirs* suggest spiritual remedies for such problems as disease, unemployment, and improving physical attractiveness; third, a column on the occult sciences, including fortune telling for individuals; and finally, to balance the requirements of the revivalist orthodox section, an *alim* replies to individual queries according to the Shari'a (Islamic law).

The same four features are present in the most widely circulated Urdu weekly magazines like the *Akhbar-i-Jahan*. Apart from these regular weekly features, the Urdu newspapers and magazines publish special articles on the death anniversaries of the prominent saints. All these articles aim to convince the reader that the saint in question was one of the great miracle workers and that his shrine today is the only place for fulfilling their desires.

If we look at the periodicals press, the evidence is even more convincing. The success of the *Sab Rang Digest*, a monthly magazine published from Karachi and with the largest circulation in the country, stimulated a boom in the monthlies' market in the early 1970s (although the *Urdu Digest* and the *Sayyarah Digest* were the monthlies with largest circulation before this). Soon there were imitators like the *Sat Rang Digest, Suspense Digest, Jassosi Digest, Soorij, Pakeeza* and *Khawateen Digest* among others. The first story in the *Sab Rang Digest* is a hagiographical sketch of a saint. The story starts with the most graphic account of the saint's miracles, and wherever possible all historical events of that period are explained as miracles of the saint. The saint of the Digest is a powerful figure, a shadow of God on earth who was sent by God especially to perform certain miracles on His behalf. The author gives a full bibliography of the sources cited in the story in order to confirm its authenticity. The story of the saint is followed by a serialised story based on Hindu mythology which reinforces the belief in superstitions, saints, spiritual power, miracles and all the paraphernalia of saint worship. It was due to the popularity of the Digest that more serious magazines like the *Urdu Digest* and the *Sayyarah Digest* also introduced stories about the saints, although in a Deobandi tradition. The *Akhbar-i-Jahan* has also followed the example of *Sab Rang Digest* and it regularly features parables based on Hindu mythology.

If we look at books published in Pakistan, the increasing popularity of saints is also apparent. One book, widely advertised and still in print in Urdu, Persian and many regional languages, is entitled *Maut*

ka Manzar ('Scene of Death') (Islam, 1975). The book is a collection
of parables from hagiographical works and provides an excellent
means of perpetuating superstitious values and belief in the power of
pirs. Even thirteen years after its first publication, an observer in
1985 described it as 'the most popular book in Pakistan' (Hoodbhoy,
1985, p. 190). The book's popularity prompted the author to write
several companion volumes like *Janat ka Manzar* ('Scene of Paradise'), *Doozakh ka Manzar* ('Scene of Hell'), *Hussun Parastoon kay
Injam ka Manzar* ('Scene from the Judgement of the Amorous') and
Marney kay Baad kia ho ga ('What Will Happen After Death')
among several others. In the late 1970s, the Urdu book publishing
industry in Pakistan expanded to meet the growing demand for all
types of books on mysticism, from the highly philosophical and
religious to the most hagiographical ones. To satisfy demand a large
number of Urdu publishers reprinted centuries-old volumes on the
subject and different publishers even published translations of the
same popular titles.

Some publishers direct their efforts specifically towards the rural
market, where one of the most popular publications is called *jantary*
(a pocket calendar book). Almost every literate villager in Pakistan
owns a *jantary* which contains three calendars in adjacent columns:
the Islamic, Christian and Hindu. The first gives the dates of religious
festivals and important *urs*, the second acts as a reminder of the dates
of court hearings, and the third is the traditional calendar of the
cultivators. The *jantary* also contains many formulas for charms and
amulets, as well as prayer formulas devised by saints. These are
interspersed with advertisements for books of charms, prayers and
new hagiographies of saints. One booklet, found in many literate
rural households, even claims that all who read it with *faith* will have
their desires fulfilled. Another booklet, called *Duaai Noor* ('Prayer
of Light'), claims that if you cannot read it, it will be sufficient to hold
it in your hand while praying to have your prayers answered. Surprisingly, in the summer of 1985, a Pakistani consultant psychiatrist
in England brought a hundred copies of this booklet for free distribution in the Friday prayers at the University of Kent.

Pirs may also be found in the fundamentalist political parties like
the Jamaat-e-Islami; Pir Muhammad Ashraf of Sahiwal is a member
of the Jamaat's high command. Maulana Abdullah Darkhawsti,
President of the Jamiat-ul-Ulema-e-Islam, was a prominent *pir*. In
1970, after addressing political meetings, he used to accept the *baiat*
(oath of allegiance to a *pir*) from many of his followers. Both these

religio–political leaders were Deobandis and distanced themselves from the Barelvi *pirs*. Their kind of *pirship* requires detailed discussion for which there is no space here. It is often assumed that only villagers and ignorant and illiterate rustics are followers of *pirs*, but this is incorrect. Ewing reports that Pir Dewal Sharif acquired a large following in the army and in the higher civil service (see Ewing, 1983, p. 265). Others in the Western-educated élite, like scientists and engineers, also adhere to the superstitious beliefs associated with *pirs*, as the following quotation illustrates: 'In a conference on Islamic sciences in 1983, an employee of the Atomic Energy Commission read out a paper arguing that, since *djinns* are spirits created by God out of fire, they could be tapped as a source of energy' (Duncan, 1987, p. 112). From this we can assume that the commission will not only solve the energy problems of Pakistan but will also succeed in producing the much publicised Islamic Bomb.

The *pirs* and the beliefs associated with them are the cause of a large number of social, economic, political and moral problems of varying magnitude in Pakistani society. Newspapers frequently report cases of fraud, deception and immorality caused by these beliefs and institutions. In 1983, the teenage daughter of a Sayyid in Punjab told her father of her dream about the *Imam*. The father, a retired junior commissioned officer of the Pakistan Air Force, was impressed and the whole family considered their daughter a great saint. In one of her frequent prophetic dreams she crosses the Arabian Sea in a box to perform pilgrimage at Karbala in Iraq. She told her father that all the family should go on pilgrimage in this manner. All the family, friends and relatives, impressed by the holiness of the young lady, decided to follow her advice and on a beach outside Karachi locked themselves into boxes which were then pushed into the open sea. Most of them perished and more than thirty bodies were recovered from the sea. The survivors were sent by air by the government to perform the pilgrimage (for further detail of this incident see Chapter 11 by Ahmed in this volume).

VIII CONCLUSION

Pakistan was demanded in the name of Islam by the secular and westernised landlords and professionals. They successfully manipulated religious sentiments to the extent that religious leadership was compelled to support their demand. Religious leadership consisted of two antagonistic classes sharply contrasted in their leadership, scholarship, outlook, establishment and popular support. The *pirs* were large landlords, often semi-literate purveyors of spiritual blessings, who claimed the allegiance of a large number of followers. Despite being religious leaders, they did not favour the religious demands put forward by the *ulema*. The *ulema* pressed hard for an Islamic constitution, while the *pirs* remained unconcerned. The government of President Ayub Khan counterbalanced the *ulema*'s opposition to its secular policies with the support of *pirs*. Since Islam is the major issue in the politics of Pakistan and the *ulema* are its interpreters, they clash with every government on many issues. In this situation all governments have sought an alliance with the *pirs* because of the large numbers of followers they can mobilise. In turn, because of their vested interests and to protect their own power and privileges, *pirs* have always supported the government in office irrespective of its policies.

Pakistani society is permeated with beliefs in *pirs*, shrines, miracles and occult powers. *Pirs* of different levels of influence are present in every corner of the country to the extent that a sample of 100 people in Multan reported allegiance to fifty-six different *pirs* (Mayer, 1967, p. 164). Not only the rustic, but highly sophisticated, highly educated, westernised and secular élite – in short all groups and classes – have their *pirs*. This is due to the persistent indoctrination in these beliefs through the mass media. Every government in search of a religious constituency further strengthens the cultural milieu which promotes the traditional institutions of *pirs* and shrines. Western scholars tend to view Pakistani governments on the basis of their secular pronouncements and the modernist stance they generally adopt for the consumption of the outside world. The institution-building under Ayub Khan, which received such high praise from Huntington, was effectively used in the most obscurantist manner as we have seen. The Bhutto regime followed in the footsteps of Ayub Khan trying to create support in the countryside and to counterbalance the opposition of the *ulema*. The government of Zia-ul-Haq in 1978, with a preponderance of the Deobandi group, encroached on very minor practices in the Barelvi mosques but the policy was soon reversed due to fear of widespread opposition. Soon the same time-tested policies of Bhutto and Ayub Khan came back into vogue. There has been a wide gap between the policy and rhetoric and the real performance of any government in Pakistan. Any kind of modernisation would demand change in traditional beliefs, practices and institutions. But in Pakistan this cannot happen, since the government manipulates these beliefs and institutions to its own advantage. Contrary to expectations, the high level of educational development and increased literacy have even strengthened these beliefs as our analysis of the publishing industry indicates. Instead of modernisation, one Pakistani scholar has even suggested that *pirs* should be licensed and taxed by the government (Chaudry, 1980, p. 166).

Notes

* I express my sincere thanks to Professor Paul Stirling, Dr J. S. Eades, Dr M. D. Fischer and Dr Hastings Donnan for their comments and criticism.
1. *Mullah* is a Persian word meaning 'a school master, doctor, learned man, judge, priest' (Steingass, 1947). Recently in Pakistan it has been used in a derogatory sense for traditional *ulema* and *imams* (prayer leaders) of the mosques.
2. According to the Household Income and Expenditure Survey 1971–2, 52.4 per cent of the rural households earned less than Rs 200 per month and 38 per cent earned between Rs 200 and 399 (Government of Pakistan, 1980, p. 7). At that time, the minimum fee charged by a mediocre specialist physician was Rs 50.
3. The All-India Muslim League was divided into two parties. One with the same name remained in India, while the leaders of the original party formed the government in Pakistan in 1947 and established the All-Pakistan Muslim League in 1948. A faction from the League separated in 1950 and formed the Jinnah Muslim League. Another split in 1952 established the Jinnah Awami Muslim League. In 1962, after the civilianisation of the military government of Ayub Khan his party became known as the Convention Muslim League, and the opposing faction as the Council Muslim League (Ahmad, 1970, pp. 125–36, 250–8). Since the late 1970s, one of the two most active factions of the League is headed by the Pir of Pagaro and is named after him.
4. These figures were obtained by the author from the office of the returning officer in April 1985.

References

Ahmad, A. (1964), *Studies in Islamic Culture in the Indian Environment* (Oxford: Clarendon Press).

Ahmad, M. (1970), *Government and Politics in Pakistan* (Karachi: Space Publishers).

Ahmad, S. (1971), 'Islam and Pakistani Peasant', *Contributions to Asian Studies*, 2, pp. 93–104.

Ali, M. M. H. (1975), *Observations on the Mussulmans of India* (Delhi: Deep Publications).

Asia 1979 Yearbook (1979), *Asia 1979 Yearbook* (Far Eastern Economic Review).

Binder, L. (1963), *Religion and Politics in Pakistan* (Berkeley: University of California Press).

Bolitho, H. (1954), *Jinnah: Creator of Pakistan* (Karachi: Oxford University Press).

Chaudry, M. I. (1980), *Pakistani Society: A Sociological Perspective* (Lahore: Aziz Publishers).

Chishti, Y. S. (1976), *Tareekhe Tassawuf – Hindi, Unani, Islami* (Lahore: Ulema Academy Auqaf Department).

Darling, M. L. (1929), *Rusticus Loquitur or the Old Light and the New in the Punjab Village* (London: Oxford University Press).

Dube, S. C. (1971), 'Modernization and Education', in A. R. Desai (ed.), *Essays on Modernization of Underdeveloped Societies* (Bombay: Thacker), pp. 505–10.

Duncan, E. (1987), 'Survey of Pakistan', *The Economist*, January 17, pp. 1–26.

Ewing, K. (1983), 'The Politics of Sufism: Redefining the Saints of Pakistan', *Journal of Asian Studies*, 42, pp. 251–68.

Ewing, K. (1984), 'The Sufi as Saint, Curer, and Exorcist in Modern Pakistan', *Contributions to Asian Studies*, 18, pp. 106–14.

Feldman, H. (1972), *From Crisis to Crisis: Pakistan, 1962–1969* (London: Oxford University Press).

Gardezi, H. N. (1973), 'Neocolonial Alliances and the Crisis of Pakistan', in K. Gough and H. P. Sharma (eds) *Imperialism and Revolution in South Asia* (London and New York: Monthly Review Press), pp. 130–44.

Geertz, C. (1968), *Islam Observed: Religious Development in Morocco and Indonesia* (New Haven: Yale University Press).

Gellner, E. A. (1982), *Muslim Society* (Cambridge: Cambridge University Press).

Gilmartin, D. (1979), 'Religious Leadership and the Pakistan Movement in the Punjab', *Modern Asian Studies*, 13, pp. 485–517.

Gilsenan, M. (1973), *Saint and Sufi in Modern Egypt: An Essay in the Sociology of Religion*. Oxford Monographs on Social Anthropology (Oxford: Clarendon Press).

Government of Pakistan (1972), *25 years of Pakistan in Statistics*. (Karachi: Central Statistical Office, Economic Affairs Division).

Government of Pakistan (1980), *Statistical Profile of Females of Pakistan* (Islamabad: Planning and Development Division).

Government of Pakistan (1984), *Pakistan Basic Facts, 1983–84* (Islamabad: Finance Division, Economic Advisor's Wing).

Government of Pakistan (1985), *Hand Book of Population Census Data* (Islamabad: Population Census Organisation).

Government of Pakistan (1987), *Pakistan Economic Survey, 1986–87* (Islamabad: Economic Advisor's Wing, Finance Division).

Government of West Pakistan (1960), *West Pakistan Yearbook 1960* (Lahore: Public Relations Department).

Government of the Punjab (1954), *Report of the Court of Inquiry Constituted under the Punjab Act II of 1954 to Enquire into the Punjab Disturbances of 1953* (Lahore: Punjab Government Press).

Haq, M. A. (1972), *The Faith Movement of Mawlana Muhammad Ilyas* (London: George Allen & Unwin).

Hoodbhoy, P. A. (1985), 'Ideological Problems for Science in Pakistan', in M. A. Khan (ed.) *Islam, Politics and the State: The Pakistan Experience* (London: Zed Books).

Huntington, S. P. (1968), *Political Order in Changing Societies* (New Haven: Yale University Press).

Islam, K. M. (1975), *Maut ka Manzar* (Lahore: Idarae Deeniat).

Kagaya, K. (1966), 'Islam as a Modern Social Force'. *The Developing Economies*, 4, pp. 70–89.

Keddie, N. R. (1972), 'Introduction', in N. R. Keddie (ed) *Scholars, Saints and Sufis* (Berkeley: University of California Press), pp. 1–14.

Maddison, A. (1971), *Class Structure and Economic Growth: India and Pakistan Since the Moghuls* (London: George Allen & Unwin).

Maniruzzaman, T. (1966), 'Group Interests in Pakistan's Politics', *Pacific Affairs*, 39, pp. 83–9.

Maududi, S. A. A. (1960), *The Islamic Law and Constitution*, translated into English and edited by Khurshid Ahmad (Lahore: Islamic Publications).

Mayer, A. C. (1967), 'Pir and Murshid: An Aspect of Religious Leadership in West Pakistan', *Middle Eastern Studies*, 3, pp. 160–9.

Meer, P. W. (1985), *Daur Jamhoor Mein Nizam-i-Badshahat ki Arzoo* (Quest for Monarchy in Republican Age), *The Daily Jang*, 17 and 18 September.

Metcalf, B. D. (1982), *Islamic Revival in British India: Deoband, 1860–1900* (Princeton: Princeton University Press).

Mortimer, E. (1982), *Faith and Power: The Politics of Islam* (London: Faber and Faber).

Muhammad, M. T. (1970), *Kashful Mahjoob* (Urdu translation) (Lahore: Islamic Publications).

Mujeeb, M. (1967), *The Indian Muslims* (London: George Allen & Unwin).

Nadwi, S. A. H. A. (1969), *Tareekh-i-Dawat wa Azeemat* (Lucknow: Majlis Tahqiqat wa Nashriatay Islam).

Nasr, S. H. (1966), *Ideals and Realities of Islam* (London: George Allen & Unwin).

O'Brien, M. A. (1911), 'The Mohammedan Saints of the Western Punjab', *Journal of the Royal Anthropological Institute of Great Britain and Ireland*, 41, pp. 509–20.

Qureshi, I. H. (1974), *Ulema in Politics* (Karachi: Ma'arif Ltd.).

Richter, W. L. (1981), 'Pakistan', in M. Ayoob (ed.), *The Politics of Islamic Reassertion* (London: Croom Helm), pp. 141–62.

Rizvi, H. (1986), *The Military and Politics in Pakistan: 1947–1986* (Lahore: Progressive Publishers).

Sayeed, K. B. (1957), 'The Jama'at-i-Islami Movement in Pakistan', *Pacific Affairs*, 30, pp. 59–68.

Sayeed, K. B. (1966), 'Islam and National Integration in Pakistan', in D. E. Smith (ed.), *South Asian Politics and Religion* (Princeton: Princeton

University Press), pp. 398–413.

Sayeed, K. B. (1967), *The Political System of Pakistan* (Boston: Houghton Mifflin).

Sayeed, K. B. (1968), *Pakistan: The Formative Phase, 1857–1948* (London: Oxford University Press).

Shahab, Q. U. (1987), *Shabab Nama* (Urdu text) (Lahore: Sang-i-Meal Publications).

Shushtery, A. M. A. (1966), *Outlines of Islamic Culture* (Lahore: Muhammad Ashraf).

Steingass, F. (1947), *A Comprehensive Persian–English Dictionary* (London: Kegan Paul).

Syed, A. (1984), *Pakistan: Islam, Politics and National Solidarity* (Lahore: Vanguard Books).

Tabatabai, S. M. H. (1975), *Shi'ite Islam* (London: George Allen & Unwin).

Talbot, I. A. (1982), 'The Growth of the Muslim League in the Punjab 1937–46', *The Journal of Commonwealth and Comparative Politics*, 20, pp. 5–24.

Talbot, I. A. (1983), 'Muslim Political Mobilization in Rural Punjab', in P. Robb (ed.), *Rural India: Land, Power and Society Under British Rule* (London: Curzon Press).

Titus, M. T. (1959), *Islam in India and Pakistan* (Madras: The Christian Literature Society).

Waardenburg, J. (1978), 'Official and Popular Religion in Islam', *Social Compass* 25, pp. 315–41.

Weekes, R. V. (1964), *Pakistan: Birth and Growth of a Muslim Nation* (Princeton: D. Van Nostrand).

Wilber, D. N. (1964), *Pakistan: Its People, its Society, its Culture* (New Haven: HRAF Press).

11 Migration, Death and Martyrdom in Rural Pakistan*

Akbar S. Ahmed

This chapter focuses on migration, its impact both on the individual and his or her society, and the social processes which may be triggered by a migrant's return home. Although several economic studies have been conducted on Pakistani migratory labour, a social anthropological or cultural perspective of this migration is, on the whole, notably missing. How do Pakistanis abroad adapt to new ideas? What do they do with them on return? Do they shift away from so-called 'traditional' culture once home again? Do they accept – or challenge – the traditional leadership, class and social structure from which they escaped? Do kinship loyalties survive or fade?

These questions raise a number of other related issues. Notions about women, status in society, sacrifice and social order may all be affected by migration. So too is the way in which people relate their daily lives to their concepts of the afterworld. The case study presented here thus also raises important issues about concepts of death, sacrifice and martyrdom among Shi'a and Sunni Muslims, a subject scarcely discussed in the anthropological literature.[1] Migration, the case shows, is only one phase which needs to be analysed as part of a migrant's total life-cycle.

In late February 1983, thirty-eight people – all Shi'a from Chakwal Tehsil in Punjab – entered the Arabian Sea at Hawkes Bay. The women and children in the group, about half the number, had been placed in six large trunks. The leader of the group, Sayyid Willayat Hussain Shah, pointing his religious banner at the waves, led the procession. Willayat Shah believed that a path would open in the sea which would lead him to Basra, from where the party would proceed to Karbala, the holy city in Iraq. A few hours later almost half the party had lost their lives and the survivors emerged in varying stages of exhaustion and consciousness.

Pakistan was astonished at the incident. Religious leaders, intellectuals and newspapers discussed the event extensively.[2] The discussions

247

revealed almost as much about those participating in them as they did about the incident. Some intellectuals saw the episode as evidence of 'insanity' (Salahuddin, 1983) and the leaders of the group were described as 'mentally unbalanced individuals with twisted and deviant personalities, the source of death and destruction' (Irfani, 1983). Sunnis dismissed the matter as yet another Shi'a deviation from orthodox Islam. The Shi'as, on the other hand, pointed to the event as a confirmation of their faith (Jaffery, 1983; Yusufzai, 1983). Only the Shi'as, they argued, were capable of such extreme devotion, of such a sacrifice. It was, undoubtedly, a case rooted in Shi'a mythology, which preconditioned the community to respond to, and enact, the drama.

I CHAKWAL TEHSIL

Willayat Shah's family lived in a small village, Rehna Sayyadan, about ten miles from Chakwal Tehsil in Jhelum District. The town of Jhelum, on the Grand Trunk Road, is about seventy miles from Chakwal Tehsil. A population of about 250 000 live in the Tehsil. Chakwal and Jhelum are areas of rain-fed agriculture, unlike the canal colonies of Lyallpur (now Faisalabad) and Sahiwal, with their rich irrigated lands. The population of the village itself is about 2000 mainly consisting of Sayyids, the upper social group, and Arain, the lower.[3] The latter are challenging the authority of the former through new channels of employment, hard work and frugality (Ahmed, 1984b). The village is somewhat isolated from the rest of Pakistan. Electricity has only recently arrived and the road to Chakwal is not yet metalled. This is one of the hottest areas in the country. Winters are short and the rainfall (about 20 inches) is unreliable. Poor harvests have pushed people off the land to look for employment outside the Tehsil. Many have joined the armed services (Jhelum District is a rich recruiting ground for the Pakistan army) and from the 1960s the Arab states offered opportunities for employment. Willayat Shah, after his service as a junior officer in the Pakistan Air Force, left to work in Saudi Arabia. He returned to Pakistan in 1981 after a stay of four years.

Rehna Sayyadan is self-consciously religious. Its very name announces a holy lineage, that of the Sayyids, the descendants of the Holy Prophet, and means 'the abode of the Sayyids'. Many of the Shi'a actors in the drama bear names derived from members of the

Holy Prophet's family: Abbass and Hussain for men, and Fatima for women. But there is tension in the area between Shi'a and Sunni, a tension made more acute by the fact that their numbers are equally balanced. The economic subordination of the Sunni by the Shi'a reinforces the tension. Conflict between Shi'a and Sunni easily converts into conflict between landlord and tenant. This opposition also runs through the local administration. The local government councillor, for example, is Sunni but the village *lambardar* (head man) is Shi'a. Even families are divided along Shi'a–Sunni lines and where individuals have changed affiliation, relationships have been severely strained. (There are at least four known cases of Sunni affiliation closely related to the main actor in the drama, Naseem Fatima.) The tension is exacerbated by the current emphasis on Sunni forms of religion by the government of Pakistan. The Shi'as, about 20 per cent of Pakistan's 100 million people, resent this emphasis. The Jamaat-e-Islami, the major orthodox Sunni political party of Pakistan, is active in the area. In the background is the larger ideological tension between the Shi'as and Sunnis in Pakistan. From 1980 onwards this tension became severe and led to clashes between the two, especially in Karachi. Beyond the south-western borders of Pakistan, a vigorous Shi'a revivalism in Iran has unsettled neighbouring Sunni states allied to Pakistan, such as Saudi Arabia.

Willayat Shah was living in Saudi Arabia when Imam Khomeini returned to Iran at the head of his revolution in 1979. Being a devout Shi'a he would have been inspired by the message and success of the Imam, but Saudi Arabia was no place to express his rekindled Shi'a enthusiasm. He would, however, have been dreaming dreams around the themes of the revolution: sacrifice, death, change and martyrdom. His first act on returning home was to begin the construction of a mosque.

II THE HAWKES BAY CASE

On 18 February 1981, Willayat Shah had been engrossed in supervising the construction of the mosque. Late that evening Naseem Fatima, his eldest child, entered his bedroom and announced she had been visited by a revelation – *basharat*. She had heard the voice of a lady speaking to her through the walls of the house. The apprehensive father suggested she identify the voice. For the first few days the voice was identified as that of Bibi Roqayya, the stepsister of Imam

Hussain, the grandson of the Holy Prophet, buried in Karbala. Some handprints next appeared on the wall of Willayat Shah's bedroom. They were made with henna mixed with clay. A handprint has highly emotive significance among the Shi'a. It is symbolic of the five holiest people in Islam: the Holy Prophet, his daughter, Hazrat Fatima, his son-in-law, Hazrat Ali, and his grandsons, Hazrat Hassan and Hazrat Imam Hussain. The news of the handprints spread rapidly in the area. The impact on the village was electric. One informant described it as follows:

> [F]or the next fifteen days or so the usual business of life came to a halt. People gave up their work, women stopped even cooking meals. Everyone gathered in the house of Willayat Hussain to see the print, to touch it, to pray and to participate in the mourning (*azadari*) which was constantly going on. (Pervez, 1983, p. 8)

The *azadari*, a recitation of devotional hymns and poems in honour of, in particular, Hazrat Hussain, was a direct consequence of the handprints. It created a highly charged and contagious atmosphere among the participants.

Sunnis, however, were cynical about the whole affair. They would remain adamant opponents of Naseem's miracles (*maujza*). Opinion was divided among the Shi'a. Established families such as the Sayyids scoffed at Naseem and her miracles and, at first, both Willayat Shah and his daughter had their doubts. As if to dispel these doubts Imam Mahdi, or Imam-e-Ghaib, the twelfth Imam, himself appeared in the dreams of Naseem. Earlier, Bibi Roqayya had announced that the Imam rather than she would communicate with Naseem. The Imam wore white clothes and was of pleasing appearance (Ansari, 1983, p. 6). All doubts in her mind were now dispelled and he addressed her as *Bibi Pak* – pure lady.

The Imam, with whom she now communicated directly, began to deliver explicit orders (*amar*). One commanded the expulsion of the carpenter who was working for Willayat in his house (ibid., p. 7) and who had overcharged him by Rs 1000, in connivance with the contractor. He was ordered never to work at a Sayyid's house again or both would be losers in the transaction. To compensate Willayat, the Imam placed Rs 500 in a copy of the Holy Qur'an and ordered the carpenter to pay the remaining 500. The orders increased in frequency and soon included matters of property and marriage. The family, at least, no longer doubted the miracles and obeyed the divine orders without question. During the revelations Naseem would demand complete privacy in her room. Her condition would change. She would quiver and tremble. Noises would sound in her head beforehand and the trauma of the revelations often caused her to faint afterwards. The orders would come to her on the days the Imams died or were made martyrs. 'The Imam', according to her father, 'had captured her mind and heart' (ibid., p. 8).

Local Shi'a religious leaders and lecturers (*zakirs*) acknowledged Naseem and visited her regularly. Of the three most regular visitors one, Sakhawat Hussain Jaffery, was particularly favoured. Naseem claimed that she had been especially ordered by the Imam to single him out. They were often alone for long periods. Naseem began to organise *azadari* regularly. These meetings were charged with emotion and created devout ecstasy in the participants. They were held next to the local primary school; so many people attended, with such noisy devotion, that the school had to close down. Naseem now completely dominated the life of the village. Before moving to the next phase of the case, let us pause to examine the effect of the revelations on some of the main actors in the drama.

Naseem was a shy, pleasant-looking girl, with an innocent expression on her face, who had a history of fits. There was talk of getting her married. Although she had only studied up to class five, her teachers recall her passionate interest in religion, especially in the lives of the Imams. She had a pleasing voice when reciting *nauhas* (poems about Karbala), many of which she composed herself. After her revelations there was a perceptible change in Naseem. She began to gain weight, wear costly dresses and use perfumes. She became noticeably gregarious and confident. In a remarkable gesture of independence, especially so for a Sayyid girl in the area, she abandoned the *purdah* or veil. According to Shi'a belief, any believer may become the vehicle for divine communications. Naseem turned to the dominant person in her life, her father, upon receiving communications and he interpreted them in his own light.

Willayat Shah now reasserted himself in village affairs after an absence of years. His daughter's religious experience had begun soon after his retirement from Arabia. He had an older brother to whom, because of the traditional structure of rural society, he was subordinate. His period in Saudi Arabia had enhanced his economic, but not his social position. Because of the miracles and revelations of his daughter, however, he gained a dominant position in the social life of the area. Sardar Bibi, Naseem's mother, was influenced by her husband and daughter and identified wholly with the latter. She was said to have been a Sunni before her marriage and this created an underlying tension in the family. In an expression of loyalty to her husband, she severed relations with her parents and brothers because they disapproved of her conversion. She unhesitatingly obeyed her daughter's revelations.

Another actor in the drama was Sakhawat Jaffery, a *zakir* of Chakwal. He was not a Sayyid and his father was said to be a butcher. He had thus risen in the social order. Willayat Shah rewarded him for his loyalty with gifts – refrigerators, televisions and fans. When he needed money for a new business he was presented with about Rs 20 000, and with this sum he opened a small shop selling general goods. He was given such gifts on the specific orders of the Imam to Naseem. In turn, he was the only one of the three *zakirs* who personally testified to the authenticity of the miracles of Naseem. Naseem was regularly visited by Sakhawat Jaffery and she visited his house. In a gesture of affection, contravening social custom, Naseem named Sakhawat's male child – a few months old – Rizwan Abbass. Such names, deriving from the Holy Prophet's family, were traditionally reserved for Sayyids.

Most people were cynical about the relationship between Naseem and the *zakir*. Sakhawat's own wife, who had complete faith in Naseem, said people had spread 'dirty talk' (*gandi batey*) about Naseem and her husband (ibid., p. 4). In spite of his belief in the revelations, Sakhawat Jaffery did not join the pilgrimage to Hawkes Bay. He had recently opened his shop and explained that abrupt departure would ensure its failure. Naseem was understanding: 'this is not a trip for *zakirs*. We want to see you prosper.'

After the visions, Naseem's followers bestowed on her the title already used by the Imam, *Pak Bibi*, or pure lady. The transformation in her appearance and character was now complete. She radiated confidence. Her following spread outside the village. In particular, she developed an attachment to the people of a neighbouring village, Mureed, who were recently converted Muslims (Sheikhs) and who wholeheartedly believed in her. Most of them were *kammis*, belonging to such occupational groups as barbers and cobblers. Naseem, as a Sayyid, represented for them the house of the Prophet while her father, being relatively well off, was a potential source of financial support. Seventeen of the villagers of Mureed would follow her to Hawkes Bay.

The normal life of the village was disrupted by the affair. The

Shi'a, in particular, 'wholeheartedly accepted the phenomenon' but, not unnaturally, 'the regular routine life of the village was paralysed.' In particular, 'women stopped doing their household jobs' (Jaffery, 1983, p. 10). Some placed obstacles in Naseem's path, teasing her family members (especially children on their way to school), and dumping rubbish in front of her house. Sayyids who did not believe in her ill-treated her followers from Mureed.

Meanwhile, a series of miracles was taking place which riveted society. Blood was found on the floor of Willayat Shah's bedroom. Naseem declared this to be the blood of Hazrat Ali Asghar, the male child of Hazrat Hussain, martyred at Karbala. On another occasion visitors were locked in a room and told that angels would bear down a flag from heaven. When the door was opened, indeed, there was a flag. On one occasion four children disappeared, to appear again later. But the greatest miracle of all remained Naseem's constant communication with the Imam. Supplicants would pray in front of Naseem's room, expressing their demands in a loud voice. The Imam would be consulted not only on profound matters but also on trivial ones, such as whether a guest should be given tea or food. Naseem, who received many of her orders during fainting fits, would then convey a reply on behalf of the Imam.

There came a time, however, when Naseem's authority was disputed. Doubts arose first from the failure of certain of her predictions and, second, from a public refusal of her kin to redistribute their property according to her orders. Naseem had been making extravagant predictions regarding illness, birth and death. Some of these came true, others did not. In one particular case she predicted the death of a certain person within a specified period. He did not die. In another case, the elder brother of Willayat was asked to surrender his house for religious purposes which he refused to do. A cousin also refused, when asked, to hand over his property to Willayat. In yet another case, Naseem, perhaps compensating for a Sunni mother in a Shi'a household ordered the engagement of her cousin to a non-Shi'a to be broken; it was not. Naseem and Willayat responded to such rebellion with fierce denunciation. The rebels were branded as *murtid*, those who have renounced Islam and are, therefore, beyond the pale. Their relatives were forbidden to have any contact with them. In some cases, parents were asked not to see their children and vice versa. While taking firm measures against those who did not believe, the followers were charged with renewed activity, calculated to reinforce group cohesiveness. The frequency of religious meetings increased as did visits to shrines. Participation was limited to be-lievers.

Naseem's physical condition now began to correspond with the revelations: she lost weight and her colour became dark when she was not receiving them; she glowed with health when she was. People freely equated her physical appearance with her spiritual condition. She lost *noor* – divine luminosity – in her periods of despondency and regained it when receiving revelations. For those who believed in her it was literally a question of light and darkness. But the crisis in Naseem was reaching its peak; so was the tension in the community.

Exactly to the day, two years after the first communication began, Naseem asked her father a question on behalf of the Imam: would the believers plunge into the sea as an expression of their faith? The question was not figurative. The Imam meant it literally. The be-lievers were expected to walk into the sea from where they would be miraculously transported to Karbala in Iraq without worldly means. Naseem promised that even the 124 000 prophets recognised by Muslims would be amazed at the sacrifice (Ansari, 1983, p. 3).

Those who believed in the miracles immediately agreed to the proposition. Willayat was the first to agree: he would lead the party (ibid.). There was no debate, no vacillation. They would walk into the sea at Karachi and their faith would take them to the holy city of Karbala. Since the revelations began, Willayat had spent about half a million rupees and had disposed of almost all his property. He now quickly disposed of what remained to pay for the pilgrimage. The party consisted of forty-two people, whose ages ranged from 80 years to 4 months. Seventeen of them were from Mureed and most of the remaining were related (see Figure 11.1). Willayat, his brother and cousin, distributed all their belongings, retaining one pair of black clothes (symbolic of mourning) only. They hired trucks to take them to Karachi. With them were six large wooden and tin trunks. They also took with them the Shi'a symbols of martyrdom at Karbala: *alam* (flag), *taboot* (picture of the mourning procession), *jhola* (swing), and *shabi* (picture of the holy images).

Stopping over at shrines for prayers in Lahore and Multan, they arrived in Karachi on the third day. Karachi was in the throes of anti-government demonstrations and the police had imposed a cur-few. The tension in the city directly reflected the rivalry between Shi'as and Sunnis in Pakistan. In spite of this, the members of the party were not stopped as they made their way to Hawkes Bay. For them this was another miracle (Ansari, 1983, p. 3). At Hawkes Bay

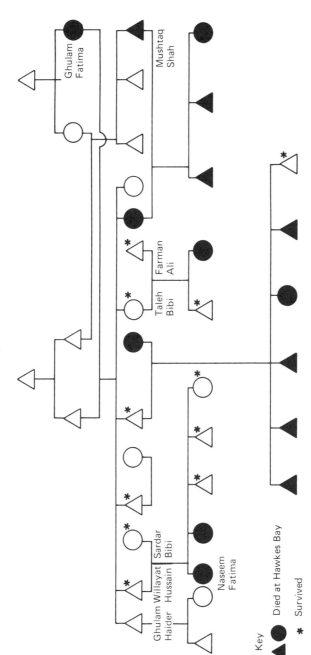

Figure 11.1   Kinship chart of Naseem Fatima

the party offered two prayers (*nafil*) and read ten *Surahs* from the Holy Qur'an including *Al-Qadr*, an early Meccan Surah, which states 'the Night of Destiny is better than a thousand months' (Surah 112, verse 3; M. Asad, 1980). The verse was well chosen: for the party, it was indeed the night of destiny.

The Imam then issued final instructions to Naseem: the women and children were to be locked in the six trunks and the virgin girls were to sit with her in one of them. Willayat was asked to hold the *taboot* along with three other men. Willayat's cousin, Mushtaq, was appointed chief (*salar*) of the party. He was ordered to lock the trunks, push them into the sea and throw away the keys. He would then walk into the water with an *alam*. At this stage four young people from Mureed, two men and two girls, became frightened. This fear, too, 'was put in their hearts by the Imam' (Ansari, 1983, p. 3). Naseem, therefore, willingly exempted them from the journey. The remaining thirty-eight entered the sea. Mothers saw children and children saw old parents descending into the dark waters. But there 'were no *ah* (cries) or *ansoo* (tears)' (ibid., p. 4). Those in five out of the six trunks died. One of the trunks was shattered by the waves and its passengers survived. Those on foot also survived; they were thrown back on to the beach by the waves. The operation which had begun in the late hours of the night was over by the early morning when police and the press reached Hawkes Bay. The survivors were in high spirits; there was neither regret nor remorse among them. Only a divine calm, a deep ecstasy.

The Karachi police, in a display of bureaucratic zeal, arrested the survivors. They were charged with attempting to leave the country without visas. The official version read: 'The incharge, FIA Passport Cell, in an application filed in the court said, it was reliably learnt that one Willayat Hussain Shah, resident of Chakwal, along with his family had attempted to proceed to a foreign country "Iraq" without valid documents through illegal route i.e. Hawkes Bay beach' (*Dawn*, March, 1983). The act came within the offence punishable under section 3/4 of the Passport Act 1974. The accused were, however, soon released.

Rich Shi'as, impressed by the devotion of the survivors, paid for their journey by air for a week to and from Karbala. In Iraq, influential Shi'as equally impressed, presented them with gifts, including rare copies of the Holy Qur'an (ibid., p. 6). Naseem's promise that they would visit Karbala without worldly means was fulfilled.

III SOCIAL CHANGE, LEADERSHIP AND KINSHIP IN CHAKWAL SOCIETY

In an attempt to find a sociological explanation of the Hawkes Bay case I shall begin by putting forward a thesis based on the so-called *Dubai chalo* (let us go to Dubai) theme in Pakistan society (Ahmed, 1984a). Briefly, the thesis suggests that Pakistani workers, returning from the Gulf with their pockets full of money, are no longer prepared to accept the status quo of the social order from which they had escaped. Those who return demand more social status and authority in society. In their own eyes they have earned the right to be respected by their long and usually hard periods abroad. But they may have little idea how exactly to go about changing society, or even whether they wish to move it 'forward' or back to older, more traditional, ways. Their new social confidence, backed by economic wealth and combined with frustration at the slow pace of change, may result in tensions and dramatic developments of which the Hawkes Bay case is an example.

Consider Willayat Shah. Belonging to the junior lineage of a Shi'a family and with a Sunni wife, he escaped to Arabia determined, it may be assumed, to make good on his return. After four hard years there, he returned with considerable wealth, but society had remained the same and there was no perceptible change in his social position. Willayat's immediate family were acutely aware of his predicament. His closest child and eldest daughter, fully grown and intelligent, and herself under pressure to get married, responded to the crisis in their lives with a series of dramatic, divine pronouncements. In her case, social crisis had triggered psychological reactions. The revelations were calculated to disturb the social equations of the village forever. Naseem dominated not only the social but also, and more importantly for the family, the religious life of the area. Willayat Shah had finally arrived. Both he and Naseem now reached out towards the better, truer world that, for Muslims, lies beyond death. Through their deaths they would gain an ascendancy which would be final and unassailable. They would triumph through the Shi'a themes of death, martyrdom and sacrifice.

For the actors in our case, society provided the stress but failed to suggest cures. We know that at least four individuals closely related to the key actor, Naseem, suffered from tension due to mixed loyalties in the Shi'a–Sunni line up; her grandmother, her mother, her uncle and her aunt's husband were rumoured to have been Sunni in the past. It was known that her grandmother's family were Sunni. By assuming the role of Shi'a medium, Naseem was socially compensating for the Sunni connections in her family. Under such complex pressures, religion is the most convenient straw to clutch. The stress thus assumes a form of illness, but the illness is both mental and physical and 'in its expression culturally patterned' (Fox, 1973, p. 180). One must look for cultural acts and symbolic forms which have local significance, including sacrifice and martyrdom. This case is certainly patterned by the religious sociology of Chakwal Tehsil.

Willayat Shah compared the sacrifice of his family to that of Karbala because 'he and his group had been assigned a duty to save the religion and the faith' (Pervez, 1983, p. 22). In an interview given to Tariq Aziz on Pakistan Television, he explained why Karachi was selected. He could have died in a pond in the village, he said. But the world would not have known of their faith. The prediction of his daughter had indeed come true. The world was amazed at the miracle of Hawkes Bay and people would talk of them as martyrs forever. Throughout the interviews he remained proud and unrepentant. His perception of those hours at Hawkes Bay is revealing. He 'insisted that he had been walking on the sea all the while like a truck driving on flat road' (Irfani, 1983). He felt no fear, no regret. Most significantly, he remained convinced that the revelations would continue, even after the death of Naseem, through a male member of the family (Ansari, 1983, p. 4). Willayat's wife, Sardar Bibi, reacted with a fervour equal to that of her husband. 'If the Imam tells us to sacrifice this baby too,' she said, pointing to an infant she was feeding during an interview, 'I'll do it' (Jaffery, 1983, p. 27).

Willayat's eldest sister, Taleh Bibi, divorced and living with her brother, lost one daughter in the incident. She herself survived because she was in the trunk that did not sink. She, too, believes the miracle will continue through a male member of their family. In relation to the Islamic concept of death, it is significant that she had mixed feelings about her own survival. Although relieved to be alive, and although she gives this as another proof of the miracle, she is none the less envious of those who died and thereby gained paradise.

Was the psychological condition of Naseem cause or effect of her religious experience? We know that her peculiarities of temperament became acceptable after the revelations. Her fits, her rapture, her ecstasy now made sense. She was touched by the divine. Even her acts defying tradition in Chakwal – such as abandoning the veil or being alone with a man – expressed her transcendent independence.

Examples of trance, spirit possession and ecstatic behaviour have been recorded among Muslim groups from the Turkmen (Basilov, 1984) to the Baluch (Bray, 1977). It is a commonplace that highly gifted but disturbed individuals adapt religious idioms to consolidate their social position or to dominate their social environment. Women have heard voices before, all over the world. Joan of Arc's voices advised her to lead her nation into fighting the English. Naseem's urged her to lead her followers into the sea. In order to understand the motives of those involved in this case, we need to combine an appreciation of religious mythology with an examination of certain sociological factors. There was more than just *jazba* (emotion, ecstasy, passion) at work in Chakwal. What did the followers think was awaiting them at Karachi?

Both local leadership and kinship helped to determine who would be on the beaches that night. The importance of a leader in an Islamic community, Shi'a or Sunni, is critical. The group is judged by its leadership (The Holy Qur'an Surah 5: 109; and Surah 7: 6–7). In different ways Willayat, Naseem and Sakhawat Jaffery played leading parts in the drama, but we look in vain for a Savonarola figure in either Willayat or Sakhawat. Leadership was by consensus. They were all agreed upon Naseem's special role in the drama. She led, as much as she was led by, her father and the *zakir*. The followers were responding not to one leader in their immediate community but to the concept of leadership in Shi'a society. They were responding to symbols centuries old and emotions perennially kept alive in Shi'a society. What is significant is the lack of ambivalence in the majority of the followers. Even the call for the ultimate sacrifice evoked an unequivocal response among most of them. Asad's interesting question, 'how does power create religion?' (T. Asad, 1983, p. 252) may therefore be turned around. The Hawkes Bay case provides an interesting example of how religion may create power.

Willayat Shah was a forceful person who mobilised public opinion behind his daughter. The *zakirs*, especially Sakhawat Jaffery, supported him and he in turn assisted Sakhawat Jaffery financially. Apart from assisting the *zakirs*, Willayat also paid sums to a variety of other people. Among the beneficiaries were members of the traditionally lower social class – mostly artisans, barbers and blacksmiths. The seventeen people from Mureed who were prepared to walk into the sea were from this class. In fact, four of this group backed out at the last minute and although thirteen entered the sea, only three of them died. The people of Mureed were recent converts to Islam and, like most converts, they were eager to exhibit their religious fervour. They looked to Willayat Shah for religious and financial support. For them he was both a Sayyid and a man of means and they were enraptured by his daughter. Through him and his daughter they found access to a higher social level.

Whatever the levelling effect of religion and the loyalties it created, the Sayyids rarely allowed their genealogy to be forgotten: the rural Punjab class structure was recognisable despite the experience at Hawkes Bay. Even in death class distinctions remained: three of the four men who held the *taboot* as they stepped into the waters were Sayyid, and the non-Sayyid was swept into the sea. Later, with a strange twist of logic, Willayat explained this by suggesting that his faith was weak (Pervez, 1983, p. 37). His faith was weak because he was not a Sayyid, while the three Sayyids who survived did so because their intentions were pure. And yet he also argued that those Sayyids who died did so because of their purity. Sayyids obviously won either way. The Sayyids, of course, provided Willayat's main support and many of them were his relatives. Of those who walked into the sea, twenty-five were related (see Figure 11.1). For these, Willayat was the elder of the family: father to one, brother to another and uncle to yet others. Of the eighteen who died, fifteen were his near relatives, while ten of his kin survived. Religious loyalty was here clearly buttressed by ties of kinship.

There was, however, structural resistance to Naseem and her revelations. The Sunni dismissed them out of hand and even the Shi'a were not unanimous in supporting her. The Sayyids, senior in the Shi'a hierarchy, ill-treated Naseem's followers, especially the poorer ones, and teased her family. The older, more established, Shi'a lineages felt threatened by the emergence of Naseem since she challenged their authority. Willayat's own brother, Ghulam Haider, suspected of having Sunni affiliation, kept away from the entire affair. The *zakir*, himself a close confidant and beneficiary of Naseem, but worldly wise, chose not to accompany the party on some pretext. And at the last moment, by the sea, four followers backed out. But, although there was opposition and resistance at every stage, thirty-eight people were prepared to sacrifice their lives on the basis of Naseem's commands and revelations. The explanation for their behaviour partly lies, I have argued, in the forces of social change, leadership and kinship in Chakwal society. But there are also other, more ideological and mythological dimensions to consider.

IV DEATH, SECTS AND WOMEN IN MUSLIM SOCIETY

There is no substantial difference between the core theological beliefs of Shi'a and Sunni. Both believe in the central and omnipotent position of Allah; both accept the supremacy of the Holy Prophet as the messenger of Allah. The Holy Qur'an is revered by both as the divine message of Allah and its arguments relating to notions of death and the afterworld are accepted by both. Discussion of death is indeed central to the Holy Qur'an which has many verses on the theme that 'every soul must taste of death'.

Death in Muslim society is seen as part of a natural preordained, immutable order, directly linked to the actions of the living and part of a continuing process in the destiny of the individual. It becomes, therefore, a means to an end, 'the beginning of a journey' (Abd al-Qadir, 1977, p. 6). Humans 'transfer' from this to the next world (the word for death in Urdu and Arabic *inteqal*, derives from the Arabic *muntaqil* to 'transfer'). The Holy Qur'an warns 'unto Him you shall be made to return' (Surah Al-Ankabut, verse 21). On hearing of someone's death, a Muslim utters the words 'from God we come, to God we shall go'. For Muslims there is no escaping the consequences of death (Muslim, 1981).

In Islam – both Shi'a and Sunni – life and death are conceptualised as binary opposites. *Al-akhira*, the end, is the moment of truth, determining the future of a person. The individual is alone in that hour; all ties including those with parents and family are repudiated (Surah 82: 19). At that time all veils between man and 'the objective moral reality will be rent' (Rahman, 1980, p. 106). *Al-akhira* is opposed to *al-dunya*, the here and now, which may mean base pursuits. Indeed, *Alam-e-Uqba*, a popular book in Urdu on death in Islam, has sections called 'Your death is better than your living' (Sialkoti, n.d., p. 50).[4] Given the awesome facts of *al-akhira*, human beings must prepare for it in this life. Together, *al-akhira* and *dunya* are a unitary whole, the latter determining the nature of the former. Life after death is explicit in Islam and central to its theology. In a general sense, this partly explains the attitudes to death shown both in the traditional religious war, *jihad*, and in contemporary events in the Muslim world. Those who killed President Sadat in Cairo and, like Lieutenant Islambuli, awaited death calmly, during the trials and those who died following Imam Khomeini's call in Iran, first against the Shah and later against the Iraqis, believed they were dying for a just, an Islamic, cause. Matters are complicated when *jihad* is freely translated as a struggle against any enemy, including Muslims (Ahmed, 1983). But the problems between Shi'a and Sunni lie in this world and are rooted in the history, not theology, of Islam. Islamic history, Shi'as maintain, began to go wrong when Hazrat Ali, married to Hazrat Fatima, daughter of the Prophet, was not made the first Caliph after the death of his father-in-law. To make matters worse Hazrat Ali was assassinated. Hazrat Ali's two sons, Hazrat Hassan and Hazrat Hussain, following in their father's footsteps, opposed tyranny and upheld the puritan principles of Islam. Both were also martyred. Hazrat Hussain was martyred, facing impossible odds on a battlefield, with his family and followers, at Karbala. Among those killed at Karbala was Hazrat Hussain's 6-month-old son, Hazrat Ali Asghar (who appeared to Naseem in Chakwal). The Prophet, Hazrat Fatima, Ali, Hassan and Hussain are the five key figures for Shi'a theology and history. These are the *panj tan pak*, 'the pure five', of Shi'as in Pakistan, including those in Chakwal. Since five of them were martyred in the cause of Islam, death, martyrdom, tears and sacrifice form a central part of Shi'a mythology (Algar, 1969: Fischer, 1980; Khomeini, 1981; Schimmel, 1981; Shariati, 1979). Members of the Shi'a community are expected to respond with fervour (*jazba*) to a call for sacrifice by the leadership. A sense of sectarian uniqueness, of group loyalty, faith in the leadership, readiness for sacrifice, devout ecstasy during divine ritual, characterise the community. It has been called 'the Karbala paradigm' (Fischer, 1980) and would have been exhibited in Chakwal.

In Pakistan today, where about 20 per cent of the population of 100 million are Shi'as, Shi'a–Sunni differences can degenerate into conflict. This is especially so during Muharram, the ten days of Shi'a mourning for the events at Karbala. During this period Shi'as mourn, flagellate themselves, organise processions symbolic of Karbala, and recite moving poems of the tragedy at Karbala which reduce those present to tears and quivering rapture. Conflict with Sunnis is often sparked as a result of overzealous Shi'as abusing figures respected by Sunnis, such as Hazrat Umar. It was one such riot which had paralysed Karachi when the party from Chakwal arrived there on its way to the Arabian Sea. Chakwal society itself is riven with Shi'a and Sunni opposition which has a long and bitter history. Local politics, marriages and economics are based on this opposition. Sectarian tension and loyalties also divide families. Some of Willayat's own nearest kin were either secret Sunnis or suspected of being sympathisers. These divided loyalties must have led to severe tension both for him and his daughter.

An appreciation of the five central figures of the Shi'as also helps us to understand the role of women in that community. The position of Hazrat Fatima is central. Her popularity among the Shi'a in Chakwal may be judged by the fact that seven women in Willayat Shah's family carry her name. Two of these are called Ghulam Fatima, or slave of Fatima. Always a great favourite of her father, Hazrat Fatima provides the link between her father and husband and between her sons and their grandfather. The Sayyids, those claiming descent from the Prophet, do so through Hazrat Fatima. So do the twelve Imams, revered by the Shi'a. In addition, Fatima's mother and the Prophet's first wife, Hazrat Khadijah, is also an object of reverence. Two other women feature in Shi'a mythology, but neither is a popular figure. They are Hazrat Ayesha and Hazrat Hafsa, both wives of the Prophet. The reason for their unpopularity is linked to the question of Hazrat Ali's succession. Ayesha was the daughter of Abu Bakar and Hafsa of Umar, the two who preceded Ali as Caliph. Ayesha is singled out as she opposed Ali actively after her husband's death.

Thus, one of the five revered figures of the Shi'a is a woman. Among the Sunnis a similar listing – of the Prophet and the first four Righteous Caliphs – consists entirely of males. In other matters, too, Shi'a women are better off than Sunnis. Shi'a women, for example, often inherit shares equal to that inherited by male kin, whereas among educated Sunni, women receive, at best, one half of what a male inherits. In the rural areas they seldom inherit at all. Shi'a women also play a leading role in ritual. The organisation of *marsyas* and *azadari*, the enactment of the death dramas of Karbala, all involve the active participation of women.

Of the eighteen people who died at Hawkes Bay, ten were women, a notably large number in view of the fact that only sixteen of the forty-two who set out on the pilgrimage were women. Willayat Shah lost both his mother and daughter. It may be argued that the women were unequivocally committed to sacrifice. By locking themselves in trunks they had sealed their own fates. For them there was no coming back from the waves. Their sense of sacrifice and passion for the cause were supreme.

The attitudes of the two communities to the Hawkes Bay incident reveal their ideological positions. Sunnis, as we saw above, condemned the entire episode as 'bizarre' and dismissed it as 'insanity'.

This, they argued, was mumbo-jumbo and quackery and not in keeping with the logic and rationality which is Islam. For Shi'as all the ingredients of high devotion were amply displayed. Through it they felt they had once again established their superior love for Islam. Here there was sacrifice, persecution, death and martyrdom, the Shi'a paradigm. Educated Shi'a, who found it awkward to explain the Hawkes Bay case, none the less applauded the *jazba* of the group. As one journalist concluded his report: 'There are millions who don't have the slightest doubt that they have demonstrated the highest degree of sacrifice by answering the call and order of the Hidden Imam' (Yusufzai, 1983). The idea of sacrificing life and property for Allah exists both in Shi'a and Sunni Islam and is supported in the Holy Qur'an. Sacrifice and its symbolism are part of Islamic religious culture. Abraham's willingness to sacrifice his son Ismail, for example, is celebrated annually throughout the Muslim world at Eid-ul-Zaha. But for the Shi'as, sacrifice holds a central place in social behaviour and sectarian mythology. Here it is necessary to distinguish between suicide – throwing away life given by God – and sacrifice, or dedication of that life to God. Suicide is a punishable offence in Islam (Islam, 1976, p. 267). Sunnis, therefore, seeing the deaths at Hawkes Bay as suicide, disapproved. They saw the episode as a throwing away of valuable lives, whereas Shi'as saw it as a sacrifice which would confirm their devotion. Willayat Shah was convinced his mission was divine and that he had proved this through a dramatic act of sacrifice. Reward, he was certain, would be paradise in the afterworld (Pervez, 1983, p. 22). In interviews after the event he expressed his wish to be martyred (*shaheed*). There was no remorse; there was only *jazba*. To a remarkable degree Shi'a tradition, and the practice of death and sacrifice, coincided in this case. For the Shi'a in Chakwal, text and practice were one.

Suffering thus became as much an expression of faith as of social solidarity. 'As a religious problem, the problem of suffering is, paradoxically, not how to avoid suffering but how to suffer, how to make of physical pain, personal loss, worldly defeat, or the helpless contemplation of others' agony something bearable, supportable – something, as we say, sufferable' (Geertz, 1966, p. 19). Suffering, martyrdom and death, the Karbala paradigm, create an emotionally receptive social environment for sacrifice. Death in our case, therefore, became a cementing, a defining, a status-bestowing act for the community. It consolidated the living as it hallowed the memory of the dead.

Through the Hawkes Bay case, we have attempted to examine complex and largely unstudied issues in Pakistan society resulting from migration. We have noted the impact of the years abroad on the migrant and his actions on his return, and how they affect those around him. We have pointed out answers to the questions raised at the beginning of the chapter. We have also discussed notions about the status of women, sacrifice, death and the afterworld.

We are thus able to note some unexpected answers to our questions. Clearly, the role of women is a much more important and central one than we are led to believe on the basis of conventional wisdom about rural Pakistan society. The Hawkes Bay case revolves around a woman.

Another interesting and perhaps unexpected observation arising from the case is that the returned villager does not necessarily shed his 'traditional' world-view for a new one. On the contrary, this traditional view becomes even more extreme, as migrants are exposed to politicised religious movements, calling for a return to a purer Islam. A returning migrant may thus call for a renewed emphasis on his society's particular culture or religion and thereby provide a lead to others in his family. In challenging the existing class and leadership structure, he invokes 'traditional' ideas. In a world of change such a migrant wishes to recreate a pure and absolute world-view. He appeals to his kinsmen and to kinship loyalties, just as he appeals to a revitalised and purified religion.

Clearly, then, an act with a pragmatic motive such as migration can generate – indirectly – an opposite move, one towards martyrdom and death. Such an act, which started with the acquisition of material wealth may end, as in the case we discussed here, with the ultimate act of sacrifice. Migrants are inevitably caught up in the course of their migratory careers in broader cultural movements. They bring this heightened consciousness back to their home villages. The mundane act of migration thus needs to be analysed in its cultural context, as it comes indirectly to impact on broader philosophic ideas about personhood and the hereafter. Inevitably, then, as Pakistani labour migration increases, so too does the polychromic complexity of Pakistani society.

Notes

*   This is a slightly revised version of a paper which first appeared in *Man* (21 (1) 1986) under the title 'Death in Islam: The Hawkes Bay Case'. I am very grateful to the editor and to the Royal Anthropological Institute for permission to use the material again here.

1.   See for example, Banton, 1966; Bloch and Parry, 1982; Douglas, 1970; Evans-Pritchard, 1937, 1965; Geertz, 1966; Keyes, 1981, 1985; Lewis, 1971; Werbner, 1977; Winter, 1966.

2.   A committee was set up by Dr M. Afzal, the Minister of Education, to examine the problem. It was chaired by Dr Z. A. Ansari and included some of Pakistan's most eminent psychiatrists and psychologists. I represented the social scientists (Pervez, 1983).

3.   The organisation of Punjab society into agricultural peasant groups, defined by ethnicity and occupation, is well documented (Ahmad, 1973, 1977; Ahmed, 1984c; Alavi, 1972, 1973; Balneaves, 1955; Darling, 1925, 1930, 1934; Eglar, 1960; Ibbetson, 1883; Pettigrew, 1975).

4.   See also Saeed, 1982. In another popular book the author promises the reader, in the subtitle, 'glimpses of life beyond the grave'. One section in the book is entitled 'the depth of hell: if a stone is thrown into hell it will take seventy years to reach its bottom' (Islam, 1976, p. 284). For discussion of *djahannam*, the Muslim hell, see Gibb and Kramers, 1981, pp. 81–2. Maulana Maududi discusses the importance of death, the afterlife and its relationship to man's life on earth, in a dispassionate analysis of Islamic society (Maududi, 1968). See also chapter 6, 'Eschatology', in Rahman, 1980.

References

Abd al-Qadir, As-Sufi (1977), 'Death, the beginning of a journey', in Abd ar-Rahim ibn Ahmad al-Qadir (ed.), *Islamic Book of the Dead* (England: Diwan Press).

Ahmad, S. (1973), 'Peasant classes in Pakistan', in K. Gough and H. P. Sharma (eds), *Imperialism and Revolution in South Asia* (New York: Monthly Review Press).

Ahmad, S. (1977), *Class and Power in a Punjabi Village* (New York: Monthly Review Press).

Ahmed, A. S. (1983), *Religion and Politics in Muslim Society: Order and Conflict in Pakistan* (New York: Cambridge University Press).

Ahmed, A. S. (1984a), '*Dubai Chalo*: Problems in the Ethnic Encounter between Middle Eastern and South Asian Muslim Societies', *Asian Affairs*, 15, pp. 262–76.

Ahmed, A. S. (1984b), 'Zia's Victory in the Field: The (Arain) Work Ethic that Keeps a President in Power', *Guardian* (London), 10 August.

Ahmed, A. S. (1984c), 'Hazarawal: Formation and Structure of District Ethnicity in Pakistan', in D. Maybury-Lewis (ed.), *The Prospects for Plural Societies* (Washington: American Ethnological Society).

Alavi, H. (1972), 'Kinship in West Punjab Villages', *Contributions to Indian Sociology* (NS), 6, pp. 1–27.

Alavi, H. (1973), 'Peasant Classes and Primordial Loyalties', *Journal of Peasant Studies*, 1, pp. 23–62.

Algar, H. (1969), *Religion and State in Iran, 1785–1906* (Berkeley: University of California Press).

Ansari, Z. A. *et al.* (1983), 'Urdu Notes for Study Based on Interviews Conducted by National Institute of Psychology, Islamabad', in S. Pervez (ed.), *Hawkes Bay Incident* (Islamabad: National Institute of Psychology).

Asad, M. (1980), Trans. and explained, *The Message of the Quran* (Gibraltar: Dar-ul-andalus).

Asad, T. (1983), 'Anthropological Conceptions of Religion: Reflections on Geertz', *Man* (NS), 18, pp. 237–59.

Balneaves, E. (1955), *Waterless Moon* (London: Lutterworth Press).

Banton, M. (ed.) (1966), *Anthropological Approaches to the Study of Religion*, ASA Monograph 3 (London: Tavistock).

Basilov, V. N. (1984), *Honour Groups in Traditional Turkmenian Society*, in A. S. Ahmed and D. Hart (eds), *Islam in Tribal Societies* (London: Routledge & Kegan Paul).

Bloch, M. and J. Parry (eds) (1982), *Death and the Regeneration of Life* (New York: Cambridge University Press).

Bray, D. (1977), *The Life History of a Brahui* (Karachi: Royal Book Company).

Darling, M. L. (1925), *The Punjab Peasant in Prosperity and Debt* (London: Oxford University Press).

Darling, M. L. (1930), *Rusticus Loquitur, or the Old Light and the New in the Punjab Village* (London: Oxford University Press).

Darling, M. L. (1934), *Wisdom and Waste in the Punjab Village* (London: Oxford University Press).

Douglas, M. (ed.) (1970), *Witchcraft Confessions and Accusations*, ASA Monograph 9 (London: Tavistock).

Eglar, Z. (1960), *A Punjabi Village in Pakistan* (New York: Columbia University Press).

Evans-Pritchard, E. E. (1937), *Witchcraft, Oracles and Magic among the Azande* (Oxford: Clarendon Press).

Evans-Pritchard, E. E. (1965), *Theories of Primitive Religion* (Oxford: Clarendon Press).

Fischer, M. J. (1980), *Iran: From Religious Dispute to Revolution* (Cambridge, Mass.: Harvard University Press).

Fox, R. (1973), *Encounter with Anthropology* (Harmondsworth: Penguin).

Geertz, C. (1966), 'Religion as a Cultural System', in M. Banton, (ed.) *Anthropological Approaches to the Study of Religion*, ASA Monograph 3 (London: Tavistock).

Gibb, H. A. R. and J. H. Kramers (1981), *Shorter Encyclopaedia of Islam* (Karachi: South Asian Publishers).

Ibbetson, D. C. J. (1883), *Outlines of Punjab Ethnography, Extracts from the Punjab Census Report of 1881, Treating of Religion, Language and Caste* (Calcutta: Government Printing Office).

Irfani, S. (1983), 'From Jonestown to Hawkes Bay', *The Muslim*, 4 March.

Islam, K. M. (1976), *The Spectacle of Death* (Lahore: Tablighi Kutub Khana).

Jaffery, S. (1983), 'Why Didn't God Take Us Too?' in *The Herald* (Karachi), March.

Keyes, C. F. (1981), 'From Death to Rebirth; Northern Thai Conceptions of Immortality' paper presented to the Annual Meeting of the Association for Asian Studies.

Keyes, C. F. (1985), 'The Interpretive Basis of Depression', in A. Kleinman and B. J. Good (eds), *Culture and Depression: Comparative Studies of Health Systems and Medical Care: Vol. 16*, (Berkeley: University of California Press).

Khomeini, Imam (1981), *Islam and Revolution* (trans.) H. Algar (Berkeley: Mizan Press).

Lewis, I. M. (1971), *Ecstatic Religion: An Anthropological Study of Spirit Possession and Shamanism* (Harmondsworth: Penguin).

Maududi, M. Abu ala (1968), *Islamic Tehzib Our Os Key Osool-o-Mobadi* (in Urdu) (Lahore: Islamic Publications, Shah Alam Market).

Muslim, Imam (1981), *Sahih Muslim* (trans.) H. Siddiqi (Lahore: M. Ashraf).

Okarvi, M. M. S. (not dated), *On Visiting a Cemetery* (in Urdu) (Karachi: Medina).

Pervez, S. (1983), *Hawkes Bay Incident: A Psycho-Social Case Study*, compiled by Seema Pervez (Islamabad, National Institute of Psychology).

Pettigrew, J. (1975), *Robber Noblemen* (London: Routledge & Kegan Paul).

Rahman, F. (1980), *Major Themes of the Quran* (Chicago: Bibliotheca Islamica).

Saeed, M. A. (1982), *What Happens after Death?* (trans.) M. H. Khan. (Delhi: Dini Book Depot, Urdu Bazar).

Salahuddin, G. (1983), 'A Glimpse of Our Insanity?' *The Herald*, (Karachi), March.

Schimmel, A. (1981), *Mystical Dimensions of Islam* (Chapel Hill: University of North Carolina Press).

Shariati, A. (1979), *On the Sociology of Islam* (trans.) H. Algar (Berkeley: Mizan Press).

Sialkoti, Maulana M. S. (n.d.), *Alam-e-Uqba* (in Urdu) (Lahore: Nomani Kutub Khana).

Smolowe, J. *et al.* (1984), 'The Strange World of Cults', *Newsweek*, 16 January.

Werbner, R. P. (ed.) (1977), *Regional Cults*, ASA Monograph 16 (London: Tavistock).

Winter, E. R. (1966), 'Territorial Groupings and Religion among the Iraqw', in M. Banton (ed.), *Anthropological Approaches to the Study of Religion*, ASA Monograph 3 (London: Tavistock).

Yusufzai, R. (1983), 'Psychiatrists' Views of Two Recent Episodes', *The Muslim*, 18 March.

Index